THE RESURRECTION OF THE MESSIAH

A Narrative Commentary on the Resurrection Accounts in the Four Gospels

Francis J. Moloney, SDB

PAULIST PRESS

New York / Mahwah, NJ

Cover image by fotogiunta/Shutterstock.com
Cover and book design by Sharyn Banks
Copyright © 2013 by Francis J. Moloney

Library of Congress Cataloging-in-Publication Data

Moloney, Francis J.
    The resurrection of the Messiah : a narrative commentary on the Resurrection accounts in the four gospels / Francis J. Moloney, SDB.
        pages cm
    Includes bibliographical references and index.
    ISBN 978-0-8091-4847-9 (alk. paper) — ISBN 978-1-58768-296-4
    1. Jesus Christ—Resurrection. 2. Passion narratives (Gospels) 3. Bible. Gospels—Commentaries. 4. Bible. Gospels—Criticism, Narrative. I. Title.
    BT482.M65 2013
    226'.06—dc23

2013024105

ISBN: 978-0-8091-4847-9 (paperback)
ISBN: 978-1-58768-296-4 (e-book)

Published by Paulist Press
997 Macarthur Boulevard
Mahwah, New Jersey 07430

www.paulistpress.com

Printed and bound in the
United States of America

Table of Contents

In Memory of Raymond E. Brown, SS

(1928–1998)

Preface

Raymond E. Brown, SS (1928–98), made a singularly outstanding contribution to New Testament scholarship, and especially to the study of the four Gospels, across a rich career. His life as a New Testament scholar and a teacher, initially at St. Mary's University and Seminary in Baltimore, and subsequently at Union Theological Seminary in New York, built a bridge from the pre-critical era into the world of contemporary biblical scholarship within and beyond the Catholic Church. His influence cannot be overestimated as his numerous publications ranged from the deeply scholarly to clear and crisp popular studies for the general reader. Not without his critics, he courageously lived his life as a scholar and a Roman Catholic priest and religious as a wonderful testimony to the richness of a life built on the Word of God. His work and the memory of his person remain a precious heritage for biblical scholars of all denominations in the United States and beyond.

The title of this volume is unashamedly modeled on two of his most famous scholarly publications, both the fruit of his mature years, almost without parallel in their depth and clarity. I refer to *The Birth of the Messiah: A Commentary on the Infancy Narratives in Matthew and Luke* (Garden City, NY: Doubleday, 1977) and *The Death of the Messiah: From Gethsemane to the Grave: A Commentary on the Passion Narratives of the Four Gospels*, 2 vols., ABRL (New York: Doubleday, 1994). In his preface to *The Death of the Messiah*, he records that many people had asked whether he was planning to complete the trilogy by writing *The Resurrection of the Messiah*. He told them that he had no such plans, and concludes: "I would rather explore that area 'face to face'" (*Death of the Messiah*, xii). Only four years later he achieved that goal.

The small volume that follows does not pretend to fill the gap left by the premature death of a great scholar. Raymond Brown's studies of the infancy narratives in Matthew and Luke, and the passion narratives of all four Gospels, were outstanding examples of historical-critical scholarship. No stone was left unturned, and no book or article (in any language) left unread, in order to uncover the world that produced the gospel texts, and the world within the Gospels of Mark, Matthew, Luke, and John. He was not only interested in the history and background of the narratives, but he also attempted to indicate the particular point of view portrayed by each evangelist. However, in my opinion, especially in his study of the passion narratives, he made choices in his allocation of the vast amount of gospel text to be analyzed that obscured what he regarded as the primary aim of these volumes: *"to explain in detail what the evangelists intended and conveyed to their audiences by their narratives of the passion and death of Jesus"* (*Death of the Messiah*, 4, stress in original). Rather than reading each narrative in its entirety, he divided the passion narrative into four acts: Jesus in Gethsemane; Jesus before the Jewish authorities; Jesus before Pilate; and Jesus' crucifixion, death, and burial. Each of the Gospels was examined within these four acts. "What the evangelists intended and conveyed to their audiences" can certainly be found within the 570 pages on the infancy narratives and the 1,524 pages on the passion narratives, but it can sometimes be hard to track down as the reader moves from the detailed analysis of narrative to narrative, and every possible exegetical and historical issue they raise, under these four headings.

The following study does not pretend to be an exhaustive study of all the questions that emerge from an attentive reading of Mark 16:1–8 (and 16:9–20), Matthew 27:62—28:20, Luke 24:1–53, and John 20:1–31 and 21:1–25, in the way that Raymond Brown would work. Although I continue his tradition in my main title, I differ in my subtitle. What follows is not a "commentary" but a "narrative commentary." This calls for a brief explanation. Since the 1980s what has been called a "narrative-critical" analysis of biblical texts has assumed a significant place in biblical scholarship, alongside the more traditional historical-critical approaches. Stated simply, this approach accepts the canonical text as it has come down to us in the tradition. Without disregarding the historical background that must be understood for an appreciation of the story, a narrative commentary attempts to trace the intended impact of that story upon its readers. This reading and interpretative process uncovers the literary structure of a passage, and then follows the unfolding of the narrative itself, allowing it to speak for itself, insofar as this is possible for an interpreter looking at a text almost two thousand years old.

Readings that focus upon the flow of the narrative must always consider the longer story. For that reason the study of the resurrection narratives that follows sketches the message of the preceding passion story and also makes links with each Gospel as a whole. The gospel accounts of Jesus' death and resurrection must be read together. What follows focuses on the resurrection narratives of Mark 16:1–8 (and 16:9–20), Matthew 27:62—28:20, Luke 24:1–53, and John 20:1–31 and 21:1–25, but they will all be read in conjunction with a briefer analysis of the respective passion narrative. We must always be aware of our personal social and religious "location," as we look back across almost two thousand years. Our particular history and social conditioning necessarily impose limitations upon our interpretations. Modesty should be a key virtue for any interpreter of ancient texts, and I trust that what follows indicates that my reading of these fundamental texts within the Christian tradition is not the only one possible. Footnotes document alternative suggestions.

A further factor must also play its part in a contemporary act of interpretation. As these stories have been read in Christian communities as part of their "Sacred Scriptures," it is taken for granted that they made an impact in their original setting and telling in the life of the Church. The evidence for that is that we still have them and still read them, even though they are centuries old, written in a distant place and time, in Greek. They have been told and retold, read and reread, heard and reheard for almost two thousand years. A narrative commentary, therefore, must also attempt to uncover a communication process that goes on between writers/tellers and readers/listeners across the Christian centuries. The study that follows is a narrative reading of the resurrection stories in Mark, Matthew, Luke, and John. Its focus is almost entirely upon the text itself. Guided by current scholarship, it aims to uncover the perennial significance of the four resurrection narratives, accepted and read as Sacred Scripture in the Christian tradition. The decision to read Mark's resurrection story as the first chapter of this book indicates acceptance of a widely held hypothesis: Mark was the earliest of the four Gospels. According to this hypothesis, the Gospel of Mark appeared about 70 AD, the Gospels of Matthew and Luke in the 80s of that century, and Gospel of John much closer to 100 AD.[1] More than a date is involved in this hypothesis. It also accepts that Matthew and Luke used the Gospel of Mark, as well as other sources, one of which they had in common (known as the Q source [Q standing for the German word *Quelle* = source]), and other sources unique to them (generally referred to as M and L, respectively). The Gospel of John does not depend directly upon any of the earlier Gospels, but the author is aware that Gospels existed. That story, however, has grown independently, nourished by its own powerful traditions and shaped by the experience of the Johannine community. The reading of the resurrection stories that follows, therefore, sometimes refers to the different directions that Mark, Matthew, and Luke have taken in their accounts, and respects the uniqueness of the Johannine Gospel.[2]

During the interpretative reading of these stories little or no attention is devoted to the question of "what actually happened." That is not the main purpose of a narrative analysis of a passage, as it has been for Raymond Brown's wonderful studies. In a closing chapter some of those issues are raised, and a theological reflection, rather than a historical one, closes the book. For those interested in historical questions, I can do no better than refer them to an early study of Raymond Brown, *The Virginal Conception and Bodily Resurrection of Jesus*, published by Paulist Press in 1973. Despite its age this book remains an illuminating and classical study of the historical-critical questions raised by the infancy and the resurrection narratives, directed to an intelligent and interested general reader. For me, no one has done this task better than Raymond Brown.

It is in memory of this great scholar and personal friend that I dedicate my own study, so different from his in so many ways, but so dependent upon his inspiration in every way.

Francis J. Moloney, SDB, AM, FAHA
Australian Catholic University, Melbourne, Victoria, Australia

Notes

1. We cannot be certain of the names of the authors of the four Gospels, as they were not present in the early manuscripts. The titles of the Gospels ("According to Mark, Matthew, Luke, and John") were added in the second century. Out of respect for tradition, and ease of reference, the authors are referred to by their traditional names, even though we cannot be sure of their identity.

2. For a very clear presentation of the relationships among Mark, Matthew, and Luke, see John S. Kloppenborg, *The Earliest Gospel: An Introduction to the Original Stories and Sayings of Jesus* (Louisville, KY: Westminster John Knox, 2008), 1–40. On John, see D. Moody Smith, *John among the Gospels,* 2nd ed. (Columbia: University of South Carolina Press, 2001).

Abbreviations

AB	The Anchor Bible
ABD	*Anchor Bible Dictionary*. Edited by David N. Freedman. 6 vols. New York: Doubleday, 1992
ABRL	The Anchor Bible Reference Library
ACR	*The Australasian Catholic Record*
AeJT	*Australian eJournal of Theology*
AnBib	Analecta Biblica
ANTC	Abingdon New Testament Commentaries
AYB	The Anchor Yale Bible
AYBRL	The Anchor Yale Bible Reference Library
BDAG	Danker, Frederick W. *A Greek-English Lexicon of the New Testament and Other Early Christian Literature*. 3d ed. Chicago: University Press, 2000
BibScRel	*Biblioteca di Scienze Religiose*
BNTC	Black's New Testament Commentaries
BT	*The Bible Today*
BZNW	Beihefte zur Zeitschrift für die neutestamentliche Wissenschaft
CBQ	*The Catholic Biblical Quarterly*
CBR	*Currents in Biblical Research*
FB	Forschung zur Bibel
GNS	Good News Studies
HTCNT	Herder's Theological Commentary on the New Testament
ICC	International Critical Commentary
Int	*Interpretation*
IRT	Issues in Religion and Theology

JB   The Jerusalem Bible

JBL   *Journal for Biblical Literature*

JSNT   *Journal for the Study of the New Testament*

JSNTSup   Journal for the Study of the New Testament Supplement Series

JSOT   *Journal for the Study of the Old Testament*

LSJ   Liddell, Henry G., Robert Scott, and Henry S. Jones. *A Greek-English Lexicon*. Oxford: Clarendon, 1968

LXX   The Septuagint

NAB   The New American Bible

NCB   New Century Bible

NIB   *The New Interpreter's Dictionary of the Bible*. Edited by Katherine Doob Sackenfeld et al. 5 vols. Nashville, TN: Abingdon, 2006

NIGTC   New International Greek Testament Commentary

NJBC   *The New Jerome Biblical Commentary*. Edited by Raymond E. Brown, Joseph A. Fitzmyer, and Roland E. Murphy. Englewood Cliffs, NJ: Prentice Hall, 1989

NRSV   The New Revised Standard Version

NTM   New Testament Message

NTS   *New Testament Studies*

PTMS   Pittsburgh Theological Monograph Series

RSV   The Revised Standard Version

SBL   Society for Biblical Literature

SBLDS   Society for Biblical Literature Dissertation Series

SHBC   Smyth and Helwys Bible Commentary

SNTIW   Studies on the New Testament and Its World

SNTSMS   The Society for New Testament Studies Monograph Series

SP   Sacra Pagina

TPINTC   Trinity Press International New Testament Commentary

TS   *Theological Studies*

WBC   Word Biblical Commentary

WUNT   Wissenschaftliche Untersuchungen zum Neuen Testament

CHAPTER ONE

The Resurrection of the Messiah according to Mark

Mark 16:1–8

Introduction

Within the overall story of each of *agapaō* the Gospels, the account of Jesus' suffering and death is the crucial climax to all that has gone before. It opens the door to the resurrection story that follows. In order to appreciate the four accounts of Jesus' resurrection, it is important to have an idea of what immediately preceded it in the story of Jesus' suffering and death. This is a feature of narrative readings of gospel texts; no passage stands alone. It always has words and events that precede it, and generally (although not the case with the resurrection narratives) words and events that follow it.

Mark's Gospel looks forward to the passion account and cannot be understood without it. This Gospel has been described as a passion story with a long introduction.[1] The Markan passion narrative is a unique story of the suffering and death of Jesus that enigmatically brings to closure the Gospel's "good news" about what God has done for us in and through Jesus. As we will see, a similar assessment can be made of the passion narratives of all four Gospels, although each evangelist has a unique appreciation and presentation of that "good news." Although not entirely true, the passion of Jesus can be said to have a strong focus upon *what happened to Jesus*, while the resurrection accounts are more about *what happened to the original disciples.*

1

Obviously, God's entering into the mystery of Jesus' death and burial is crucial for a Christian appreciation of what happens to Jesus![2] Jesus' death is not "for himself," as he explains in the words that accompanied his gift of the wine "poured out for many" at the final supper in Mark (14:24) and Matthew (26:28). More intensely, at the sharing of the bread and wine moment in Luke Jesus explains that the bread is his body "given for you," and the wine is "poured out for you" (22:19–20).[3] The passion narrative is not *only* about what happened to Jesus. Equally true, the resurrection stories are not *only* about what happens to disciples, as they bring to closure God's action in and through Jesus. At the head of the following chapters, therefore, dealing in turn with each of the four Gospels, a brief presentation of the passion narrative outlines what Mark, Matthew, Luke, and John tell us of God's action for Jesus and "for us" in and through Jesus' passion and death. We will thus be well situated to read and interpret the four resurrection narratives, the primary focus of this book.

Mark's Passion Story

Mark's passion narrative (14:1—15:42) is made up of two major sections. The first section comprises 14:1–72. It is made up of a continuous interplay between Jesus and the disciples, located almost entirely among disciples, Jewish leaders, and the crowds.[4] As Jesus moves steadily toward his ironic condemnation by the Jewish leaders, the disciples' failure intensifies, despite their privileged sharing of a final Passover meal with Jesus, at which he tells of future betrayal and denials (14:17–31). At the arrest in Gethsemane, the disciples flee, fearful and naked in their separation from Jesus (v. 50). Their situation is caught in the episode of the young man who "followed him" but fled naked when danger threatened (vv. 51–52).[5] At the Jewish trial Jesus is ironically proclaimed Christ, Son of God, whose suffering will be vindicated by the coming of the Son of Man (14:61–62). Only Peter remains, following at a distance. But he associates himself with Jesus' enemies and denies him three times (vv. 53–54, 66–72). Yet, at the center of 14:1–72, the sixth of eleven scenes that alternate between fragile disciples and Jesus' movement toward the cross, Jesus shares a meal with his weak and failing disciples (vv. 22–25).[6] The disciples are told that the shepherd will be struck, and they will all fall away. But they are promised that, despite their denials and betrayals, fear and flight, Jesus will go before them into Galilee. There they will see him (14:27–28).

The second section (15:1–47) is a further interplay of other characters with Jesus. Romans, however, replace the disciples as Jesus' major dialogue partners. The disciples, with the exception of Peter, who will deny him, have disappeared from the story in 14:50. They will not be active characters in the story, although they are mentioned significantly in 16:7. The Romans are his judges and his executioners throughout this section, although the Jewish leaders are never far away. The ironic christological proclamation of the Jewish trial (see 14:61–62) is extended into the Roman hearing and the crucifixion. Jesus is proclaimed "the King of the Jews" by Pilate (15:2, 9), by the crowd (v. 12 [indirectly]), by the Roman soldiers (v. 18), and in the title the Romans place on the cross (v. 26). Alone in his agony, he is proclaimed Savior by the passers-by (v. 30) and by the Jewish leaders (v. 31), and ironically recognized as the Christ, the King of Israel, in the mockery of the Jewish leaders (v. 32). They ask that he come down from the cross. The reader/listener is made aware that it is only *on the cross* that Jesus can lay claim to be Savior, Christ, and King of Israel, as his enemies demand that he come down from the cross that they might see and believe (vv. 30, 32).[7] Crying out an anguished question of abandon to his God (v. 34), Jesus cries out again in desperation as he expires (v. 37).[8] The christological high point of the Gospel arrives as a consequence of Jesus' agonizing death: the Temple of Jerusalem is symbolically destroyed, and the Sanctuary once reserved to the Jewish priests is laid open for all to see. A new Temple, built upon the rejected cornerstone, is founded (see 12:10–11), and the Roman centurion, standing before Jesus and having seen the manner of his death, is the first of many to proclaim that Jesus is the Son of God (vv. 38–39). The promise of the voice from heaven in 1:11 has been realized in 15:39. At the center of 15:1–47, the fifth of nine scenes, vv. 20b–25 tell of the silent and merciless account of Jesus' crucifixion, the event so long anticipated by the Gospel of Mark (see 2:20; 3:6). Women watch, and Jesus is hurriedly buried in scenes that bring the traditional passion story to an end. But they have been shaped to point the reader/listener toward the resurrection promised by Jesus during his journey to Jerusalem (8:31; 9:31; 10:33–34), and demanded by Jesus' question of God in his moment of death (15:34). Has God abandoned his Son?

As the first half of the passion narrative closed, the disciples moved tragically toward the denials of Peter (14:66–72). As the second half ends, the Romans' participation in Jesus' agony closes with one of them accepting that Jesus is the Son of God (15:39). The simplicity of the literary structure combined with the depth of the dramatic irony used to proclaim the truth of Jesus, Christ, King, and Son of God on the cross reflect a finely tuned Christian author.[9] This passion narrative has prepared the reader/hearer for the Gospel's climax: the much-anticipated account of the resurrection of Jesus (see 8:31; 9:9–13, 31; 10:32–34).[10] There, one would expect, the failure of the disciples and the apparent failure of Jesus will be resolved. God will become the major agent in what follows, but there is a twist to the end of the tale. God will show that he has never abandoned his Son (see 15:34), but the expected restoration of discipleship to those fearful and frightened men who fled from Jesus at Gethsemane (14:50) will receive something of a setback. The women must become the major players. They have courageously remained with Jesus, present at the crucifixion, looking on "from afar" (14:40–41), and they will see where the dead body is laid in a tomb (v. 47). Surprisingly, they will join the disciples in fear and flight (16:8).[11]

Mark's Resurrection Story

After this rapid overview of the passion story, we can now focus more closely upon the details of Mark's account of the resurrection. The events that took place on the day after the Sabbath are closely linked with the story of Jesus' passion. The indication of time, "And when the Sabbath was passed," of 16:1a looks back to 15:42, "It was the day of Preparation, that is, the day before the Sabbath." The explicit naming of the characters, Mary Magdalene, Mary the mother of James, and Salome (16:1b), brings back on stage all the women mentioned watching the death of Jesus from afar (15:40). Two of them (Mary Magdalene and Mary the mother of Joses) had also seen where the body of Jesus was laid (15:47). A tight connection, linking the time of the week and the people from the passion story with the events of the first day of the week, is established. On the basis of this connection the final page of the narrative of the Gospel of Mark is told in three steps:[12]

1. vv. 1–4: The setting: an empty tomb

2. vv. 5–7: The Easter proclamation

3. v. 8: The failure of the women

These steps in the unfolding narrative need to be read attentively, as they contain problems that have bothered scholars and readers of all generations. But the first major problem is external to the text itself. A textual problem must be resolved: did the original Gospel of Mark end with 16:8?

Our present printed English translations indicate a number of possible continuations to a story that might have originally followed on from the surprising response of the women in v. 8. For example, the RSV separates v. 8 from vv. 9–20 and indicates in a note that "the most ancient authorities bring the book to a close at the end of v. 8." Other endings are provided in the commentary provided below the text. The NRSV closes the Gospel with v. 8 and then provides two further endings, in parentheses, with separate headings: "The shorter end of Mark" (vv. 9–10) and "The longer ending of Mark" (vv. 9–20). The confusion that faces the modern reader at the end of the Gospel of Mark reflects difficulties that emerged in the earliest days of Christian tradition. Where did the original Gospel of Mark end? Once the written gospel texts were passed from generation to generation, scribes were faced with a Markan story that (unlike the Gospels of Matthew, Luke, and John) apparently closed with the women fleeing from the empty tomb (v. 8). The most ancient manuscripts bring the story to an end at that point: the women flee from the tomb, afraid. They had heard the Easter message (v. 6) and have been commissioned by the young man in the tomb to tell Peter and the disciples of Jesus' going before them into Galilee, as he had promised (v. 7; see 14:28). How is it possible that the Gospel ended at 16:8?

Over the early decades of the Christian Church and its mission, as the written text was passed on to newer generations, scribes provided more satisfactory endings to make the Gospel of Mark conform to the conclusions of the Gospels of Matthew, Luke, and John. In Matthew and

Luke, women receive the Easter message and report it to the disciples (Matt 28:1–10; Luke 24:1–12). In the Gospel of John, there is only one woman, Mary Magdalene, but the story of the empty tomb is reported to Peter and the Beloved Disciple (John 20:1–3). The imaginative gathering of a number of Easter appearance stories from the other Gospels and the Acts of the Apostles generated the longer ending (vv. 9–20). The shorter ending merely affirms that the women reported the message, and from then on salvation was proclaimed from east to west (vv. 9–10). However, these are only two of several textual traditions that have come down to us, and none of them has serious claim to authenticity.[13] They are the work of scribes, unhappy with the silence of the women in v. 8. The *textual* problem was created by a *theological* problem. Is it possible that, for Mark, the women did not proclaim the Easter message, with the result that the relationship between Jesus and the faltering disciples was never restored?

Given the agreement that the present endings (both vv. 9–20 and vv. 9–10) are the work of later scribes, those who claim that the original Gospel of Mark did not end at 16:8 suggest that the original ending was lost. In the light of the promise of a future encounter in Galilee (v. 7), and the agreement of Matthew, Luke, and John that the women announced the Easter message, these scholars claim that there must have been a further page to resolve the tension created by vv. 7–8.[14] However, the suggestion of a lost ending creates more difficulties than it resolves. The "lost ending" solution depends upon a number of well-nigh impossible hypotheses. Perhaps the original ending was contained in a self-standing page in what we call a codex, an ancient predecessor of what we now recognize as a book. It was formed by sewing a number of separate pages down a spine so that the pages could be opened, just as we open a modern book.[15] As with our much-loved and often-used books, wear and tear may detach the first or the last page. How often the front or the back cover of our favorite book suffers damage. But it is very unlikely that the Gospel of Mark was originally written in a codex. That form used for the preservation of texts came into Christian usage very early, but probably not for the original autographs of the New Testament texts.[16]

It is more likely that the very first "Gospel of Mark" was written on a scroll, not a codex. A scroll is an unbroken long piece of smoothed and specially prepared papyrus, forming one sheet.[17] It was stored as a roll and read by unrolling the scroll to find the relevant passage, as Jesus is reported to have done in the synagogue in Nazareth (see Luke 4:16–20). It is possible that the last part of the original manuscript, a scroll, was torn off or became worn and tattered from continual unfolding and folding, just as the last page of a codex might have become detached. Although it's more difficult to lose the end of a scroll than the last page of a codex, wear and tear on a much-used scroll may have damaged its final several inches. If the original ending of the Gospel of Mark was lost in this way, then we must accept that the loss of the closing section of the scroll would have taken place *with the original autograph of the Gospel of Mark*. It is unlikely that the community that received the original scroll containing the Gospel of Mark would inadvertently allow the ending of this precious document to disappear. It had to have happened with the original scroll because, even if there was only one other scroll that contained a copy of the whole Gospel, including the supposed "lost ending," some trace of it would be found in later copies. It is difficult to imagine that before even a single copied version of the original Gospel of Mark came into existence, the ending of *the original* was *inadvertently* torn off and nothing was done to retrieve it. Is it possible that no one noticed the loss of the Gospel's ending? It would only take one copy of the original Mark, containing the so-called "lost ending," to be in existence for something of that ending to be present in an ancient manuscript tradition, but we have no such evidence.[18]

We must thus face the fact that our present "endings" to the Gospel of Mark, vv. 9–20 or vv. 9–10 in our printed translations, were not part of the original manuscript, and that the idea of a "lost ending" is very difficult to imagine. Thus, for the purposes of our narrative reading of Mark's resurrection account, we must make sense of Mark 16:1–8 as a self-standing literary unit bringing the Gospel to conclusion. Every effort must be made to understand the author's literary and theological reasons for closing his Gospel with the fear, flight, and silence of the women (v. 8).[19]

The Setting: An Empty Tomb (vv. 1–4)

The link between the time and the characters in the passion account and the events that take place "when the Sabbath was past" has already been noticed. The narrator reports that they brought spices so that they might go and anoint Jesus' dead body. Joseph of Arimathea had buried Jesus without the usual washing and anointing of the body in 15:46. A hint of Jesus' burial without anointing appeared in Jesus' interpretation of the unknown woman's gesture in 14:8: "She has anointed my body beforehand for burying." However, the notion of returning, some thirty-six hours after a death by crucifixion, to anoint a body that has been entombed without embalming has been seized upon by the critics as an indication of the implausibility of the motivation for the women's visit to the tomb. Historically speaking, the objection is sound, and the issue of the anointing disappears immediately from the narrative. Both Matthew (28:1) and Luke (24:1) eliminate the bringing of spices *to anoint the body*, although Luke retains a reference to spices.

But these historical-critical objections devote too little attention to Mark's narrative agenda. A motivation flowing from earlier parts of the narrative, especially Jesus' anointing before his passion (see 14:8) and his hurried burial (15:46), has been introduced by Mark to bring the women to the site of Jesus' burial.[20] Mark has the women come to the tomb to render respect to the person whom they have seen slain (15:40–41) and buried (15:47), and in this they show that they are not prepared for what they discover. "For all its strangeness, from the Markan standpoint this notice serves to show that motivated as they were by ordinary desires, they had not the slightest expectation from the human side of the amazing divine sequel."[21]

The women proceed to the site of the tomb "very early on the first day of the week." The day is Sunday, thus fulfilling the repeated use of "third day" language across the Gospel (see 8:31; 9:31; 10:34; 14:58; 15:29). The time of the day is just after sunrise: "when the sun had risen" (v. 2). The remark about the in-breaking of daylight may be more than an innocent remark to inform the reader/listener on the time of day. The rising of the sun might indicate that something more than the women imagine, quite outside their control, is about to be revealed. Mark 16:2 is a first indication to a reader/listener that the darkness that enveloped the earth as the agonized Son called out to the Father asking why he had abandoned him (see 15:33–37) has been overcome. The close connection between the passion narrative and the report of the Easter events is maintained: light is dawning as God enters the story.[22] On their way to the tomb the women ask one another who will roll away the stone covering the opening into the tomb (v. 3; see 15:46). Why did they not ask this question before they set out on their journey with the express purpose of anointing the body (see v. 1)?[23] The narrative provides the answer in v. 4: if three women were aware that they would not be able to roll back the stone, it must have been very large.[24] The narrator announces that such was the case (see v. 4b).

God's action has already overcome the women's difficulty. Raising their eyes, they saw that the stone *had been rolled back* (v. 4a). The passive form of the perfect tense of the verb indicates that God had already entered the story. Biblical narratives often use the passive mood of a verb, without mentioning the agent, to hint that God, who remains unnamed, is active in what is described: "the stone has been rolled back." By whom? Grammarians call this use of the verb the "divine passive." There is no one else who could have rolled back the stone except God, to whom Jesus cried out in anguish in his dying moments (15:34). The divine passive is used to extend the first hint provided by the rising of the sun as the women went to the tomb. The exaggerated use of two verbs to tell of the women's raising their eyes and seeing (16:4a: "and looking up they saw") heightens the solemnity of the moment. This is no ordinary seeing. The women may not be aware of it, but the reader/hearer senses in this exaggerated "seeing" the hint of a sight of the revelation of God's action.[25] The narrator then confirms what the reader/listener suspected on overhearing the women's discussion over who would roll back the stone: "it was very large" (v. 4b; see v. 3). The event of God's intervention is in the past. The women see what God has already done. The scene is set for the second step in the Markan resurrection account. The most important character has entered the narrative. Not named, God has overcome the darkness and has opened the seemingly impossible to open (vv. 2–4).[26]

The Easter Proclamation (vv. 5–7)

Three stages mark the central section of the brief narrative: a description of the young man in the tomb and the women's reaction (v. 5), the proclamation that God has raised Jesus (v. 6), and the women's commission to tell the disciples of Jesus' going before them into Galilee (v. 7). On penetrating the tomb, the women see a young man seated on the right side of the tomb, dressed in a white robe. The response of the women is amazement. The Greek verb used is already strong, and Mark has added a prefix to it to further strengthen the impact of the verb *to be amazed.* Literally, the women are "amazed out of themselves." The sense of something that is greater than the human mind and experience can grasp is conveyed as the women's reaction matches traditional responses to the presence of God in a theophany.[27] The young man, and only the young man, on the right side of the tomb, announces that the tomb is empty, before even a word is spoken.[28] They do not find the body of Jesus but a young man.

It is almost universally accepted that the young man dressed in a white robe is an angelic figure (see 2 Macc 3:26, 33; Tob 5:9; Mark 9:3; Acts 1:10; 10:30; Rev 6:11; 7:9, 13; Josephus, *Ant.* 5.277).[29] He is a messenger from God. This is no doubt true, but the reader/hearer recalls the earlier reference to the "young man" in 14:51–52. He was a symbol of the failed disciples who fled from Gethsemane in fear, naked in their nothingness as they separated themselves from Jesus at his arrest. Unable to deny themselves, take up the cross, and follow him (see 8:34), despite their protestations that they would die for him (see 14:31), they abandon Jesus to his solitary death.[30] The clothing of the young man in 16:5 is different. The young man in Gethsemane left "a linen cloth" (Greek: *sindonē*) in the hands of Jesus' assailants when he ran away in fear (14:52). The young man in the tomb is dressed in "a white robe" (16:5; Greek: *stolēn leukēn*). But the dead body of Jesus was wrapped in a *sindonē* (15:46), and now there is no sign in the tomb of this garment of death. The young man in the garden was initially "clothed" (14:51) but ran away "naked" (14:52). The young man in the tomb is "clothed," and the verb used in 14:51 returns in 16:5. At this stage of the story, however, there is no indication that his white robe will be snatched from him.

The verbal links are too many, and the passages follow one another too closely within the story, for these links between the "young man" (Greek: *neaniskos*) who ran away and the "young man" (Greek: *neaniskos*) in the empty tomb to be totally irrelevant for a careful reader/listener (14:51–52; 15:46; 16:5). No doubt the primary meaning of the text is that the women encounter a heavenly figure in an empty tomb, and this figure announces the Easter message to them (see v. 6). However, it also contains a hint that the disciples, whose flight and fear have been judged in the story of the young man who fled naked in 14:51–52, have not been dismissed from the story. God has entered the story, and his messenger, dressed in a white robe, will announce what

God has done to the one who had been laid in the tomb (v. 6). As God has transformed the death of Jesus by raising him from the dead, discipleship may be reestablished and nakedness covered (see 14:51–52). The reader/listener will find that the disciples and Peter are named in v. 7, called to "see" Jesus in Galilee, just as he promised they would in the midst of their earlier confusion and failure (see 14:28). The case must not be overstated, as the function of the young man is not to act as a symbol of "restored discipleship" but a hint that God's action can reverse failure.[31] As God has done with the apparent failure of Jesus, so can he do for the disciples who have failed as they fled in fear (14:51–52), as they betrayed their Master (14:10–11, 43–46), and as they denied him (14:53, 66–72).[32]

The young man announces an Easter message that focuses upon the transforming power of God. Paralleling biblical theophanies, he urges the women not to be afraid (v. 6a). In a carefully constructed sentence the pre-Easter Jesus, known by the women who followed him from Galilee and who watched his death (see 15:40–41), is described: "You are seeking Jesus, the Nazarene, who was crucified" (16:6a). They have known Jesus, and they have witnessed his crucifixion, but that situation has changed. Two of them who watched the crucifixion from afar (15:40–41) also saw where they laid him (15:47). They are asked to look again: "He is not here; see the place where they laid him" (v. 6c). At the center of the proclamation, explaining the transformation of the women's experience of the death (15:40–41) and the burial (15:47), lies the action of God: "He has been raised!" (v. 6b). Another divine passive appears in the story (see v. 4). The aorist tense of the verb, indicating a decisive action that has already taken place, announces that God had entered the story of Jesus before the women appeared on the scene. Human experience and expectation have been transcended by the action of God.[33]

The question asked of God by Jesus from the cross, "My God, my God, why have you forsaken me?" (15:34), has been answered. Jesus has not been forsaken. Unconditionally obedient to the will of God (see 14:36), Jesus has accepted the cup of suffering. On the cross he is Messiah, King of Israel, and Son of God (see 15:32, 39). God's never-failing presence to his obedient Son leads to the definitive action of God: he has been raised! The apparent failure of Jesus has been reversed by the action of God, who has raised Jesus from death. The women are told to look at the place where they laid him. The opponents of Jesus crucified him, and they placed his body in a tomb ("look at the place where *they* laid him"). It could appear that *they* have had their victory, but *they* have been thwarted. He has been raised, and the existence of the Gospel indicates that there is a community of believers whose coming into being depends upon God's action. Jesus' prophecy that the rejected stone would become the foundation stone of a new Temple of God has proved true (see 12:11–12; 14:58; 15:29).

The existence of a future Markan community, promised by Jesus in the passion narrative as a "new Temple" (14:57–58; 15:29, 38–39; see 11:20–25; 12:10–11) depends upon those who have carried the story of Jesus away from the time of Jesus into the time and place of the Markan community and beyond. During the life and ministry of Jesus the disciples were commissioned for that task (see 3:13–14; 6:7–13) and told that before the end of time the Gospel would be preached to all nations (13:10).[34] They have disappeared from the story, fleeing in fear, naked in their nothingness (14:50–52). The young man commissions the women to announce a message to failed disciples. The promise of the restoration of these disciples was first made by Jesus to his disciples as they walked away from their last meal: "After I am raised up, I *will go* [future tense] before you into Galilee" (14:28). A hint that this promise was to be realized was found in the presence of a young man in the empty tomb (16:5), reversing the parabolic comment upon the fleeing disciples (see 14:50) in the episode of the young man who fled in fear, naked (14:51–52). The future tense of 14:28 is now rendered as a present tense in the young man's instruction to the women. They are to tell the disciples of Jesus and Peter that "he *is going* [present tense] before you into Galilee, as he told you" (v. 7). Jesus' ministry began in Galilee (1:14–15). He called the disciples, and they began their mission in Galilee (2:13–14; 3:13–14; 6:6b–30). They are to return to the place of their enthusiastic beginnings and resume their mission in the place that Isaiah called "Galilee of the Gentiles" (Isa 9:1).[35]

In 10:32 the reader/listener learned that the disciples were on the way toward Jerusalem because Jesus "was going before them," leading them to the place of his passion, death, and resurrection. His promise, that he would later lead them away from the city of their fear and failure so that they might see him (14:28), will be fulfilled (16:7).[36] The stage is set for an encounter in Galilee where failure will be forgiven and discipleship restored.[37] Despite their fear (4:40; 6:50; 9:32; 10:32), failure (4:35–41; 5:16, 31; 6:7–30, 35–36, 45–52; 8:4, 14–21, 31–33; 9:5–6, 28–29, 32–34, 38–41; 10:35–41; 11:9–10), and flight (14:50), they will see him there, as he had promised (16:7; see 14:28).

The Failure of the Women (v. 8)

This promise appears to be thwarted by the last line of the Gospel: "And they went out and fled from the tomb; for trembling and astonishment had come upon them; and they said nothing to anyone, for they were afraid" (v. 8). The women, who had overcome the scandal of the cross, by looking on from afar as Jesus died (see 15:40–41), and had watched where he was buried (15:47), have not been able to overcome the scandal of the empty tomb and the Easter proclamation. They have joined the disciples in flight (see 14:50, 52) and fear (see 4:41; 6:50; 9:32; 10:32). Like Peter, they have graduated, following "from a distance" (15:40; see 14:54), to final failure (16:8; see 14:66–72). Does this mean that there is, in Mark's view of things, no vision of the resurrected Jesus, and that the disciples are still waiting for his return?[38] The very existence of the Markan community, receiving and passing on this gospel story, makes that option unlikely. Many have suggested that the silence of the women is a form of Markan apologetic, allied to the idea of the messianic secret. On the basis of the Pauline evidence (see 1 Cor 15:3–5), it is claimed that nothing was known of the empty tomb in earlier traditions. Mark invented the silence of the women to explain this lack of knowledge. Others have focused upon the emotional experience of the women: "trembling and astonishment had come upon them." These emotions often accompany the experience of the grandeur of the divine. In this understanding the fear and flight are an indication of holy awe in the face of the numinous wonder of the resurrection.[39]

The women's sharing of the fear and flight of the disciples must be given its full importance. Before them, the disciples in the story had steadily increased in their experience of fear (see 4:41; 5:36; 6:50; 9:32; 10:32), and they finally broke their oneness with him when they fled (14:50; see 3:14). The association of the experience of the women with that of the disciples is too important and too obvious to be subsumed into the themes of the absence of Jesus, an apologetic for general ignorance concerning the tomb, or the more theological explanation of fear and trembling in the face of the action of God in Jesus. There is doubtless an important element of the numinous in the reaction of the women to the words of the young man in vv. 6–7, but there can be no missing Mark's primary intention. The odd but dramatic ending of a book with the words "for they were afraid" is not an indication that there must have been a longer ending.[40] It drives home, with considerable force, the women's sharing in one of the fundamental aspects of the disciples' failure to follow Jesus to the cross: fear (see 4:41; 6:50; 9:32; 10:32). Mark indicates that, in the end, the women who have followed Jesus through the experience of the cross to the grave finally join the other disciples in the fear and flight of their failure (14:50–52).

Does that mean that the Gospel ends in unresolved failure on the part of all who have followed Jesus? In one sense, such is the case, but to read this failure independently of the earlier parts of the story would lead to a misunderstanding of the Gospel of Mark. The ending of the Gospel must be understood in the light of the story as a whole, and especially as a return to the prologue (1:1–13). As the Gospel opened, the reader/hearer was provided with all the information necessary to understand who Jesus was and what God was doing through him for humankind. The prologue to the Gospel is unashamedly full of confessions of faith in the person of Jesus of Nazareth. However, *the reader/listener* is the only one who hears these confessions. The characters in the story are not standing by, listening. The narrator tells *the reader/hearer* that Jesus is the Christ (1:1), the Lord (v. 3), the mightier one (v. 7), the one who will baptize with the Holy Spirit (v. 8), the beloved Son in whom God is well pleased (v. 11). Only the reader/hearer recognizes that Jesus' presence in the wilderness, with the wild animals and served by angels, recalls God's original design for humankind, told in the story of Adam and Eve. God's original created order has been restored in the person of Jesus of Nazareth (vv. 12–13).[41]

The beginning (1:1–13) and the end (16:1–8) of the Gospel of Mark address the reader/listener. Throughout the story the reader/listener has followed the disciples, as they steadily fell further from the design God had for his Son and for those who follow him (see 8:34—9:1). They have abandoned him (14:50), betrayed him (14:43–45), and denied him (14:66–72). They have ignored Jesus' command to "watch" with him across the passion (13:35–37). Jesus has unflinchingly accepted God's will, cost what it may (see 14:36). The voice of God, summoning the disciples to listen to his obedient Son (9:7), has gone unheeded. Only the women, who have been with him since his days in Galilee, have been present at the cross (15:40–41), at the burial (15:47), and at the empty tomb (16:1–7). But in the end they join the disciples in their trembling, astonishment, fear, and flight (v. 8; see 14:50). In the light of the information provided in 1:1–13 *the Christian reader* is asked to reassess God's design, outlined in 1:1–13, on arrival at the conclusion of the story of Jesus in 16:1–8. If 1:1–13 served as a prologue to the Gospel of Mark, 16:1–8 is its epilogue. The action and the design of God are again at center stage.

Mark 16:1–8 is the masterstroke of a storyteller who, up to this point, has relentlessly pursued the steady movement to failure of all the male disciples. The evidence of the tradition (seen in the Gospels of Matthew [Matt 28:1–10], Luke [Luke 24:1–12] and John [John 20:1–3]) indicates that women were the first witnesses of the Easter event and reported an Easter message to the unbelieving and discouraged disciples. This was well known by members of early Christian communities. In this, Matthew, Luke, and John (each in his own way) are closer to what happened on that Sunday morning. Well before the Gospel of Mark appeared, Paul had passed on an even earlier tradition that described appearances of the risen Jesus (1 Cor 15:3–8).[42] *But Mark has changed the story.* Why has Mark taken a well-known tradition and altered it so radically?

There is something profoundly Pauline in what Mark is trying to do as he takes away all initiative from human beings and places it with God.[43] As with the promises of Jesus' forthcoming death and resurrection (8:31; 9:31; 10:33–34), the promises of 14:28 and 16:7 will be fulfilled. *What Jesus said would happen, will happen.* Challenged by his enemies to prophesy (14:65), the failure of the disciples (14:50; see v. 27), the betrayal of Judas (14:43–46; see vv. 17–21), and the denials of Peter (14:66–72; see vv. 30–31), his arrest, his trials, and his crucifixion have all shown that Jesus' predictions come true. The *reader/hearer* has every reason to believe that the promises of 14:28 and 16:7 *have already come true*. But Jesus' meeting with the disciples and Peter in Galilee does not take place within the limitations of the story. It cannot, because the women do not obey the word of the young man. They, like the disciples, fail. As with the disciples, they flee in fear (16:8).

When and how does Jesus' meeting with the failed disciples, women and men, take place? The answer to that question cannot be found *in the story*, but the *very existence of the story* tells the reader/hearer that *what Jesus said would happen, did happen.* The Gospel of Mark, with its faith-filled prologue telling of God's design for the human situation in the gift of his Son (1:1–13) addresses a believing community. The young man repeats the promise of Jesus, first made in 14:28. He instructs the women that the disciples "will see" the risen Jesus in Galilee (16:7). The readers and listeners know that what Jesus says will happen, does happen. The disciples and Peter did see Jesus in Galilee, as he had promised (14:28; 16:7). As Jesus' prophecies come true (see 8:31; 9:31; 10:32–34; 12:11–12; 14:17–21, 27–31), the believing reader accepts that the promise of 14:28 and 16:7 also came true. There is no record of any such encounter *within the narrative*. It is not required, as the believing community has the Word itself: "Jesus has been raised" (16:6). If the promise of 14:28 and 16:7 had been thwarted, there would be no Christian community, and thus no Gospel of Mark, read and heard within the community. "This is the end of Mark's story, because it is the beginning of discipleship."[44]

Explanation of the Enigma of Failure

The explanation of the enigma of the failure of the women in 16:8 lies in Mark's desire to instruct his readers/listeners that the encounter between the risen Jesus and the failed disciples did not take place because of the success of the women. As the disciples failed (14:50–52), so also the women failed (16:8). In the end, *all human beings fail*...but God succeeds. God has raised Jesus from the dead (16:6); the Father has not abandoned the Son (15:34). The same God will also raise the disciples, men and women, from their failure. They will see the risen Lord in Galilee, but not because the disciples or the women succeed. The event that bridged the gap between the end of the Gospel of Mark and the community that heard it and read it took place because of the initiative of God, and not the success of men or women. The Christian community that produced and received the Gospel of Mark existed because of the initiative of God. The promise of the Gospel's prologue (1:1–13) is fulfilled in the action of God described in its epilogue (16:1–8) and experienced by believing readers of the Markan story.

The epilogue to the Gospel of Mark maintains its relevance. The Easter proclamation, "He has been raised" (v. 6), the promise that Jesus was going before his disciples into Galilee (v. 7), and the failure of the women to speak to anyone because they, like the disciples before them, fled in fear (16:6–8; see 14:50), point beyond the limitations of the Markan story to the existence of a believing Christian community. The prologue to the Gospel (1:1–13) informed the reader/hearer that Jesus was the Christ (1:1), the Lord (v. 3), the mightier one (v. 7), one who would baptize with the Holy Spirit (v. 8), the beloved Son of God (v. 11), restoring God's original creative design (vv. 12–13). The original Markan community accepted this confession of faith and attempted to live as authentic disciples of Jesus, taking up their cross, receptive servants of all, in imitation of Jesus (see 8:31—10:44), who came to serve and not be served, and to lay down his life (10:45). Yet, in human terms, the disciples, both men and women, fail to follow Jesus through the cross to resurrection. In the same human terms even Jesus failed, crying out in anguish from the cross (15:34). But Jesus' apparent failure is his victory. On the cross he is King, Messiah, and Son of God (see 15:26, 31–32), and God has entered the story by raising his Son from the dead: "He has been raised" (16:6b). He is no longer in the place where they laid him (v. 6c).

Mark believes and wishes to communicate that the christological claims of the prologue (1:1–13) have been vindicated by the story of the suffering and crucified Jesus, especially by means of the Easter proclamation of the epilogue (16:1–8). The affirmation of God's project by means of the prologue (1:1–13) and the epilogue (16:1–8) also points to God's vindication of failed disciples.[45] The original readers of the Gospel of Mark, aware of their fragility, were encouraged by a story that told of the inability of the original disciples, men and women, to overcome their fear and follow Jesus through the cross to resurrection (14:50; 16:8). But as God has transformed the failure of Jesus by the resurrection (16:6), his promise to the failing disciples of a meeting in Galilee (14:28; 16:7) has also come about. God, and not human beings, generated the new Temple, built upon the rejected cornerstone (see 12:10–11; 14:57–58; 15:29, 38). The existence of the Gospel and its original intended readership are proof of that fact.[46]

The accomplishment of Jesus' promises is not found *in the text*. The existence of the Markan community and its story of Jesus indicate that it is taking place *among the readers and hearers of the text*, in the experience of the original readers and hearers of the Gospel of Mark. But that is not the end of the process. The proclamation of the Gospel of Mark in fragile Christian communities, experiencing their own versions of fear and flight, for almost two thousand years, suggests that the accomplishment of the promise of 14:28 and 16:7 continues in the Christian experience of the subsequent readers (and hearers) of the Gospel. What Jesus promised (14:28; 16:7), happened for the Markan community and continues to happen among generations of fragile followers of Jesus. As Christian disciples continue to fail and flee in fear, they are told that God's action in and through the risen Jesus overcomes all such failure. Jesus is going before them into Galilee. There they will see him. The conclusion to Mark's Gospel is not a message of failure but a resounding affirmation of God's design to overcome all imaginable human failure (see 16:1–8) in and through the action of God's beloved Son (see 1:1–13). Words addressed to the struggling disciples at the transfiguration are addressed to all who take up this Gospel: "Listen to him" (9:7).

An Appendix: Mark 16:9–20

The Gospel of Mark closed with the flight of the frightened women in 16:8. Paradoxically, although it is certain that the author of Mark 1:1—16:8 played no part in the composition of 16:9–20, many Christian lectionaries use this passage, added late in the second century to the original Gospel, as the Gospel Reading for the Feast of St. Mark on April 25.[47] The presence of the passage in the lectionaries, therefore, calls for a comment, despite the fact that the aim of this study is to trace the literary and theological argument of the resurrection of the Messiah in the Gospel of Mark that originally concluded with 16:1–8.[48] What follows serves as a guide to understand and interpret the "appendix" to the Gospel of Mark.[49]

The Christian communities of the second century that received the Gospel of Mark also received the other Gospels and the Acts of the Apostles. These narrative proclamations of the saving action of God through the life, death, and resurrection of Jesus witnessed to resurrection appearances and to Jesus' commissioning of the founding disciples.

The Gospels were transmitted from one generation to another, and from one location to another, in both a written and an oral form, as many early Christians would not have been "readers" in the modern sense of being able to read texts (if they could afford to have them). They were thus "listeners" to the story as it was told or even performed.[50] The desire to preserve and transmit texts regarded as important to the emerging Christian Church sometimes led to the further desire on the part of the copyists to improve upon the text they received. Most alterations to the texts are not deliberate, but rather the result of human error that naturally creeps into the arduous task of copying a long script by hand. At worst, they reflect the desire of a scribe to make the text grammatically or logically more consistent.[51]

Mark 16:9–20 has been added to a narrative that originally concluded with 16:1–8. It is the only example of such an interpretative addition to any of the Gospels. The only other passage that might be suggested as a parallel to Mark 16:9–20 is John 21:1–25. But the final chapter of John's Gospel is not an "appendix," added to a narrative that originally closed with John 20:1–31. There is no evidence in our ancient textual witnesses that the Gospel of John ever circulated without 21:1–25. As we will have occasion to see in chapter 4, it was added to a narrative that had originally concluded with 20:30–31 by those responsible for John 1:1—20:31 before the Gospel ever appeared. There has never been a Gospel of John without 21:1–25. It is not an appendix, added by a later scribe, but an "epilogue," added later to respond to issues left unresolved by 1:1—20:31.[52]

The author of Mark 16:9–20 selected from across the other Gospels and the Acts of the Apostles. He developed a synthetic description of many actions of the risen Lord reported elsewhere: the response of the disciples, a final commission, a report of Jesus' ascension, a summary description of the success of the disciples' mission, and the validating signs that accompanied it.[53] The most obvious elements are:

v. 9: The appearance to Mary Magdalene alone (see John 20:11–18), and her description as "from whom he [Jesus] had cast out seven demons" (see Luke 8:2).

v. 10: The mourning of the disciples, whose hopes have been dashed (see Luke 24:19–24).

vv. 11: The disciples display lack of belief in the risen Lord (see Luke 24:11, 41; Matt 28:17).

v. 12: Two disciples on the road (see Luke 24:13–35).

v. 14: Jesus reproaches the disciples for their lack of belief (see Luke 24:25, 37; John 20:19, 26).

v. 15: Jesus gives the disciples a commission (see Matt 28:19; Luke 24:46–49; Acts 1:8; see also John 20:21–23).

v. 16: Belief brings salvation and unbelief leads to condemnation (see John 3:18, 36; 12:44–50; 20:22–23, and passim).

v. 17: Jesus promises the gift of tongues to future missionaries (see Acts 2:4; 10:46).

v. 18: He also promises that they will be protected against the dangers of serpents and poisoning (see Acts 28:3–5).

v. 19: Jesus ascends (see Luke 24:51; Acts 1:2, 9).

v. 20: A general summary of the activity of the missionaries that betrays knowledge of the missionary activity reported in Acts (see the detail of Acts 2:5–13; 28:3–5, and the many similarities across Acts as a whole).[54]

The Lukan Emmaus story (Luke 24:13–35) and the Matthean great commission (Matt 28:16–20) have played an important role in the development of vv. 9–20. In addition to this systematic exploitation of the themes of failure, presence of Jesus to those who are failing, and the commission, which have their origins in Luke 24 and Matthew 28, there are also indications of contact with a number of details only found in John 20.[55]

The Purpose of Mark 16:9–20

The author was not unintelligent. Despite his culling of episodes from other narrative material in the New Testament, in vv. 9–20 he has extended certain themes that appeared regularly across the Gospel of Mark. Most obvious are the themes of the failure and lack of faith of the disciples (see vv. 11, 13, 14), and the theme of mission (vv. 15–18, 20).

However close to Matthew 28:19 Jesus' words in Mark 16:15 may appear, they continue (with a Matthean flavor) the words of the Markan Jesus: "First the gospel must be preached to all the nations" (Mark 13:10). A further, perhaps more subtle theme that continues into the conclusion is the ultimate success of Jesus' never-failing presence to the ever-failing disciples (v. 20).

There were at least three major "purposes" for the construction and addition of Mark 16:9–20:

1. The most fundamental purpose was to overcome the scandal of the flight and the silence of the women. Matthew, Luke, and John all report the commission given to women (a woman in John) at the tomb (in Luke by two men, in Matthew and John by Jesus himself). In all cases the women fulfill their commission: they announce the Easter message. The absence of this sequence of events in the Gospel of Mark was unacceptable. It was clear from the other Gospels, and from Paul (see 1 Cor 15:3–8) that Mark's ending, as it came to a second-century author, was factually incorrect. He resolved the problem by means of the addition of 16:9–20.

2. He has continued themes from the Gospel of Mark (the fragile disciples and the theme of mission) but is strongly determined by his own situation in a second-century Christian Church, increasingly involved in the Gentile mission. The silence of the women in v. 8 had to be transformed to give authoritative missionary instruction from the risen Jesus to fragile disciples now involved in that mission.[56]

3. The missionaries must be encouraged. For this reason the Gospel of Mark, as handed on by the author responsible for vv. 9–20, concludes with a passage that reports three resurrection appearances, but which, in effect, is articulated in five stages, all ultimately directed to the missionary situation of the second-century Christian Church:

a. A first resurrection appearance to Mary Magdalene, leading to the unbelief of the disciples (vv. 9–11).

b. A second resurrection appearance to two disciples on the road in the country, which also leads to the unbelief of the disciples (vv. 12–13).

c. An appearance of Jesus to the disciples during which he upbraids the disciples for their continuing failure (v. 14).

d. At this final appearance, Jesus commissions his disciples for a universal mission, promising salvation, charismatic gifts, and protection for all who believe (vv. 15–18).

e. Jesus ascends to heaven, to the right hand of the Father, and the disciples go forth and preach everywhere, supported by the presence of Jesus from the right hand of the Father (vv. 19–20).

The Message of Mark 16:9–20

Fundamental to the missionary activity of the early Church was the conviction that the missionaries were doing the work of the Lord. Thus, the first step in addressing the missionary Church is to show that (contrary to the silence and flight of 16:8) the conclusion to the Gospel of Mark established contact between the risen Lord and the disciples, however fragile they have appeared to be across the Gospel of Mark as a whole. This is achieved with a certain clumsy skill. The clumsiness comes from the author's dependence upon already existing gospel narratives. But the theological relevance of vv. 9–11 and the repetition of the motif of appearance, announcement, and failure in vv. 12–13 must not be undervalued. These two reports of appearances of the risen Jesus address second-century missionaries (and no doubt Christian missionaries of all time), who struggle with their failures in faith and the ambiguities of the mission itself. Not even the disciples of Jesus believed in the proclamation that Jesus was alive, risen from the dead.

Borrowing from the Johannine (see John 20:19, 26) and perhaps the Lukan (see Luke 24:25, 37; Acts 1:10–11) traditions, the author reports that these disciples are so caught up in their mourning and weeping that they do not believe the proclamation of Mary Magdalene, to whom Jesus first appeared. They will not believe that he is alive and has been seen (vv. 9–11). This must have been an important matter as the author penned these lines. One failure to believe in an authentic witness to the risen Lord does not suffice. Using different characters, this time taken from the Lukan tradition, he reports a second time that the first disciples did not believe the witness of two disciples who meet Jesus while they are walking in the country (vv. 12–13; see Luke 24:13–35). The adroit repetition of appearance, proclamation, and lack of belief in vv. 9–11 and vv. 12–13 indicates the importance of belief that Jesus "was alive" (v. 11). The use of repetition makes the point forcibly: Jesus *is risen*, he *is alive*, and he *has appeared* to certain witnesses. However, the original disciples of Jesus do not believe these "first" witnesses (see v. 9).

In a fashion that recalls the Lukan and the Johannine resurrection appearances (Luke 24:36–43: an appearance and a meal in a room; John 20:19–23: an appearance in a room; 21:9–14: an appearance and a meal by the side of the lake), Jesus comes to the Eleven (the Twelve, less Judas) while they are at table. Despite the presence of the theme of the failure of the disciples in vv. 11–13, where it was highlighted twice, it appears here for a third time. There may well be a reminiscence of the disciples' response to Jesus' appearance to them on the mountain in Galilee in Matthew 28:17: "And when they saw him they worshiped him, but some doubted." The persistence of this theme, so central in the Gospel of Mark, into these verses added both to close the Gospel and to encourage and exhort missionaries reflects the ever-present reality of failure among believers (v. 14), perhaps present in vv. 9–20 because of the ongoing presence of sin, despite the saving events reported in the Gospel of Mark. Not only do the disciples refuse to believe in the witnesses of Jesus' resurrection, but succeeding generations also refuse to believe.

The commissioning of the disciples, reported in different forms across all other Gospels (see Matt 28:16–20; Luke 24:44–49; Acts 1:8; John 20:19–23), now follows. The command to go into the whole world and to preach the gospel to all creation is close to Matthew 28:16–20, where the universal lordship of the risen Lord lies behind the command to go out and teach everyone what Jesus has taught them (v. 15). Matthew 28 is under the eyes of the author who penned these verses, as baptism is seen as an important element in the response to the preaching of the gospel. However, baptism is something more than an initiation rite; it is an expression of belief.

The second-century missionary activity of the Church would have influenced the risen Lord's indication to the disciples of the fruits of their mission. There are no verbal links, but a Johannine ring sounds behind his words concerning the salvation of those who believe and whose faith is manifested in baptism. They will be saved, while those who do not believe will be condemned (see, for example, John 3:11–21, 31–36; 12:44–50). As vv. 9–20 will conclude with Jesus' departure from the disciples, his commission must also assure the missionaries, by means of signs, that despite Jesus' physical absence they are acting with his authority.[57] These signs are not unknown in the rest of the New Testament. Phenomena reported in the ministry of the disciples in Mark 6:7–13 (healing and casting out demons), the experience of Paul in Acts 28:3–5 (picking up serpents), the charismatic experiences of early Christian communities reflected in 1 Corinthians 12—14 (speaking in tongues), and other parallel experiences reported in the Acts of the Apostles (see Acts 2:5–13), are provided in vv. 17–18. Belief leads to the believers' ability to cast out demons and to speak in tongues, to be free from the poisonous bite of the serpent and from the poisonous potions made by human beings. Belief produces a security that only the risen Lord can assure. The language and experiences may come from the experience of Christians in the second Christian century, but they are not without a continuing relevance.

Aware that Jesus is no longer present to them as he was during his days on earth, the author tells of his departure to heaven (see Luke 24:50–53; Acts 1:1–2, 9), to sit at the right hand of God (see Ps 110:1; Mark 12:36; 14:62). From this position Jesus exercises the authority of his universal lordship and assures the ultimate success of those who believe in him (v. 19). Thus, there is a logical link between the statement on Jesus' ascension to the right hand of God in v. 19 and the report of the success of the preaching of the disciples "everywhere." Jesus may be absent, but his fragile disciples are empowered by signs that are evidence of the authority of the risen Lord, enabling them to perform successfully what they have been commanded to do. This is only possible because their absent Lord (see v. 19) is, in fact, "working with them" (v. 20). Looking back to vv. 17–18, the author recalls the prodigious signs that the believers were able to do and indicates that the authority of the absent Lord to his missionary Church is certified by these and other signs (v. 20).

Conclusion

The author responsible for vv. 9–20 must have spoken effectively to the Christian communities of the second century. Among several candidates, it is the Markan ending most widely represented in the textual tradition and accepted into the Christian canon. It resolved the enigmatic ending of the Gospel of Mark at 16:8; continued some of the themes central to the Gospel, especially disciples, failure, and mission; and finally, spoke effectively to a missionary Church of the second century. The enigmatic silence of the women is replaced by Jesus' appearances to Mary Magdalene, two disciples, and then the Eleven. Despite the weakness of their belief (vv. 9–14), vv. 9–20 assure success, the ongoing authority of the risen and ascended Jesus, and his constant protection for themselves and their converts (vv. 15–20). This is a comforting message.

The author used existing accounts of the risen Jesus' appearances, the commissioning of the disciples, and the missionary activity of the early Church to speak to the missionaries of his own time. But the author of 16:9–20 has betrayed one of the fundamental purposes of Mark, the original evangelist, whose version of the story of Jesus closed with the fear, flight, and silence of the women in 16:8. Rather than ask the *readers of the Gospel* to "fill the gap" left by the failure of the women in 16:8, especially by means of the promises of Jesus in 14:28 and 16:7, he provides all the "filling" that second-century readers might have needed. The message of vv. 9–20 is not without significance in the contemporary Christian Church, but the original author's fundamental point of view has been lost. Indeed, one could say that it has been betrayed by this added ending.

We must allow Mark to close his Gospel in the way he intended. The ending of the original Gospel at 16:8 comes as something of a shock to us, as it was to the first generations of Christians *and their scribes.* They knew of other endings to Jesus' story, and a pastiche of those endings now forms 16:9–20. But the original Mark has it right. The flight and silence of the women force the readers and listeners to ask where they stand, depending only upon the action of God to make divine sense of human nonsense. This message is challenging, and not particularly comforting...in the light of our ongoing failed attempts to determine our own future and God's ways within that future. Given that, it would be appropriate if we looked elsewhere in the Gospel of Mark for a reading that might better represent the shadowy figure behind this first and remarkable story of Jesus' life, teaching, death, and resurrection as we celebrate the Feast of St. Mark in our liturgies.

Notes

1. This statement was first made in 1892, in a footnote. It has been repeated time and again ever since. See Martin Kähler, *The So-Called Historical Jesus and the Historic, Biblical Christ*, trans. Carl E. Braaten (Philadelphia: Fortress, 1964), 80 n. 11.

2. The final chapter of this book reflects upon what the evangelists say about what the resurrection meant for Jesus, and what it meant for his followers.

3. Another important word of Jesus indicating the purpose of his self-gift in death is found in Mark 10:45: "For the Son of Man also came, not to be served, but to serve, and to give his life as a ransom for many." See also Gerald O'Collins, *Believing in the Resurrection: The Meaning and Promise of the Risen Jesus* (Mahwah, NJ: Paulist Press, 2012), 43–46. The English translations of the Greek are my own but depend heavily on my default text, the RSV.

4. See Francis J. Moloney, *The Gospel of Mark: A Commentary* (Grand Rapids, MI: Baker Academic, 2012), 276–79. Although not identical to what follows, see also the structure of 14:1—15:47 proposed by Joel Marcus, *Mark: A New Translation with Introduction and Commentary*, 2 vols., AB/AYB 27–27A (New York: Doubleday; New Haven, CT: Yale University Press, 1999–2009), 2:924–27. He also sees the interplay between Jesus and others in alternating scenes.

5. See Moloney, *Mark*, 299–300. Not all would agree with this assessment of the flight of the young man, and some exaggerated interpretations have appeared over the centuries. For a survey, see Marcus, *Mark*, 2:1124–25.

6. On the supper narrative in Mark, see Francis J. Moloney, *A Body Broken for a Broken People: Eucharist in the New Testament*, rev. ed. (Peabody, MA: Hendrickson, 1997), 31–56.

7. I am introducing here the cumbersome use of "reader/listener." I sometimes also refer to the reader and the hearer of the story. The Gospels emerged in a dominantly oral culture, as very few people "read." However, the stories were communicated effectively through an "audience." A few may have read, but most "listened" or "heard." The experience of *both* the reading and the listening "audiences" guaranteed the ongoing life of the gospel narratives. For an excellent summary of this issue, see Kelly R. Iverson, "Orality and the Gospels: A Survey of Recent Research," *CBR* 8 (2009): 71–106.

8. On the anguish of these cries from the cross, see Craig A. Evans, *Mark 8:27—16:20*, WBC 34B (Nashville, TN: Thomas Nelson, 2001), 506–8.

9. Although Matthew 26:1—27:66 depends heavily on Mark's simple structure of alternating scenes, first between the disciples and Jesus and then between the Romans and Jesus, this structure will be disturbed by some important Matthean additions. Luke's passion story is presented quite differently.

10. There is an exquisite interplay between the disciples *in the story* and the readers/hearers *of the story* in 9:10. The disciples are "discussing what rising from the dead meant," while the readers/hearers know that Jesus rose from the dead.

11. For a detailed reading of Mark 14:1—15:47, see Moloney, *Mark*, 275–336. Copious references to scholarly debates surrounding the Markan text and its interpretation can be found there.

12. This structure, with slight variations around vv. 7–8, is widely accepted. See Craig A. Evans, *Mark 8:27—16:20*, 533; Marcus, *Mark*, 2:1079–82; Brendan Byrne, *A Costly Freedom: A Theological Reading of Mark's Gospel* (Collegeville, MN: The Liturgical Press, 2008), 254–59.

13. The longer ending (vv. 9–20) is found in most manuscripts of the Gospel, but not in the oldest witnesses. Clement of Alexandria (ca. 150–ca. 215) and Origen (ca. 185–ca. 254) show no knowledge of it, and Eusebius (ca. 260–ca. 339) and Jerome (ca. 340–ca. 420) already regarded it as inauthentic. The shorter ending (vv. 9–10) is found in a considerable number of manuscripts of the seventh to the ninth century, generally as a preface to the longer ending. A third ending, called the "Freer Logion," is a gloss on 16:14 (in the longer ending) and is quoted by Jerome (347–420). It was also early, but not original.

14. For an up-to-date survey of the discussion, see Adele Y. Collins, *Mark*, Hermeneia (Minneapolis, MN: Fortress, 2004), 797–801.

15. See the brief description in David J. Trobisch, "Codex," *NIB* 1:697.

16. For a brief history of the use of the scroll and the codex in early Christian transmission of texts, see Jack Finegan, *Encountering New Testament Manuscripts: A Working Introduction to Textual Criticism* (London: SPCK, 1975), 27–29.

17. See the brief description in Joel E. Lemon, "Scroll," *NIB* 5:138.

18. A most important study that details the argument pursued here is James A. Kelhoffer, *Miracle and Mission: The Authentication of Missionaries and Their Message in the Longer Ending of Mark*, WUNT 2.112 (Tübingen: Mohr Siebeck, 2000).

19. See also Collins, *Mark*, 780–81, 799–801. Most contemporary critics accept that Mark intended to end his Gospel at 16:8. There are still a few dissenting voices. See, for example, John R. Donahue and Daniel J. Harrington, *The Gospel of Mark*, SP 2 (Collegeville, MN: The Liturgical Press, 2002), 460.

20. See Adele Y. Collins, *The Beginning of the Gospel: Probings of Mark in Context* (Minneapolis, MN: Fortress, 1992), 134–35.

21. Hugh Anderson, *The Gospel of Mark*, NCB (London: Oliphants, 1976), 354.

22. See also Marcus, *Mark*, 2:1083–84; Byrne, *Costly Freedom*, 254.

23. See Donahue and Harrington, *Mark*, 457–58.

24. As Craig A. Evans, *Mark 8:27—16:20*, 535, notes: "The three women assume that they do not possess the size and strength to roll the stone aside."

25. So also Marcus, *Mark*, 2:1084.

26. See Marcus, *Mark*, 2:1084; Byrne, *Costly Freedom*, 254–55. Eduard Schweizer, *The Good News according to Mark* (London: SPCK, 1971), 371, comments: "For man the large stone closes the tomb now and forever, and this makes the miraculous intervention of God which has already occurred so much more impressive." See also R. Alan Culpepper, *Mark*, SHBC (Macon, GA: Smyth & Helwys, 2007), 585.

27. See Marcus, *Mark*, 2:1085; Collins, *Mark*, 795–96; Donahue and Harrington, *Mark*, 458.

28. The origin of an empty tomb tradition is at the heart of many debates surrounding Mark 16:1–8. An empty tomb does not generate Easter faith. But, as we will consider in chapter 5, the antiquity of an empty tomb tradition is likely. See especially Dale C. Allison, Jr., *Resurrecting Jesus: The Earliest Christian Tradition and Its Interpretation* (London: T & T Clark, 2005), 198–375. For a contrary opinion (Mark invented the empty tomb tradition) see Collins, *Mark*, 781–82, and Allison's response in *Resurrecting*, 300–2.

29. See the evidence for this assembled in Raymond E. Brown, *The Death of the Messiah: From Gethsemane to the Grave: A Commentary on the Passion Narratives in the Four Gospels*, 2 vols., ABRL (New York: Doubleday, 1994), 1:299–300. See also Craig A. Evans, *Mark 8:27—16:20*, 536; Collins, *Mark*, 795–96; Marcus, *Mark*, 2:1085.

30. For this interpretation of 14:51–52, see Moloney, *Mark*, 299–300. On a possible connection between 14:50–51 and 16:5, see Collins, *Mark*, 795; Craig A. Evans, *Mark 8:27—16:20*, 535–36. Donahue and Harrington, *Mark*, 458,

make the connection but take it no further. Most reject the connection because of some of the exaggerated claims that have been made for the young man in 14:50–51. For a survey of those claims, see Marcus, *Mark*, 2:1124–25.

31. This is further enhanced if Marcus, *Mark*, 2:1085, is correct in suggesting that there is evidence that the location of the young man on the right side "is traditionally associated with power, victory, and auspiciousness."

32. This is nothing more than a hint. See also Culpepper, *Mark*, 585–87. Because too much is sometimes read into the parallels between 14:51–52 and 16:5 (see Brown, *The Death of the Messiah*, 1:299: "flights of imagination"), mainstream scholarship tends to reject any connection. Some have attempted to link the uses of the young man in 14:51–52 and 16:5 with baptismal symbolism. This is not called for. Collins, *Mark*, 795–96, claims that the "young man" represents Jesus symbolically and is also an interpreting angel.

33. Full strength must be given to the passive mood: "He has been raised" (Greek: *ēgerthē*). Mark's focus is upon the proclamation that God has raised Jesus, not on the fact of the empty tomb. The words of the young man in the tomb reflect a pre-Markan early Christian confession. See Marcus, *Mark*, 2:1085; Donahue and Harrington, *Mark*, 458.

34. Mark insists that the disciples are to leave Jerusalem as that is not where they are to exercise their ministry. They will be witnesses to the risen Jesus in Galilee, and this will lead them into a Gentile mission. See Donald Senior, "The Struggle to Be Universal: Mission as Vantage Point for New Testament Investigation," *CBQ* 46 (1984): 63–81.

35. See Senior, "The Struggle to Be Universal," 74–81; Marcus, *Mark*, 2:1086 (see also 1:171); Craig A. Evans, *Mark 8:27—16:20*, 539–40; Byrne, *Costly Freedom*, 256–57.

36. Sometimes too much is made of the use of the Greek verb *proagain*. Against a popular suggestion that the disciples are gathered in Galilee, waiting for the Parousia in the absence of Jesus, others have claimed that Jesus is going ahead of them as a shepherd (for example, Ernest Best, *Following Jesus: Discipleship in the Gospel of Mark*, JSNTSup 4 [Sheffield: JSOT Press, 1981], 199–203). Its primary meaning is to "lead forward" or to "go before," BDAG, 864, s.v. *proagō*). LSJ, 1466, s.v. *proagō*, also gives examples from classical literature of "escort on their way," but the meaning of "leading" is primary, and the only meaning given in BDAG. See also Collins, *Mark*, 796. That is what Jesus does in 10:32, promises to do in 14:28, and is announced as doing in 16:7 (see also 6:45; 11:9).

37. The singling out of Peter in v. 7 looks back to his denials and thus highlights the theme of failure. The women are to tell the disciples "and especially Peter." See Craig A. Evans, *Mark 8:27—16:20*, 537; Marcus, *Mark*, 2:1085–86.

38. This is the position followed by a number of recent scholars, especially Theodore J. Weeden, *Mark—Traditions in Conflict* (Philadelphia: Fortress, 1971), 111–16; Norman Perrin, *The Resurrection Narratives: A New Approach* (London: SPCK, 1977), 17–40.

39. This is the traditional solution to the problem, generally with reference back to the fear of the disciples at the transfiguration (see 9:6). See, for example, Vincent Taylor, *The Gospel according to St. Mark*, 2nd ed. (London: Macmillan, 1966), 609; Ronald H. Lightfoot, *The Gospel Message of St. Mark* (Oxford: Clarendon Press, 1950), 96–97. Most recently, see Collins, *Mark*, 801. She refers back to the presence of awe and the numinous throughout the Gospel.

40. It has often been claimed that a book could not end with the word *for* (Greek: *gar*). It is certainly a strange ending but should not be taken as impossible. Among many, see Lightfoot, *Gospel Message*, 80–97, and especially the study of Kelly R. Iverson, "A Further Word on Final *Gar*," *CBQ* 68 (2006): 79–94.

41. See Moloney, *Mark*, 38–41.

42. Paul's First Letter to the Corinthians was written from Ephesus about AD 54.

43. Fundamental to Pauline thought is the belief that God has saved sinful humankind by his free gift of grace, made available in and through the death and resurrection of Jesus Christ (see Rom 3:21–26). It is not so much a question of how good the believer might be, or how well he or she performs (although a life modeled on that of Jesus is demanded [see the "ethical excursus" of Romans 5:1—8:39]). What ultimately changes the relationship between God and the human story, lost since the fall of Adam, is the boundless goodness of God (Rom 5:12–21), made visible in Jesus Christ (see Rom 8:31–39).

44. Morna D. Hooker, *The Gospel according to St. Mark*, BNTC (London: A. and C. Black, 1991), 394. For a similar interpretation, see Robert C. Tannehill, "The Gospel of Mark as Narrative Christology," *Semeia* 16 (1980): 82–84; Thomas E. Boomershine, "Mark 16:8 and the Apostolic Commission," *JBL* 100 (1981): 234–39; Susan R. Garrett, *The Temptations of Jesus in Mark's Gospel* (Grand Rapids, MI: Eerdmans, 1998), 137–69; Sharyn Dowd, *Reading Mark: A Literary and Theological Commentary on the Second Gospel,* (Reading the New Testament (Macon, GA: Smyth & Helwys, 2000), 167–71; Byrne, *Costly Freedom*, 258–59.

45. See Morna D. Hooker, *Endings: Invitations to Discipleship* (Peabody, MA: Hendrickson, 2003), 3–4: "Tidy endings take us back to where we began: a skilful use of what literary critics call *inclusio* reminds us that it was, after all, the writer's purpose all along to lead us to precisely this point....The end which brings us back to the beginnings forms a satisfying conclusion."

46. On the perennial nature of the Markan message of the tension between success and failure among disciples, both women and men, see Elizabeth S. Malbon, "Fallible Followers: Women and Men in the Gospel of Mark," in *In the Company of Jesus: Characters in Mark's Gospel* (Louisville, KY: Westminster John Knox, 2000), 41–69.

47. In the Roman Catholic Lectionary, it is also the gospel reading for the commemoration of St. Francis Xavier, an optional Gospel for the Common of Pastors, the Mass for the Catechumenate and the Initiation of Adults to the Faith, and for occasional Masses for Priests, for ministers of the Church, for the spread of the gospel, and for the sick.

48. In 1546 the Council of Trent declared that Mark 16:9–20 was part of the Catholic canon of Sacred Scriptures. See the discussion of the relevance of this declaration in Eugene LaVerdiere, *The Beginning of the Gospel: Introducing the Gospel according to Mark*, 2 vols. (Collegeville, MN: The Liturgical Press, 1999), 2:332–33.

49. We will attend neither to the shorter ending added to 16:8, often printed in Bibles, nor the so-called Freer Logion. See above, note 13.

50. On the emerging discipline called "performance criticism," see the fine survey of Kelly R. Iverson, "Orality and the Gospels: A Survey of Recent Research," *CBR* 8 (2009): 71–106. See also Francis J. Moloney, "Mark as Story: Retrospect and Prospect," *Pacifica* 25 (2012): 1–11, especially 7–9.

51. See Kurt and Barbara Aland, *The Text of the New Testament: An Introduction to the Critical Editions and to the Theory and Practice of Modern Textual Criticism*, trans. Erroll F. Rhodes (Grand Rapids, MI: Eerdmans, 1987), 275–92.

52. See Francis J. Moloney, *The Gospel of John*, SP 3 (Collegeville, MN: The Liturgical Press, 1998), 545–68, and below, 17–26.

53. For a comprehensive study of the characteristics of the passage that display an author's deliberate attempt to bring the Gospel of Mark to a satisfactory conclusion, in greater conformity with Matthew, Luke, and John, see Kelhoffer, *Miracle and Mission*, 177–244. See also Collins, *Mark*, 802–18; Craig A. Evans, *Mark 8:27—16:20*, 540–51. For the purposes of this book I limit references to scholarship. Detailed discussion can be found in Moloney, *Mark*, 355–62, and in the fine study by Kelhoffer.

54. This list has been developed from Craig A. Evans, *Mark 8:27—16:20*, 546, and especially the comprehensive analysis of Kelhoffer, *Miracle and Mission*, 65–122. For a summary and an excellent chart, see 121–22. Kelhoffer argues that the author of vv. 9–20 had the other Gospels in front of him as he developed the ending.

55. See also Kelhoffer, *Miracle and Mission*, 123–50.

56. On the nature of the longer ending as an exhortation to missionaries, see Kelhoffer, *Miracle and Mission*, 473–80. See also William R. Telford, *The Theology of the Gospel of Mark*, New Testament Theology (Cambridge: Cambridge University Press, 1999), 144–45: "While the text has Jesus upbraid the disciples for their unbelief and hardness of heart, it has him commission the twelve nevertheless, and give them authority to carry out a mission to all the world, to Jews and Gentile alike."

57. For documentation indicating that miracles performed by believers, under instruction by the apostles, authenticated the preaching of the missionaries, see Kelhoffer, *Miracle and Mission*, 245–338.

CHAPTER TWO

The Resurrection of the Messiah according to Matthew

Matthew 27:62—28:20

Introduction

Matthew used the Gospel of Mark as a source and model for his story of Jesus. But Matthew has his own story to tell and his own theological perspective. This Gospel was designed to address other readers and listeners. But there is a strange tension within the Matthean story that is either resolved—or rendered more complex—by the narrative of Jesus' passion and resurrection, the concern of this chapter.

As the public life of Jesus opens, he appears to embrace the traditions of late-first-century Judaism, forging a close bond between his followers and the observance of the Law. He announces:

> Think not that I have come to abolish the law and the prophets; I have not come to abolish them, but to fulfill them. For truly, I say to you, till heaven and earth pass away, not an iota, not a dot will pass from the law until all is accomplished. (Matt 5:17–18)

The matter becomes more complex as we read further into the Gospel's report of Jesus' ministry. Jesus limits his disciples' mission to Israel alone. At the beginning of a long discourse that deals with the mission of the Church (10:1—11:1), he instructs his disciples, as he

33

sends them out: "Go nowhere among the Gentiles, and into no town of the Samaritans, but go rather to the lost sheep of the house of Israel" (10:5–6). A little later in the story he responds to the pleas of a Canaanite woman to heal her daughter: "I was sent only to the lost sheep of the house of Israel" (15:24). During his public ministry the Matthean Jesus limits his mission to Israel and exhorts his followers to live and teach with exactitude the Law of Israel (5:17–18). None of this was present in the Gospel of Mark.

But this view is compromised by Matthew's report of the healing of the Gentile centurion's servant (8:5–13). Although Jesus cures the servant of a Gentile soldier, the miracle is worked within the context of the lack of belief that Jesus finds in Israel (see 8:1–27). Jesus warns Israel:

> Truly, I say to you, not even in Israel have I found such faith.
> I tell you, many will come from east and west and sit at the
> table of Abraham, Isaac and Jacob while the sons of the king-
> dom will be thrown into the outer darkness; there men will
> weep and gnash their teeth. (vv. 10–12)

Despite Jesus' personal mission to Israel alone (15:24), he looks to a later time when God's chosen people will be "thrown into outer darkness" while others will "come from east and west." A regular reader of the Gospel of Matthew senses a tension between the ministry of Jesus, his limitation of mission and ministry to the Gentiles—even though a threat of eventual disappointment hangs over that ministry (8:10–12)— and the final words of the Gospel, where the risen Jesus sends out his disciples to "all nations" (28:16–20).

An important feature of any narrative is the way an author uses various aspects of "time" as the plot of the story unfolds. Matthew exploits this with skill.[1] The events in a narrative normally follow the chronological order in which they happen in any human story. This use of time is generally called "narrative time." But sometimes events from the past are recalled and drawn into the story to enrich the events of "narrative time" as they unfold. Two well-known examples of this are found in the story in the Gospel of John that tells of John the Baptist's experience at Jesus' baptism (John 1:32–34) and the fact that a man was born blind (9:1–5). The chronologically determined reporting of events (narrative time) is enriched by recalling events that took place *outside* that chronology, and *prior to it*. This practice of looking back into a time prior to the "narrative time" of the regular passing of events in a story is called "analepsis." Matthew, however, tells his story by introducing elements into his story that give a hint of something that *will happen in the future*. In all the Gospels, Jesus' predictions of his oncoming passion and resurrection (Mark 8:31; 9:31; 10:32–34; and parallels; John 3:14; 8:28; 12:32) interrupt the day-to-day events to look to Jesus' future. The technical term used for these interruptions into "narrative time" is "prolepsis."[2]

Jesus' words to his disciples in 5:17–18 come very early in Jesus' story. They open his Sermon on the Mount. However, these words look beyond the time line of the Sermon on the Mount and point to the future.

> Think not that I have come to abolish the law and the prophets; I have come not to abolish them but to fulfill them. For truly, I say to you, *till heaven and earth pass away, not an iota, not a dot, will pass from the law until all is accomplished.* [italics mine]

Some future "time" will come. There is the "now" of Jesus' preaching during his public ministry, but there is a moment "yet to come" when the present order of things will be changed: heaven and earth will pass away and all will be accomplished (v. 18). There is a time in the future *until* which every detail of the Mosaic Law must be observed: "*till heaven and earth pass away...until* all is accomplished."[3] When might that future time be? In the light of our understanding of Jesus' eschatological teaching, beginning in the Christian narrative tradition in Mark 13 and strongly affirmed in Matthew 24—25, most scholars read 5:17–18 as a reference to the Jewish notion of the end of all time. For the Matthean Christians, therefore, the Law must be observed in its entirety till the end of all time.[4]

This understanding of the future events referred to in 5:17–18 strengthens Jesus' limitation of his disciples' and his own preaching to the lost sheep of Israel (10:5–6; 15:24) and his hesitation before working two miracles for Gentiles (8:5–13; 15:21–28). All Christians are to observe every detail of the Jewish Law till the end of time.[5] But as we turn to a reading of Matthew's resurrection story, prefaced by the passion narrative, we will find some awkward contradictions within the narrative as Jesus dies (27:45–54), at his resurrection (28:2–4), and in Jesus' commissioning of the disciples (28:16–20). The risen Jesus' final words in the Gospel of Matthew send the disciples on a mission to the ends of the earth, promising that he will be with them till the close of the age. If the future time of 5:17–18 referred to the end of all time, the command of Jesus that the Jewish Law be perfectly observed, without changing even the tiniest detail, should still be in force in the post-Easter Matthean community, awaiting Jesus' final coming.[6] But something happens between Jesus' ministry and his final words that changes the perspective of 5:17–18: the death and resurrection of Jesus.[7]

Matthew's Passion Story

Matthew's passion narrative depends on his main source, the Gospel of Mark. "The Markan passion and Easter narrative is the only written source for Matthew 26—28 as a whole."[8] As this is the case, it is surprising that most major commentaries "give up" on an attempt to trace a possible literary and theological structure for the narrative.[9] This difficulty arises from a desire, on the part of the interpreters, to find neat divisions of approximately equal length, based on chronological and geographical changes. However, once the literary dependence upon Mark is recognized, the narrative drama generated by that literary shape can be recognized: Jesus' interaction with other characters in the story. Matthew *accepts* the Markan account and all that it suggests. Into this basic structure Matthew has inserted some passages not found elsewhere. He has also rewritten Mark's story on several occasions. These elements in the passion narrative give the story its unique Matthean twist.[10]

A schematic presentation of the story, based upon Mark's structure, and indicating the uniquely Matthean additions to Mark and reshaping of Mark can guide us.[11]

26:1–2: *Uniquely Matthean introduction*

[A] 26:3–5: The plot of the Jewish leaders.

    [B] vv. 6–13: The anointing of *Jesus.*

[A] vv. 14–16: Judas, *one of the Twelve*, joins the plot.

[B] vv. 17–19: *Jesus* prepares for a Passover meal.

[A] vv. 20–25: *Jesus* predicts the betrayal of Judas. **Only Matthew has Judas ask if he is the betrayer, and Jesus affirms that he is the one** (v. 25).

[B] vv. 26–30: *Jesus* shares the meal *with his disciples*. **Only Matthew adds to Jesus' words over the cup: "for the forgiveness of sins"** (v. 28).

[A] vv. 31–35: *Jesus* predicts the denials of Peter and the flight of the disciples.

[B] vv. 36–46: The prayer of *Jesus* in Gethsemane.

[A] vv. 47–56: The betrayal of *Judas* and the flight *of the disciples*. **Only Matthew has Jesus address Judas as "friend," and asks why he is there** (v. 50). **Only Matthew has Jesus telling Peter to put away his sword, indicating that he could ask God for help, but that this must happen to fulfill the scriptures** (vv. 52–54).

[B] vv. 57–68: *Jesus* reveals his identity at the Jewish trial.

[A] vv. 69–75: *Peter* denies Jesus three times. **Only Matthew adds the comment: "Then Peter remembered what Jesus said: 'Before the rooster crows, you will betray me three times.' And he went outside and wept bitterly"** (v. 75).

After describing the plot to execute Jesus and the handing over of Jesus to Pilate (27:1–2), **only Matthew describes Judas's despair and suicide** in 27:3–10 (side by side with the report of Peter's sorrow [26:75]).

This first section of Matthew's passion story calls for brief comment. The most important feature of Matthew's storytelling is his acceptance of Mark's indication that the first part of Jesus' passion was marked by his interaction with his disciples and their descent into tragic failure (marked by [A]), despite his care for them (marked by [B]). It is introduced by Matthew's use of a final passion prediction in 26:1–2. It marks the end of Jesus' ministry and his acceptance of what lies ahead.[12]

Across eleven scenes, six of them are negative [A]. One of the Twelve (only Matthew has this focus on "the Twelve") joins the plot of the Jewish leaders and agrees to betray him (26:3–5, 14–16); Jesus predicts that Judas will betray him (vv. 20–25); Jesus predicts that Peter will deny him and all the disciples will flee (vv. 31–35); the betrayal takes place (vv. 47–56); the denial and the flight take place (vv. 69–75). This tragedy is accompanied by gestures of love and Jesus' self-revelation in five scenes [B]: the anointing in preparation for burial (vv. 6–13);[13] Jesus prepares for a final meal with his disciples (vv. 17–19); Jesus shares a meal with his disciples (vv. 26–30); Jesus demonstrates unconditional obedience to the Father, cost him what it may (vv. 36–46); and Jesus reveals himself as the Christ, the Son of God and the Son of Man, at the Jewish trial (vv. 57–68). What is noteworthy in this literary and theological structure lies at the heart of the passage.

Flanked by prophecies of betrayal (vv. 20–25: fifth scene), denial and flight (vv. 31–35: seventh scene), in the central sixth of eleven scenes, Jesus breaks bread and shares wine with these fragile disciples.[14] Only Matthew inserts into this otherwise almost verbatim repetition of Mark 14:17–31 words from Jesus indicating that this meal not only looks forward to his forthcoming death but is "for the forgiveness of sins" (Matt 26:28), perhaps under the influence of Jeremiah 31:34 or Exodus 24:8, or both.[15] The new covenant is founded in the blood of Jesus. Matthew's account of Jesus' final encounter with his disciples before his death is marked by understanding, love, forgiveness, and compassion.[16] This is the feature of the other Matthean additions to Mark. Apart from his solemn introduction in vv. 1–2, where Matthew has a fourth passion prediction, marking that Jesus has now finished all that he will say to his disciples (v. 1: "when he had finished saying all these things"), he announces his forthcoming passion without any reference to the resurrection (see Matt 16:21; 17:22–23; 20:17–19). In his prophecy of Judas's betrayal, he indicates to Judas that he is already aware of his identity (v. 25), and in the actual event of the betrayal, as well as the Markan kiss (see Mark 14:45; Matt 26:49), he addresses Judas as "friend" and asks why he finds himself in that situation (v. 50). He tells Peter and the disciples that there is no call for a sword, as "all this" is happening "that the scriptures of the prophets might be fulfilled" (vv. 52–54). Most poignantly, the juxtaposition of the weeping of Peter and the despair and suicide of Judas, who has been called "friend" to the last, indicates two alternatives to the rejection of Jesus that no doubt spoke to the readers and hearers of this dramatic account. Sorrow and repentance lead to forgiveness; despair and loss of all hope can only produce a senseless suicide (vv. 26:75; 27:3–10).[17] "For Matthew, the forgiveness of sins stands at the center of Jesus' mission."[18]

Although briefer, Matthew's account of Jesus' execution as the crucifixion of the King also continues this staged presentation of scenes that alternate from one situation to another, developed in different settings and with different characters. One is as affirmation of who Jesus is and the meaning of his suffering and death, marked [B], the other the abuse and execution of Jesus, often ironically presenting the truth about Jesus, marked [A].

> [B] 27:1–2, 11–14: *Jesus* reveals himself as King to the Roman authority.

> [A] vv. 15–23: The question of Barabbas, and the choice of a false messianic hope. *Matthew adds the intervention of Pilate's wife, asking that he have nothing to do with this righteous man* (v. 19).

> [B] vv. 24–26: Pilate proclaims *Jesus innocent* and *King. Matthew adds Pilate's washing of his hands, claiming innocence in the face of turbulence, and the terrible cry of "all the people": "His blood be on us and upon our children"* (vv. 24–25).

> [A] vv. 27–31: The Roman soldiers mock Jesus (ironically as King!).

> [B] vv. 32–37: The crucifixion of "the King of the Jews".

> [A] vv. 37–44: The crucified is mocked (ironically as King, Son of God and Savior).

> [B] vv. 45–54: The death of Jesus. *The report of this event is marked by Matthew's introduction of apocalyptic signs to accompany Jesus' death* (27:51–54).

> [A] vv. 55–56: The women at the cross.

> [B] vv. 57–61: Burial of Jesus, watched by the women.

Matching the literary and theological structure of 26:1–75, Matthew's account of the Roman trial and Jesus' death is centered upon the moment of the physical crucifixion of Jesus.[19] The fifth of nine scenes, the episode is reported entirely without any direct speech (vv. 32–37). The actual crucifixion is not reported but referred to as "when they had crucified him" (v. 35), and closes with the title on the cross: "This is Jesus, the King of the Jews" (v. 37). Like the centerpiece of Jesus' final presence with the disciples, it is framed by scenes that repeat the same action and theme. In the fourth scene the Roman soldiers abuse Jesus and ironically announce the truth that he is "King of the Jews" (vv. 27–31). In the sixth scene passers-by and the Jewish leaders abuse him, and ironically proclaim him as God's Son, Savior, and King of Israel (vv. 38–44). Set between this ironic use of abuse by all who surround him to proclaim the truth, this wordless crucifixion scene is the grim enthronement of the Son of God, the King of Israel, Savior.

The elements unique to Matthew continue themes that have been present across his story of Jesus.[20] He goes to some lengths to ease the responsibility of Pilate for the death of Jesus (the intervention of his wife, and his washing his hands of the guilt), and locates the Jewish leaders, and eventually "all the people," as the driving force for the crucifixion of the innocent King of Israel, Son of God, and Savior. Beyond the scope of these few reflections, this stance brings a central theme of Matthew's story to a climax. The life of Jesus is presented as the perfection of the Davidic messianic promises, the Son of God, the perfection of Torah and the prophets, the living out of all righteousness in Israel (see 3:15; 5:6, 10, 17–18, 20; 6:1, 33; 21:32).[21] But the opposition to Jesus from the leaders of Israel steadily increases. It begins with tension between Jesus and Israel (11:2—16:12) that becomes public antagonism (16:13—20:34), concluding with final rejection (26:1—27:66). In the Roman trial "all the people" join the rejection of Jesus in their cry that his blood be upon them and upon their children (27:24–25). Written for a Christian community that has been thrust out of its Jewish home in the synagogue,[22] Matthew uses his story of Jesus to show that Jesus fulfilled Israel's Sacred Scriptures, fulfilling all righteousness in his mission to "the lost sheep of Israel." He is the perfect continuation of God's design for the true Israel. However, the historical Israel has rejected Jesus, and it has rejected Matthew's Christian community, the ongoing presence of Jesus (see 1:23; 28:20). As we will see in our study of

Matthew's resurrection story, it is the Christian community that has become the true Israel, while the historical Israel that rejected and crucified its King has lost its way.[23]

Most important for this study, however, is the surprising description of events drawn from Jewish apocalyptic texts that immediately follow the death of Jesus, found only in Matthew:

> Now from the sixth hour there was darkness over all the earth until the ninth. ....And behold, the curtain of the temple was torn in two, from top to bottom, and the rocks were split; and the tombs were opened, and many bodies of the saints who had fallen asleep were raised, and coming out of the tombs after his resurrection they went into the holy city and appeared to many. (27:45, 51–54)

Not only the centurion (as in Mark 15:39), but also those keeping watch with him (vv. 35–36: Roman soldiers) "saw the earthquake and what took place, they were filled with awe, and said, 'Truly, this was the Son of God'" (v. 54). In Mark 15:37–39, Jesus' death is immediately followed by the tearing of the Temple veil. The sight of Jesus' death and the torn veil lead only the centurion to confess that Jesus was the Son of God. The collection of apocalyptic phenomena that accompany Jesus' death and lead to the confession of the centurion and his companions, all those present, are found only in Matthew: the splitting of the rocks, the opening of the tombs, the resurrection of the deceased holy ones, and their appearance in the holy city after the resurrection of Jesus.

Is this the beginning of the promise made by Jesus in 5:17–18: the Law must be observed in all its detail *until heaven and earth pass away*? Some of Mark's imagery is retained: the darkness over the earth and the tearing of the veil, but Matthew has added to this scenario considerably.[24] He has drawn upon "apocalyptic" symbols from Jewish tradition, but he has *shifted their timing*.[25] The events described—darkening of the skies, splitting of the rocks, and the rising of the dead—are events that were expected at the end of all time when God would return as Lord and Judge (see Amos 8:9; Joel 2:10; Hag 2:6; Zech 14:5; Dan 12:2; Jer 15:9; Ezek 37:7, 12–13; Isa 26:19; Dan 12:2). Matthew indicates that these events will take place *not only* at the end of all history, as was held by Jewish tradition. They have *already happened* at the death of Jesus.[26] Heaven and earth are passing away! But this is only the beginning.[27]

A forward-looking tension emerges as the passion narrative draws to a close. The reader/listener is told that the holy ones who rise from their open graves go into the city "after his resurrection." The story has not come to closure as the reader/listener has been advised—already at the moment of Jesus' death—that he will rise (v. 53).[28] Matthew continues to follow Mark's description of the aftermath of Jesus' death: the presence of the woman at the cross, the burial by Joseph of Arimathea, watched by women. The Christian reader is aware that this is not the end of the story. Matthew opens the narrative to the resurrection story by means of a "bridge episode," not found anywhere else in the Gospels. In 27:62–66 he reports the request of the Pharisees that a guard be set at the tomb. Recalling Jesus' words from his ministry, that he would rise on the third day (v. 62; see 16:21; 17:22–23; 20:17–19), the setting of a guard will ensure that his disciples do not come, steal the body, and then announce that Jesus has risen from the dead (v. 64). The guard is set, but a Christian reader and listener waits for the resolution of the story, and part of that waiting is a resolution of the apocalyptic expectation initiated at the moment of Jesus' death and the indication that he would rise from the dead (27:51–54).[29]

Matthew's Resurrection Story

The passion story closed with the burial of Jesus, in the company of the waiting and watching women (27:57–61). The resurrection story begins with a uniquely Matthean passage that serves as a bridge out of the passion story into the resurrection story. It is a "bridge" because the location is still at the tomb of Jesus. However, by reminding the reader and the listener of Jesus' earlier promises that he would rise on the third day, the expectation of that event is heightened. As throughout the passion story, Matthew uses the Gospel of Mark as his major source. However, he is far more creative in his use of other traditions and his own initiative to offer his readers and listeners a further interpretation of the significance of Jesus' death and resurrection. This is already obvious in the way Matthew presents the material in his passion narrative. We have already seen that he has adopted Mark's structure of alternating scenes that move from the darkness of rejection and failure (marked [A], above) to a positive, at times ironic, presentation of the person of Jesus as King, Son of God, and Savior (marked [B], above).[30] This pattern disappears in Mark's enigmatic resurrection story of Mark 16:1–8. But it is maintained in the literary structure of Matthew 27:62—28:16 to create a "leap-frogging" from the negative to the positive in the following fashion:

[A] 27:62–66: Negative: *The Matthean account of the setting of the guard at the tomb, to ensure that no "fraud" will be perpetrated by Jesus' disciples.*

[B] 28:1–10: Positive: The resurrection of Jesus. The essential elements of the Markan account are found in vv. 1, 5–7. However, Matthew rewrites Mark 16:8, as the women set off from the tomb full of joy, to announce the Easter message to the disciples. Into this account *Matthew inserts a description of what took place at the resurrection of Jesus in a further description of apocalyptic events (vv. 2–4). He adds an appearance of the risen Jesus to the women (vv. 9–10).*

[A] 28:11–15: Negative: *The Matthean account of the report of the guard to the authorities, and their being paid not to say anything to anyone, so that the saying remains abroad that the disciples stole the body.*

[B] 28:16–20: Positive: *Jesus' final commission to the eleven disciples on "the mountain." This commission, which has no parallel anywhere else in the New Testament, releases the disciples from keeping essential elements of the Mosaic Law, sends them out to all nations, and promises the presence of Jesus till the end of time.*

Setting of the Guard (27:62–66)

Matthew's negative attitude to the leaders of Israel drives the first addition of special material to the Markan source: the request of "the chief priests and the Pharisees" to Pilate that the tomb be guarded.[31]

Their rejection of Jesus continues, as they call him an "imposter," and ironically recall his predictions, during his life and ministry, that he would rise again on the third day (vv. 62–63; see 16:21; 17:22–23; 20:17–19). They must put a stop to any possible continuation of this fraudulent behavior on the part of any of his disciples, who might steal the body and then tell the people that "he has risen from the dead." This would only make matters worse (v. 64). "The Jewish leaders, being self-deceived, deceive others. While they call Jesus a deceiver, it is he who warns against deception: 24:4, 5, 11, 24."[32] Pilate, as detached from the events as he can possibly be, allows them to have the guard of soldiers, but it is the Jewish leaders who must see to it that the tomb is made as secure as possible (v. 65). Their response is to make the sepulcher secure by sealing the stone, and to set a guard (v. 66).[33] There are several reasons for Matthew's addition of this tradition to his narrative. In the first place it heightens the authority of God's action in breaking through the seals and guard set by Jesus' opponents. No human contrivance can stand in the way of God's action.[34] Second, it sets the scene for the subsequent report of the behavior of the soldiers who must tell the chief priests what had taken place in the interim. Behind all of this lies a problem for Matthew's community: "This story has been spread among the Jews to this day" (v. 15). There are close logical and narrative links between 27:62–60 and 28:11–15, but a crucial passage lies between them: 28:1–10.[35]

The Resurrection of Jesus (28:1–10)

Matthew provides the only attempt in the New Testament to offer a description of events that surrounded the resurrection of Jesus. Matthew 28:1 opens the resurrection story with a rewriting of Mark 16:1–2.[36] Matthew focuses on the fact that what follows takes place "after the Sabbath...on the first day of the week," thus three days after the death of Jesus.[37] He changes the Markan names of the women making the journey to the tomb to "Mary Magdalene and the other Mary" to generate a tight internal logic between the names of the women who saw where he was buried (27:61: "Mary and the other Mary").[38] He eliminates any reference to the anointing of a body that, after three days, should already be in a state of decay. He has reshaped Mark 16:2, with its reference to the time of the day and the rising of the sun, with an elegant insertion in Matthew 28:1: "toward the dawn of the first day of the week."[39] As Davies and Allison have rightly commented: "The literal dawning of a new day signals a new period of history."[40]

Having set the scene in this very precise fashion, Matthew describes the events of that moment in a way reminiscent of the apocalyptic language used at the moment of Jesus' death in 27:51–54.

> And behold, there was a great earthquake; for an angel of the
> Lord descended from heaven and came and rolled back the
> stone, and sat upon it. His appearance was like lightning, and
> his raiment white as snow. And for fear of him the guards
> trembled and became like dead men. (28:2–4)

As the death of Jesus was marked by language associated with the end of the ages, the same apocalyptic language returns at the moment of Jesus' resurrection. Yet another earthquake takes place (see Hag 2:6; Zech 14:5), an angel of the Lord with an appearance like lightning descends from heaven (see *1 En.* 1:3–9; 20:17–19),[41] and trembling and fear possess the guards (see Dan 10:7–9, 16; 12:2). "Matthew extends into the empty tomb story the apocalyptic atmosphere that erupted at the moment of Jesus' death."[42] There can be no mistaking Matthew's intentions. By associating events that traditionally were predicted to mark the end of all time, Matthew points to the death and resurrection of Jesus, not as the end of all time, but as the turning point of the ages.[43] Everything that has been in place until this *time* is being transformed, because heaven and earth are passing away (see 5:18a). Everything has been accomplished (see 5:18b). "The essential link between the death-resurrection of Jesus and the beginning of the new age strains Matthew's narration. He wants to show that God's acts of salvation come immediately as a response to the obedient death of Jesus."[44]

As we will see in our reading of 28:16–20, Matthew does not claim that the world as we know it has come to an end; there is still much to be done, and much to be endured (see 24:9–14, 36–51). However, by marking Jesus' death (27:51–54) and resurrection (28:2–4) with events that were traditionally associated with the end time, he insists on what could be called an "anticipated eschatology." Eschatology has been transformed. No longer will God enter definitively into human history *only* at the end of all time; he has anticipated that entry in Jesus' death and resurrection. After all, as the reader/hearer learned in the infancy story, Jesus of Nazareth is the Emmanuel, God with us (1:23). Time, human history, and the ups and downs of human experience will continue, but—for Matthew—everything has been transformed by Jesus' death and resurrection. This suggests to the reader/listener that Jesus' earlier instructions that all details of the Law must be observed (5:17–20) and that *the time* of his disciples' limitation of their mission to Israel (see 10:5–6) have come to an end. He had come only to the lost sheep of Israel, and there he has lived out the righteousness of God in its fullness (see 15:2–4). Another *time* is at hand, and the crucified and risen Jesus *now* sends out his disciples to all nations (see 28:16–20). As he said, programmatically, to John the Baptist, in his very first words in the Gospel as the Baptist objected to Jesus' submission to his baptism: "Let it be so for now; for thus it is fitting for us to fulfill all righteousness" (3:15). That "for now" has come to an end at the death and resurrection of Jesus, for Matthew and his community, the turning point of the ages.[45] One era has come to an end; another is dawning.

The narrative returns firmly to its Markan source in 28:5–8, with an important rewriting of Mark 16:8. There is a slight tension in Matthew's editing, as in v. 4 he reported that the guards were almost struck dead with fear. Resuming his Markan source, the women are told not to fear, even though there is no indication in Matthew that they were afraid. It can, of course, be presumed! The angel, a heavenly being, knows that they seek Jesus of Nazareth, the crucified One. The angelic figure takes on the role of a heavenly messenger. The women knew Jesus of Nazareth, and they have seen him crucified (27:55–56). The Easter proclamation follows: he is no longer in the tomb. He has been raised, as he said would happen. The women are to look at the place where those who killed him allowed him to be buried (28:6). They are then commissioned to go quickly to the disciples and announce that he has been raised from the dead and is going ahead of them to Galilee (v. 7). In Matthew the angel takes on a divine authority not found in the "young man" in Mark. In Mark the women are reminded of what Jesus said to them about going into Galilee (Mark 16:7). Even though, in Matthew, Jesus has told the disciples, in the context of their failure during their last night with Jesus, that he would go before them into Galilee (Matt 26:32), the angel takes on the authority of Jesus, instructing them to go into Galilee. It is his word, and not that of Jesus, that sends them on their way to Galilee: "I have told you" (v. 7). The emotional response of the women repeats the Markan description. They depart from the tomb "with fear." But they do not flee and say nothing to anyone because of their fear (see Mark 16:8). The Matthean women may be afraid, but they also full of great joy, and they run to tell the disciples. They are the first to announce the Easter message (Matt 28:8).[46]

Another Matthean addition to Mark 16:1–8 closes the episode of the woman at the tomb. In a way that has parallels with the encounter between the risen Jesus and Mary Magdalene in John 20:11–18,[47] on their way to announce the message to the disciples the risen Jesus met them, greeting them with a salutation that catches the "great joy" (Greek: *charas megalēs*) that marked their departure from the tomb: "Rejoice" (Greek: *chairete*).[48] Their response is that of a respectful "going to him." Matthew uses one of his favorite verbs to report the women's approach to Jesus (Greek: *proserchomai*). It has appeared across the story to tell of the approach of the sick or other petitioners who see Jesus (see 8: 2, 5, 19, 25; 9:14, 20, 28; 13:10, 36; 15:30; 17:14; 18:21; 19:16; 20:20; 21:14; 26:7). Their approach leads to an affectionate taking hold of his feet and a humble bowing down before him.[49] The Greek verb used to indicate their bowing down (Greek: *proskuneō*) is another of Matthew's favorite words to indicate recognition of the presence of the divine in Jesus' story (see 2:2, 8, 11; 4:9, 10; 8:2; 9:18; 14:33; 15:25; 20:20; 28:17).[50] Despite their reverence and attachment to him, although not as vigorous as Jesus' command to Mary Magdalene not to cling to him (see John 20:17), Jesus sends them on their mission to announce the Easter message to the disciples (Matt 28:10).

It is often claimed that he repeats the words of the angel at the tomb from v. 7. This is true, except for one important detail. The angel sent the women to announce the Easter message to "the disciples" (v. 7). Jesus' words to the women are identical to those of the angel, but he does not send them to "the disciples" but to "my brethren" (Greek: *tois adelphois mou*). This is important and shows another contact with John 20:11–18. Because of the transforming events of Jesus' death and resurrection, the recipients of the Easter message are no longer his "disciples" but his "brethren." There is a new equality between Jesus and his followers that approaches that of the Johannine message that Mary Magdalene must announce the Easter message to Jesus' brethren. She was told to announce that he is going to his Father and God, who is also their Father and God (John 20:17). Although Matthew has not reached that theological trajectory, the essential newness in the nature of the relationship between Jesus and his disciples, generated by his death and resurrection, is made clear.[51] They are no longer his "disciples" but his "brethren." This is one of the results of the fact that the death and resurrection of Jesus has marked the turning point of the ages.[52]

To this point the resurrection narrative has moved from the *negative* indication of the placing of a guard to avoid all fraudulent preaching about the risen Jesus (27:62–66), to the *positive* account of the dramatic events that surrounded the event of the resurrection and the encounter between the women and the angel at the tomb, and Jesus (28:1–10). This leap-frogging process continues as the narrative returns to the guard set at the tomb, and the *negative* consequences of their experience of the resurrection events, recounted in 28:2–4 (28:11–15).

The Guards Report to the Jewish Authorities (28:11–15)

The final *negative* scene, with its crucial statement in v. 15, tells of the report of the guards to the chief priests in vv. 11–15. As the women are on their way to announce the resurrection to the disciples, some of the guards from 27:61–66 are simultaneously on their way to the chief priests. They, like the women, will also tell "all that had taken place" (v. 11). The two reports, one a lie (vv. 13–14), and the other the truth (vv. 7–8), will produce different fruits.[53] The meeting between the guards and the chief priests is solemn, an assembly at which the priests take counsel with the elders: the Jewish leadership. They decide that they will bribe the soldiers with money (v. 12). As Judas was led astray with the promise of money (26:14–16), so are the soldiers. They are instructed to tell a lie: "His disciples came by night and stole him while we were asleep" (v. 13). The unlikelihood of this happening and the severe punishments that would be meted out to any soldier who fell asleep on guard do not bother the leaders of the Jews (chief priests and elders [vv. 11–12]).[54] They are happy to tell a further lie so that the lie of the guards will not be exposed: if any of this comes to the Roman authority (the governor), they will also keep him happy. The suggestion of the further bribe can be read between the lines![55] "The entire episode presents the leaders in the worst possible light."[56]

The result of the soldiers' acceptance of the money and telling the story of the stolen body leads to the point of this final negative report: "This story has been spread among the Jews to this day" (v. 15). The

Matthean community tells the story of the resurrection of Jesus and his appearances; the Jews tell the story of a body stolen by his disciples. "All players in the narrative are agreed that the tomb was empty."[57] The reason for the women's story is their Easter experience of the risen Jesus. The reason for the story told by the Jews is corruption among the leaders of the Jews. Again, Matthew's pastoral prejudice against the Jews is in evidence. Speaking into the situation of Jewish Christians alienated from their Jewish home, he lays the blame for this lie firmly on the shoulders of the Jewish leadership, and the acceptance of this lie by the leaders of the Jews. "Clearly Matthew's community knew and cared about what the synagogue across the street was saying."[58] The Jews are the ones continuing the ongoing presence of untruth. Matthew's Christians are living in the truth of the risen Jesus, while the Jews are living and telling a lie.[59]

The Risen Jesus Commissions the Eleven Disciples (28:16–20)

The climactic *positive* scene stands alone. As Jesus opened the Sermon on the Mount, he told his disciples, "*Until heaven and earth pass away, not one letter, not one stroke of a letter, will pass from the law until all is accomplished*" (5:18) [italics mine]. The signs that marked the death (27:45–54) and the resurrection (28:1–10) of Jesus indicate that heaven and earth are passing away and all is accomplished. Much still lies ahead (see 24:1—25:46), but Jesus' restriction of his own mission and the mission of his disciples to the lost sheep of Israel (see 10:5–6; 15:25) has come to an end, as the disciples must face a future that reaches beyond Judaism and Israel. The command to observe all the details of the Mosaic Law (5:17–20), impossible in the Gentile mission (28:19), is also at an end. The death and resurrection of Jesus mark the turning point of the ages, and the Gospel concludes with Jesus' final commission to his disciples to go to all the nations (28:16–20), like 5:17–20, delivered on the mountain in Galilee. Conditions that have been in force across the ministry of Jesus have now ceased, as heaven and earth have passed away; all is accomplished in the death and resurrection of Jesus. But a new challenge, and a new presence of Jesus, are promised in 28:16–20.

It is universally recognized that the final scene in the Gospel of Matthew, the commissioning of the disciples for mission, and Jesus' promise to be with them, is a key to the interpretation of the Gospel itself. "All of the basic theological statements of the Gospel of Matthew seem to be gathered up in these forty words at the end of the Gospel."[60] We have seen that Jesus' ministry was directed uniquely to Israel (15:25), and that he also limited his disciples' ministry to the lost sheep of the house of Israel (10:5–6). As he opened his programmatic Sermon on the Mount, he taught that every detail of the Law and the Prophets must be taught and observed (5:17–20). However, in the final commission this limited mission program and the agenda of the Law and the Prophets seem to have been abandoned. The key to understanding 28:16–20 lies in the interpretation of the death and resurrection of Jesus as the turning point of the ages, as only now have heaven and earth passed away, and all is accomplished (see 5:18). With the dramatic events of the death of Jesus (27:51–54) and the resurrection of Jesus (28:2–4) behind him, Jesus can go to the mountain in Galilee to meet his eleven disciples. The "prolepsis," that tension in the temporal aspect of narrative that must look further into the story for its "time," has now been resolved. But Matthew 28:16–20 does more than resolve the prolepsis initiated in 5:17–20. It takes the reader/listener into a new time that lies outside the time limitations of the story of the Gospel, a time that could be called, in pseudo-Matthean language, "the time of the Church" (see Matt 16:18; 18:17).[61]

It is impossible fully to appreciate the vigor of 28:16–20 without understanding the setting within which this Gospel was being proclaimed. The Matthean community, as we have already had reason to suggest in the analysis of the rejection of Jesus, and the terrible cry from "all the people" that Jesus' blood be upon them and their children (27:25), is in a difficult situation of rejection from the traditional Jewish world and its familiar ways.[62] Matthew's response to this pastoral situation is to present Jesus as the one who continues and fulfills God's design. The people in the Synagogue, who reject Matthew's Christians, continue the tradition of the Jewish leaders and the people in the story of Jesus who rejected him. They not only rejected him, but in the end they crucified him, crying out for his death to a vacillating Pilate, who preferred to wash his hands of the whole business (Matt 27:15–26). The Matthean Christians were struggling to establish their identity, in the light of their rejection by their former Jewish neighbors and kinsfolk, whose predecessors had been associated with the crucifixion of Jesus. But Jewish religion at this period was also searching for its post-war and post-Jerusalem religious identity. Gradually, Jews were generating a firm adherence to the Law that would eventually produce what later came to be known as Rabbinic Judaism. It is most powerfully articulated in the third-century Mishnah, and the Jerusalem and Babylonian Talmuds (fourth and fifth centuries, respectively). The Jewish community at the time of Matthew's Gospel was an embryonic form of what later became one of the world's great religions.

The Gospel of Matthew emerges in a time when two religions, once identified as one religion, were searching for their identity. On the one hand, the Matthean Christians are being told a story that affirms that Jesus is the perfection of all righteousness, the one who generates the true Israel. This tradition eventually becomes Christianity, and the Gospel of Matthew becomes part of its "Sacred Scripture." On the other hand, an emerging post-war Judaism attaches itself closer to the observance of Torah and its ordinances, finding there a path of truth and life. This tradition eventually became Judaism, based upon Torah and its interpretation in the other books of the Bible and later Jewish Rabbinic commentary. In this setting, as paths separated, hostility and rejection were an understandable part of a tense relationship between Jews and Christians. What we find in Matthew 28:16–20, however, is not hostile; it transcends all such concerns as the Matthean community moves further away from Judaism into a Gentile mission. The separation is behind them, and these words direct the Matthean disciples, and those reading and hearing the words of the risen Jesus, into a way of life that looked beyond the religious thought and practice of late-first-century Jews. With this historical and religious background in mind, Matthew's final episode speaks eloquently to the new Israel, sent out on mission to all the nations (28:16–20).

Eleven disciples (as Judas has left the Twelve in despair [27:3–10]) went into Galilee, to the mountain, already instructed by Jesus to meet him there (v. 16).[63] This is not the first time Jesus has summoned his disciples to the top of a mountain to give them important instructions. Earlier in the Gospel (5:1—7:28) he began his ministry of teaching by gathering his disciples on a mountain (see 5:1) to give them a new Law (see 5:17–20, 21–22, 27–28, 31–32, 33–34, 38–39, 43–44). On a new Sinai a new and perfect Moses gave a new people of God a new Law. The situating of the giving of the new Law on a mountain was important for Matthew (see 4:8–9; 5:1–2; 7:28–29; 17:6–7).[64] On mountains, closer to God, the human can touch the divine. As Jesus began his

Sermon on the Mount, he insisted that, for the moment, the Law and the Prophets had to be lived perfectly (5:17-20). There will be a time, however, when heaven and earth pass away, when all is accomplished. At that time all such limitations to traditional Jewish life and practice could no longer hold sway. As we have seen, for Matthew (and only Matthew), heaven and earth are rocked and the signs of the end of all time are present at Jesus' death (27:45, 51-52) and resurrection (28:2-4). One era has come to its perfection in Jesus; another is about to start. Thus, again on the mountain in Galilee, the risen Lord commissions his Church.

The reaction of the disciples to the sight of Jesus is ambiguous.[65] Some worship him. As we have already seen, Matthew makes regular use of the verb *to worship* (Greek: *proskuneō*) to indicate the correct attitude of faith. Some of the Eleven demonstrate this faith in the risen Jesus. However, Matthew reports: "But some doubted" (v. 17). The hesitation of the disciples in the presence of the risen Lord is one of the hallmarks of the Synoptic resurrection accounts, each in its own way (see Mark 16:8 and Luke 24:10-11, 13-35, 36-37). It is also reported in the experience of Mary Magdalene and Thomas in the Gospel of John (John 20:11-17, 24-29). This theme continues to be an important part of Matthew's theology of the Church. All the Gospels have a realistic understanding and presentation of the disciples of Jesus. They believe, yet they falter in their belief. This situation of fragile belief, or what Davies and Allison helpfully understand as "divided belief," is recorded across the Gospels because it retains its power in all experiences of post-Easter believers.[66] The presence of the risen Jesus, in whatever form, is never guaranteed unconditional acceptance of faith and subsequent action in the post-Easter Christian experience.

Jesus opens his final instructions with a declaration about himself and then spells out the consequences of such a declaration for his disciples and their mission. The man whom they had known as Jesus of Nazareth claims that all authority in heaven and on earth has been given to him (v. 18). The Jesus who had been crucified is now exalted to have power and authority over the whole of creation. This is nothing less than to claim that Jesus has taken over the authority and dignity that traditional Israel allowed only to YHWH. Passages indicating this are innumerable. An example, and perhaps the most important Old Testament passage on the oneness of God and his complete authority, is found in Deuteronomy 6:4–9, which begins: "Hear, O Israel, the Lord our God, the Lord alone" (Deut 6:4). Behind Jesus' claim to absolute authority, there is probably also a reference to the giving of all authority to the "one like a son of man" in Dan 7:14: "To him was given dominion and glory and kingship, that all peoples, nations and languages should serve him." A careful reader or listener to the Gospel of Matthew should not be surprised. Jesus has regularly promised that this would be the case. As recently as 26:64 he announced to hostile Jewish leaders that the Son of Man would be exalted to the right hand of God (using words from Ps 110 and Dan 7:14).[67] "The entire world was turned upside down by the resurrection of Jesus."[68]

On a mountain with his hesitant disciples, Jesus claims to have been given all the authority that, according to traditional Judaism, belonged to YHWH alone. Flowing from the uniqueness and universality of his authority, the Matthean Jesus breaks through three further elements basic to Jewish belief and practice in vv. 19–20. There is a close logical link between Jesus' absolute authority, articulated in v. 18, and the commands that follow, generated by the expression *therefore* (Greek: *oun*). Only on the basis of his claims in v. 18 can Jesus *therefore* issue the commands that follow.

1. He commands his disciples: "Go therefore and make disciples of all nations" (v. 19a). They are to make "disciples." Matthew is almost the only New Testament author to use the verb *make disciples* (see 13:52; 27:57; see also, only Acts 14:21). He is also the evangelist who most frequently calls Jesus' disciples by the Greek expression for "disciple" (*mathētēs*), which means "one who engages in learning through instruction from another," across the gospel story.[69] The Eleven are "disciples" and have been learning from Jesus to this point. They are now to draw others into this circle of people who learn from Jesus, as v. 19 will indicate. Scholars have long debated whether Jesus' command to make disciples of "all nations" (Greek: *panta ta ethnē*) means "to all nations," including the nation of Israel, or "to all Gentiles," excluding Israel.[70] This is an important question for the theology of Matthew. Does the Gospel of Matthew "give up" on the possibility of a

Christian mission among Jews, and thus definitively move away from the Jewish roots of Christianity, or are attempts still being made to reach out to them? There is sufficient evidence throughout the Gospel of a mission to Israel to claim that it cannot be excluded (see 10:23), and it must always be remembered that the majority of Matthew's community would still have been Jews, for whom Matthew is a Jewish scribe taking from their treasures, and revealing things both new and old (see 13:52). Ulrich Luz is most likely correct in his acceptance of the majority position, aware of the difficulty pastoral realities that faced Matthean Christians. "While it does not exclude a continuing mission to Israel, Matthew probably no longer had great hopes for it; that is shown by 22:8–10; 23:39–24:2, and 28:15. For him and his churches the separation of Israel into a majority hostile to Jesus and a minority consisting of disciples of Jesus is definitive."[71] Whatever one makes of that important debate, something astonishingly new in Jewish religious practice is commanded by Jesus. There had been openness to the idea of a universal salvation in the Prophets (see, for example, Isa 2:1–4), but it had always meant a movement from the Gentile world toward Zion. There is only one people of God, with its Father Abraham, and its Law from Moses, the nation Israel. This is reversed: the disciples, already a new people of God, founded by Jesus of Nazareth, are to "go out" to make disciples *of all nations.*[72]

2. The disciples are further instructed to "baptize" in the name of the Father and of the Son and of the Holy Spirit (v. 19b), thus introducing a new initiation rite for the new people of God, setting out on its mission. The Christian missionary is told to replace the initiation of circumcision with baptism. This interpretation of v. 19b depends upon the interpretation offered in this chapter, that the restrictions of the Jewish Law (see 5:17–20) have now been overcome by the anticipated "end time" of the death and resurrection of Jesus. Some major scholars, who do not accept this position, argue that the Matthean Church still

lived the detailed observance of the Law,[73] while others are amazed that, in the light of 5:17–20, there is no mention of circumcision in 20:19.[74] It is not mentioned because it has been replaced by the universal Christian practice of baptism. Neither Jews nor Gentiles who enter into the Christian community generated by the missionaries that follow this injunction of the risen Jesus do so by means of circumcision. Such a situation must have been extremely difficult for many Matthean Christians, themselves Jewish Christians, and totally alien to their Jewish neighbors, for whom circumcision was the sign of the uniqueness of the Jewish male.[75] But this was the radical nature of Christianity, by the time of the Gospel of Matthew affirming its uniqueness. Baptism in the name of the Father, the Son, and the Holy Spirit anticipates but does not teach the doctrine of the Trinity, which came much later (at the Council of Nicaea in AD 325). As in Jesus' baptism, the voice of the Father comes from heaven and the Spirit of God descends upon Jesus (3:16–17): the baptism practiced in the Matthean Church must have used a formula over the newly baptized that is recorded here.[76] As Luz describes that process: "On the one hand it expresses the belonging that is constitutive of the baptized persons, on the other hand it reminds them of the Baptism itself in which these three names were 'proclaimed' over the person who was being baptized."[77]

3. The final command broadens the basis of traditional Jewish faith, built upon the teaching and the learning of the Torah. It remained as the heart of the Jewish understanding of God's ways among his people and his people's approach to him. Jesus does not "replace" the Torah, but he "perfects" it (see 5:17–18). Jesus uses words commonly found in passages on the importance of the Torah: "to teach," "to observe," "commandments" (see, for example, Deut 5—6, esp. 6:1, where all these terms appear) to indicate a new teaching: "teaching them to observe all that I have commanded you" (v. 20a). No longer does the command to teach and observe look to the Torah but rather to

the teaching of Jesus. The Law of Moses has been perfected by the teaching of Jesus, but Jesus does not instruct his disciples to abandon the Law and replace it with the teaching of Jesus. From this point on, the Law will be interpreted through the teaching of Jesus. "Jesus not only was, he always is the 'only teacher' of his church (23:8). His proclamation makes the church's proclamation plain."[78]

But there is more to this final command. The teaching of Jesus that must be taught by the disciples is the teaching found in this story of Jesus, especially as it has been magisterially expounded in his great discourses on the ethical organization of the community (5:1—7:29), on the mission and lifestyle of the disciples (10:1–42), on the nature of the kingdom (13:1–52), on the quality of life and care within the community (18:1–35), and on the end of time and the purpose of history (24:1—25:46).[79] These final words of the risen Jesus are a canonization of the Matthean Gospel, and it is quite possible that Matthew already understood himself as writing "Sacred Scripture." The Christian canon was under way.[80]

Jesus' final words are not words of departure, but words assuring that he will always be with his disciples (v. 20b). These words point back to 1:23, where Jesus was promised as the Emmanuel, "God with us." The theme of the presence of Jesus has sounded across the entire story (see 9:15; 17:17; 18:20), with special intensity in the passion narrative (26:11, 18, 20, 23, 29, 36, 38, 40, 51, 69, 71). There are repeated stories of Jesus' helping presence among his disciples (see 8:23–27; 14:13–21, 22–23; 15:29–39; 17:1–8; 26:26–29). "Jesus' promise to be with his disciples to the end of the world again points back to the story of the earthly Jesus."[81] In the Gospel of Luke the idea of ascension is a pictorial image of Jesus leaving this earth and returning to his Father, but in the Gospel of Matthew there is no trace of any such event. In fact, one could say that the opposite is the case. Matthew's Gospel ends with Jesus' promise that he will never leave them. Of course, theologically, Luke is saying the same thing through his message of a return to the Father and his eventual sending of the Spirit. But whether it is Jesus' Spirit sent by the

Father (Luke) or the abiding presence of Jesus who will never leave his Church (Matthew), the message of God's purposes to found and sustain a holy people in and through Jesus rings true.[82]

Although the story ends here, the reader/hearer knows what will take place after this concluding commission, thanks to Jesus' parable discourse (13:1–52) and his eschatological discourse (24:1—25:46). In these discourses Jesus told several parables that explained what would happen in the period between his resurrection and his return as the Son of Man at the close of the age. There will be periods of persecution when many will fall away (13:21). There will be a mixture of good and bad within the Church (13:24–30). Many will grow weary waiting for his return (25:1–13), but at the end of the age Jesus will come as the Son of Man to judge the nations (25:31–46). Thus the great commission (28:16–20) is not an ending but a beginning that invites the reader/hearer to discipleship and to the evangelization of the nations in the period between the death and resurrection of Jesus, the turning point of the ages, and the final coming of the Son of Man.[83]

Conclusion

As far as Jesus is concerned, the Law and the Prophets have been brought to their perfection. Thus, as risen Lord to whom all authority on earth and in heaven has been given, he can send his disciples to all nations, teaching what he taught them (28:16–20). This final missionary commission, sending the disciples to all the nations, does not stand in conflict with Jesus' own life and ministry but forms the culminating point of the Gospel's structure and message. As Ulrich Luz has commented: "The final passage in the Gospel of Matthew is like a large terminal railway station in which many lines converge."[84] The image is effective, as long as this railway station is not understood as "the end of the line." The eschatological turning point of the ages takes place because of the death and resurrection of Jesus. His death and resurrection anticipate the end time and open a new era in the life of the Christian community, but the traditional Jewish expectation of a final "day of the Lord" is still an important part of the Matthean historical and theological agenda (see especially 24:1—25:46). Jesus may have responded perfectly to God's design, and thus heaven and earth pass away, and all things are brought to their perfection (5:18). But much still lies ahead for his disciples.

As far as the disciples are concerned, the heavens are still above, the earth is still firmly in place under their feet, and the end time still lies somewhere in the unknown future. The crucified and risen Jesus will be with his community till the end of the age (28:20), but, sent by the Lord of heaven and earth (28:18), they are to carry out their mission in the in-between-time, in a bold new way that is different from their Jewish roots, until the end of the age (28:19–20). No doubt many of them were resisting this mission, preferring to stay with former, well-practiced ways. This may be the reason for Matthew's placing such a powerful statement, sending his Christians out into mission, at the end of his story.[85] But it is not new. Their responsibilities have been made clear to them across the Gospel, as Jesus instructed them by both deed and word (see especially 8:1—11:30; 13:54—18:35). In his final discourse, on the eve of his death and resurrection (24:1—25:6), he instructs his disciples: "And this gospel of the kingdom will be preached throughout the whole world, as a testimony to all nations; and then the end will come" (24:14). But none of this would have been possible if God had not acted decisively among us in the death and resurrection of Jesus. The Church is living "the in-between time," gifted by the "turning point of the ages" by means of Jesus' death and resurrection, living and proclaiming the Gospel of Jesus, making disciples of all nations until God's final gift that will come at the end of the age.

> In Matthew...this age and the age to come seemingly overlap. Although the consummation lies ahead, although this age is still full of tribulation, and although the Christian casts his hope in the future coming of the Son of Man, saints have already been raised, the Son of Man has already been enthroned in the heavenly places, the resurrected Jesus is ever present with his followers (28:20). If we may so put it, Matthew's eschatology is, in some ways, more realized than that of Mark.[86]

Notes

1. For more detailed presentation of the narrative theory that follows, see Gérard Genette, *Narrative Discourse: An Essay in Method*, trans. Jane E. Lewin (Ithaca, NY: Cornell University Press, 1980), 33–85, and the excellent summary of Genette's contribution in Shlomith Rimmon-Kenan, *Narrative Fiction: Contemporary Poetics*, New Accents (London: Methuen, 1983), 43–58.

2. For more detail on the nature, variety, and effect of analepses and prolepses in narratives, see Genette, *Narrative Discourse*, 48–67 (analepses) and 67–79 (prolepses).

3. See John P. Meier, *Law and History in Matthew's Gospel*, AnBib 71 (Rome: Biblical Institute Press, 1976), 48: "It is important for the subsequent exegesis that 'until' is the *only* possible meaning. There are no solid grounds for changing the meaning to 'in order that.'"

4. See, for example, the authoritative interpretations of William D. Davies and Dale C. Allison, *The Gospel according to Saint Matthew*, 3 vols., ICC (Edinburgh: T & T Clark, 1988–97), 1:482–503; and Ulrich Luz, *Matthew*, trans. James E. Crouch, 3 vols. (Minneapolis, MN: Fortress, 2001–7), 1:213–19.

5. See Davies and Allison, *The Gospel according to Saint Matthew*, 3:685, and Luz, *Matthew*, 3:631–32. The strongest advocate of this position is David Sim, *The Gospel of Matthew and Christian Judaism: The History and Social Setting of the Matthean Community*, SNTIW (Edinburgh: T & T Clark, 1998).

6. This is argued by Luz, *Matthew*, 1:218: "If the Matthean Jesus had temporarily limited the validity of the Torah, that would have been a completely surprising message for the Jewish Christian readers of the Gospel. It would not at all have been in keeping with the one who wants to keep the same Torah down to its last iota." But that is what he seems to do in 28:16–20.

7. Undergirding the interpretation that follows is the study of Meier, *Law and History in Matthew's Gospel*, 1–40. See also John P. Meier, *The Vision of Matthew: Christ, Church, and Morality in the First Gospel*, Theological Inquiries (New York: Paulist Press, 1978), 26–39.

8. Luz, *Matthew*, 3:301. See also Donald Senior, *The Passion of Jesus in the Gospel of Matthew*, The Passion Series 1 (Wilmington, DE: Michael Glazier, 1985), 10–11.

9. See, for example, Luz, *Matthew*, 3:299: "It is futile to try to find a systematic structure in the Matthean story of the passion." See also Davies and Allison, *The Gospel according to Saint Matthew*, 3:436–691. They structure each unity in their exegesis but offer no overall literary structure. Donald Senior, *Matthew*, ANTC (Nashville, TN: Abingdon, 1998), 287–88, divides 26:1—27:66 into seven sequences, following chronological and narrative crite-

ria. John Paul Heil, *The Death and Resurrection of Jesus: A Narrative-Critical Reading of Matthew 26—28* (Minneapolis, MN: Fortress, 1991), structures Matt 26—28 around three large sections that are then divided and further subdivided into threes. Some divisions are too forced. See Luz, *Matthew*, 3:299.

10. For an accurate synthesis of Matthew's particular thrust in his passion narrative, see Brendan Byrne, *Lifting the Burden: Reading Matthew's Gospel in the Church Today* (Collegeville, MN: The Liturgical Press, 2004), 200–201.

11. I indicate the major interpretative Matthean additions by printing them in bold. There are many other minor changes. Matthew corrects Mark's Greek, shortening or lengthening what Mark says. He omits Markan detail and even some important Markan passages (for example, the flight of the naked young man in Mark 14:51–52). He pays closer attention to Jewish practices (e.g., in the process of the Jewish trial) and continues his practice, found throughout the Gospel, of inserting an indication that what is happening is the fulfillment of scripture, that is, part of God's design for Jesus (see 26:28, 31, 38, 56, 64; 28:9–10).

12. On the role of 26:1–2 in the passion narrative, see Senior, *The Passion of Jesus in the Gospel of Matthew*, 49–52. "The Son of Man, committed to the way of justice, moves forward to the final act of fidelity to his Father. His opponents, oblivious to the moment of grace and intent on their opposition to Jesus, will become instruments of death" (52).

13. It is not all "good news." In Mark 14:4 "some" of the bystanders complain about the waste. In Matt 26:8–9 the disciples become indignant.

14. On the supper narrative in Matthew, see Francis J. Moloney, *A Body Broken for a Broken People: Eucharist in the New Testament*, rev. ed. (Peabody, MA: Hendrickson, 1997), 57–83.

15. See Luz, *Matthew*, 3:279–81; Davies and Allison, *The Gospel according to Saint Matthew*, 3:474–75.

16. See the treatment of Byrne, *Lifting the Burden*, 204–6. For Donald M. Gurtner, *The Torn Veil: Matthew's Exposition of the Death of Jesus*, SNTSMS 139 (Cambridge: Cambridge University Press, 2007), 133–37, the addition of "for the forgiveness of sins" to Jesus' words over the cup is "the most important statement about Jesus' death in Matthew" (133).

17. Senior, *The Passion of Jesus in the Gospel of Matthew*, 102: "The failure of the leading apostle not only serves as a foil to the courageous testimony of Jesus but Peter's testimony of remorse on remembering the words of Jesus will contrast with the despair of another apostle who also bitterly regrets his failure but does not choose repentance."

18. Luz, *Matthew*, 3:381. See also Senior, *The Passion of Jesus in the Gospel of Matthew*, 66–71. "His death would be the final expression of his

entire life and mission: it was a body broken and given, it was a cup poured out, to be taken and consumed. It was a life of service for the other, a renewed covenant between God and God's people, a pledge of freedom. It was an act of gracious forgiveness" (71).

19. For a succinct, accurate, and helpful interpretation of 26:11–31, see Senior, *The Passion of Jesus in the Gospel of Matthew*, 108–55. Senior is especially skilled in drawing out the subtle use of irony that exposes Matthew's presentation of Jesus as King and Son of God.

20. On the preparation for the passion across the story of Jesus' ministry, see Senior, *The Passion of Jesus in the Gospel of Matthew*, 17–45.

21. For more on this, see Francis J. Moloney, "Matthew 5:17–18 and the Matthean Use of *dikaiosunē*," in *Unity and Diversity in the Gospels and Paul: Essays in Honor of Frank J. Matera*, ed. Christopher W. Skinner and Kelly R. Iverson, Early Christianity and Its Literature 7 (Atlanta: SBL, 2012), 33–54; and Roland Deines, "Not the Law but the Messiah: Law and Righteousness in the Gospel of Matthew—An Ongoing Debate," in *Built on the Rock: Studies in the Gospel of Matthew*, ed. Donald M. Gurtner and John Nolland (Grand Rapids, MI: Eerdmans, 2008), 53–84.

22. On this, see the classic studies of William D. Davies, *The Setting of the Sermon on the Mount* (Cambridge: Cambridge University Press, 1963); Krister Stendahl, *The School of St. Matthew*, 2nd ed. (Philadelphia: Fortress, 1968).

23. This theological thrust of Matthew's narrative lies behind the terrible words of "all the people," which has been used so often to motivate persecution of the Jewish people (see Luz, *Matthew*, 3:506–11). This cry from the Jewish people was never uttered. It reflects the bitter animosity between Matthew's community and the ongoing Synagogue-centered Judaism after the destruction of Jerusalem. Writing in the mid-80s, Matthew no doubt looked upon the destruction of Jerusalem, its Temple, and the disintegration of the traditional Jewish way of life in AD 70 as part of their punishment for rejecting Jesus (see Luz, *Matthew*, 503). This is *not* theologically sound but rather the result of late-first-century polemics between Matthean Christianity and the Synagogue across the road. It should remain there! See especially Byrne, *Lifting the Burden*, 212–14, and the important remark of Senior, *The Passion of Jesus in the Gospel of Matthew*, 122: "There is little doubt that the Roman trial scene and its climactic choice by the people is an integral part of Matthew's theology of history. It bears as well scar tissue from the friction between the Jewish Christian community and Pharisaic Judaism. Both dimensions must be kept in mind if this controversial, and dangerous, biblical text is to be interpreted in a responsible way."

24. For a rich study of the history of the interpretation of Matthew 27:45, see Dale C. Allison, "Darkness at Noon (Matt. 27:45)," in *Studies in Matthew: Interpretation Past and Present* (Grand Rapids, MI: Baker Academic, 2005), 79–105.

25. The expression *apocalyptic* is used to describe events that are traditionally associated with the final and definitive intervention of God *at the end of time*. As it is about the action of God, highly symbolic language is found. See John P. Meier, *Matthew*, NTM 3 (Wilmington, DE: Michael Glazier, 1980), 350–53; Senior, *The Passion of Jesus in the Gospel of Matthew*, 142–49.

26. For a fine study, reaching these conclusions, see Gurtner, *The Torn Veil*. Gurtner's impressive study focuses upon the tearing of the veil, and especially upon the background of Ezek 37. However, his detailed study of Matt 27:51b–53 (see 138–98) shows conclusively that the language and imagery used in this uniquely Matthean passage indicates "the turning point of the eschatological ages which is occasioned by the death of Jesus" (169). I am surprised that Gurtner never refers to John Meier, who is especially fond of the expression "the turning point of the ages" to describe Jesus' death and resurrection.

27. The genuinely great commentary of Ulrich Luz struggles at this point. Unable to accept that the death and resurrection of Jesus mark a "turning point of the ages," as he believes that the demands of 5:17–20 are still in place for the post-Easter Matthean community, he finds it difficult to explain the non-apocalyptic nature of these obviously apocalyptic events associated with the death of Jesus. See Luz, *Matthew*, 3:560–71. The same must be said for the fine commentary of Davies and Allison, *The Gospel according to Saint Matthew*, 3:628–43. They recognize a link with traditional eschatology but do not develop that motif further (3:660–68). They simply state that "the present earthquake also probably has eschatological content" (664–65) but take that observation no further.

28. This is another example of Matthew's use of prolepsis sending the reader/listener further into the story, seeking resolution. Luz, *Matthew*, 3:567–69, is unable to explain this and reluctantly suggests that v. 53 is a careless post-Matthean gloss. For a better solution, see Byrne, *Lifting the Burden*, 219.

29. As Senior, *Matthew*, 336, succinctly comments: "As signs of the end time erupt on Golgotha, Jesus' rejection by the leaders and the 'people as a whole' is thwarted, God's judgment against the Jerusalem temple is anticipated, and a new people who acclaim Jesus as God begin to appear. Matthew lays the groundwork for the final words in the Gospel when the Risen Jesus will extend the mission of the disciples to the ends of the earth and the End of time." See also Nils Alstrup Dahl, "The Passion Narrative in Matthew," in *The Interpretation of Matthew*, ed. Graham Stanton, IRT 3 (London: SPCK, 1983), 42–55.

30. On this alternation between "Jesus' opponents" and "Jesus," see Luz, *Matthew*, 584–85. Craig S. Keener, *A Commentary on the Gospel of Matthew* (Grand Rapids, MI: Eerdmans, 1998), 699, suggests that this presentation of the true and the false forces the readers/hearers "to declare their choice." The elements in the narrative found only in Matthew are again printed in bold.

31. This is the only time the Pharisees are associated with the chief priests, and the only time they are mentioned in the passion narrative. Ironically, the Pharisees, who believed in resurrection from the dead, join the priests in constructing a lie about Jesus' resurrection. See John Nolland, *The Gospel of Matthew*, NIGTC (Grand Rapids, MI: Eerdmans, 2005), 1236.

32. Davies and Allison, *The Gospel according to Saint Matthew*, 3:654.

33. On the guards being Roman soldiers, see Davies and Allison, *The Gospel according to Saint Matthew*, 3:655; Nolland, *The Gospel of Matthew*, 1238–39. This adds to the irony of their making their report to the Jewish leaders in 28:11.

34. See Nolland, *The Gospel of Matthew*, 1237. Donald A. Hagner, *Matthew*, 2 vols., WBC 33-33B (Dallas, TX: Word, 1993–1995), 2:863–64, makes the pertinent comment: "The incongruous, ironical result is that the opponents took Jesus' words about rising from the dead more seriously than did the disciples."

35. Raymond E. Brown, *The Death of the Messiah: From Gethsemane to the Grave: A Commentary on the Passion Narratives in the Four Gospels*, 2 vols., ABRL (New York: Doubleday, 1994), 2:1301–05, suggests that 27:62–66 and 28:11–15 were once a unified narrative, into which Matthew has inserted 28:1–10.

36. On Matthew's creative use of Mark 16:1–8, see Timothy A. Friedrichsen, "The Commissioning of Women Disciples: Matthew 28:9–10," in *Transcending Boundaries: Contemporary Readings of the New Testament: Studies in Honor of Francis J. Moloney*, ed. Rekha M. Chennattu and Mary L. Coloe, BibScRel 187 (Rome: LAS, 2005), 266–70.

37. Jewish "days" are counted by the presence of daylight. There was daylight on Friday, Saturday, and "the dawn" of Sunday: three days. What happens takes place "on the third day," or "after three days."

38. This is typical of Matthew's careful editing. Mark has a list of names who are at the cross (Mark 15:40), and a different list for those who see the burial (15:47). He then returns to the names of the woman at the cross when he tells of the journey to the tomb (16:1). Matthew, more logically, has the women who see the burial (Matt 27:61) as the ones who go to the tomb (28:1). See Senior, *Matthew*, 338.

39. There are grammatical problems with the Greek original, but this is what it means. For detail, see Luz, *Matthew*, 3:594–95.

40. Davies and Allison, *The Gospel according to Saint Matthew*, 3:664.

41. The more eschatological Matthew is the only Synoptic Gospel to report the presence of an "angel of the Lord" at the tomb. In Mark 16:5 he is a "young man." Luke 24:4 has two men. This feature of Matthew is almost universally neglected by commentators, as they claim that the "young man" (Mark) or the two men (Luke) are angels. This may be so, but why are they not called "angels," as in Matthew?

42. Senior, *Matthew*, 340. See also Meier, *Matthew*, 359–63.

43. See Meier, *Law and History in Matthew's Gospel*, 30–35; Eduard Schweizer, *The Good News according to Matthew* (London: SPCK, 1976), 524: "All the elements [of vv. 2–4] thus recall the signs expected to accompany the coming of the Lord at the end of the world and the irruption of the Kingdom of God." See also Donald Senior, "The Death of Jesus and the Resurrection of the Holy Ones (Matthew 27:51–52)," *CBQ* 38 (1976): 312–29; Dale C. Allison, *The End of the Age Has Come: An Early Interpretation of the Death and Resurrection of Jesus* (Philadelphia, PA: Fortress, 1985), 40–50. Again, Luz, *Matthew*, 3:595–96, and Davies and Allison, *The Gospel according to Saint Matthew*, 3:660–68, note the "eschatological content" (3:665) but take that observation no further.

44. Senior, *The Passion of Jesus in the Gospel of Matthew*, 147.

45. See Moloney, "Matthew 5:17–18," 42–45.

46. As we saw in our analysis of Mark 16:1–8, it was most likely well-known that women (a woman: Mary Magdalene?) were the first to witness to the risen Jesus. The traditions behind the Gospels of Matthew, Luke, and John, and 1 Cor 15:3–8 (our earliest resurrection witness) indicate that the woman announced Easter (Matthew, Luke, and John), and that the risen Jesus appeared (Matthew, Luke, John, and Paul). Mark is the only voice that does not report this. We have suggested that he has changed a well-known traditional ending for his pastoral and theological reasons. See above, 14–16.

47. On the parallel, see Dale C. Allison, "Touching Jesus' Feet (Matt. 28:9)," *Studies in Matthew*, 107–8.

48. The continuation between v. 8 and v. 9 should be noticed, even though the Greek verb could be a simple greeting and is regularly translated "Hail." The theme of joy at the announcement of the resurrection should be maintained. See Luz, *Matthew*, 3:607.

49. See Nolland, *The Gospel of Matthew*, 1252: "To take hold of the feet is at one and the same time intimate and profoundly self-subordinating." See also Hagner, *Matthew*, 2:874; Senior, *Matthew*, 342. For Allison, "Touching Jesus' Feet," 107–16, the patristic interpretation of this episode to argue that the human Jesus was risen, and was not a phantom, should also be added to the themes of humble affection and worship.

50. On Matthew's use of *proskuneō*, see Davies and Allison, *The Gospel according to Saint Matthew*, 1:236–37.

51. On the relationship between the Matthean and the Johannine accounts, see Davies and Allison, *The Gospel according to Saint Matthew*, 3:668–69.

52. See Luz, *Matthew*, 3:607; Byrne, *Lifting the Burden*, 222. Friedrichsen, "Commissioning of the Women Disciples," 270–76, convincingly argues that there are two commissionings at the end of Matthew: the famous commission of 28:16–20, and the commissioning of the women in 28:9–10. On the pastoral importance of this literary parallel between the commissioning of the women (28:9–10) and the men (28:16–20) for the Matthean community (and in the Christian community), see 276–79.

53. For an imaginative reconstruction of a possible debate between Jew and Jewish Christian that could lie behind this schematic presentation of truth countered by a lie, see Davies and Allison, *The Gospel according to Saint Matthew*, 3:652–53.

54. On this, see Keener, *Matthew*, 713–15, especially nn. 334–35.

55. As suggested by Davies and Allison, *The Gospel according to Saint Matthew*, 3:672. See also Nolland, *The Gospel of Matthew*, 1257.

56. Senior, *Matthew*, 343.

57. Byrne, *Lifting the Burden*, 223.

58. Davies and Allison, *The Gospel according to Saint Matthew*, 3:670.

59. See the very helpful remarks of Luz, *Matthew*, 3:611–13. This passage, especially v. 15, is sometimes drawn into discussions of the historicity of the empty tomb. Both the Christians and the Jews know of an empty tomb, but they have different stories to explain it. Behind both—Christian (the resurrection) and Jewish (a stolen body)—lies a common fact: an empty tomb. See, for example, Keener, *Matthew*, 713–15: "The empty tomb tells us about the *nature* of the resurrection (and of the body and history), but the witnesses attest to its facticity" (713). Against this, see Allison, *Resurrecting Jesus*, 312.

60. Luz, *Matthew*, 3:621; Byrne, *Lifting the Burden*, 221: "The programmatic conclusion to the whole Gospel." See also Davies and Allison, *The Gospel according to Saint Matthew*, 3:687–89, and the extensive bibliography of studies dedicated to it (689–91). Joachim Lange, *Das Erscheinen des Auferstandenen im Evangelium nach Matthäus: Eine traditions- und redaktionsgeschichtliche Untersuchungen zu Mt 28:16–20*, FB 11 (Würzburg: Echter Verlag, 1973), dedicates 573 pages to this passage!

61. Senior, *Matthew*, 344, comments: "The resurrection marks the beginning of the final age of the world."

62. See above, 40–41 and note 22.

63. The promise that Jesus would go before them into Galilee has been made in 26:32 (by Jesus) and in 28:7 (by the angel). There is no earlier instruction of Jesus to go to a mountain. But the use of the Greek verb meaning "to instruct" looks back to the first scene on the mountain in 5:1-2 where Jesus had taught them, although a different verb is used there. See Davies and Allison, *The Gospel according to Saint Matthew*, 3:681.

64. See the very helpful study of Terence R. Donaldson, *Jesus on the Mountain: A Study in Matthean Theology*, JSNTSup 8 (Sheffield: JSOT Press, 1985). See also the more general article of Mark D. Green, "Mount, Mountain," *NIB* 4 (2009): 159-60.

65. The "sight" of Jesus continues an important element of the resurrection traditions in the New Testament, beginning with the regular use of the verb *to be seen* or *to appear* in the earliest report of separate post-Easter appearances in 1 Cor 15:5, 6, 7, 8. See Davies and Allison, *The Gospel according to Saint Matthew*, 3:681.

66. Davies and Allison, *The Gospel according to Saint Matthew*, 3:681-82. See also the excellent discussion of this "doubt" and its function in Matthew's narrative in Luz, *Matthew*, 3:622-23, and Hagner, *Matthew*, 2:884-86.

67. On the foreshadowing of this promise across Jesus' ministry, see Luz, *Matthew*, 3:623-24.

68. Luz, *Matthew*, 3:624.

69. BDAG, 609, s.v. *mathētēs*. See also Hagner, *Matthew*, 2:886-87; Senior, *Matthew*, 346.

70. In support of the former (majority) opinion, see John P. Meier, "Nations or Gentiles in Mt 28:19," *CBQ* 39 (1997): 94-102, and in support of the latter (minority) position, see Douglas R. Hare and Daniel J. Harrington, "'Make Disciples of all the Gentiles' (Mt 28:19)," in Daniel J. Harrington, *Light of All Nations: Essays on the Church in New Testament Research*, GNS 3 (Wilmington, DE: Michael Glazier, 1982), 110-23.

71. Luz, *Matthew*, 3:631. See his excellent discussion of the debate (628-31). See also Keener, *Matthew*, 720-21.

72. See Davies and Allison, *The Gospel according to Saint Matthew*, 3:683: "The prophecy that in Abraham all the families of the earth will be blessed (Gen 12:3) comes to fulfillment in the mission of the Church."

73. See, for example, Sim, *The Gospel of Matthew and Christian Judaism*, 252-55.

74. See, for example, Luz, *Matthew*, 3:631-32. See Davies and Allison, *The Gospel according to Saint Matthew*, 3:685, who attempt to explain away the tension (which is resolved in the interpretation adopted here) by claiming that Matthew would insist upon circumcision for Jews but not for Gentiles. There

is no indication in the text that such is the case. For a justified criticism of the ambiguity of Luz and Davies and Allison, see Sim, *The Gospel of Matthew and Christian Judaism*, 252.

75. It is sometimes pointed out that the practice of baptism in the early Church extended the initiation rite to women as well as men. This is true, but hardly in the mind of Matthew at this point of his story of Jesus.

76. See Luz, *Matthew* 3:632; Hagner, *Matthew*, 2:887–88; Byrne, *Lifting the Burden*, 228. For a fine discussion of the origins of Matthew's use of the expression, see Jane Schaberg, *The Father, the Son and the Holy Spirit: The Triadic Phrase in Matthew 28:19b*, SBLDS 61 (Chico, CA: Scholars Press, 1982). She argues that it is a development of the triad of the Ancient of Days, the one like a son of man, and angels in Daniel 7. The use of the formula containing the names of Father, Son, and Spirit is also found in Paul. See 1 Cor 6:11; 12:4–6; 2 Cor 13:13; Gal 4:6, and beyond: 1 Pet 1:2. For indications of the earlier links among Jesus, the Father, and the Holy Spirit in the Gospel, see Nolland, *The Gospel of Matthew*, 1269.

77. Luz, *Matthew*, 3:632.

78. Luz, *Matthew*, 3:633. Davies and Allison, *The Gospel according to Saint Matthew*, 3:680, suggest that, like 1 Chr 22:1–16 (David's commissioning of Solomon) and Jer 1:1–10 (commissioning of the prophet), traditions about Moses are being borrowed in 28:16–20. As Moses commissioned Joshua, so does the new Moses. He further promises his "assisting presence." If this is true, then Matthew's theme of the "perfection" of the Mosaic Law (see 5:1–2, 17) continues into the final episode in the narrative. See also Dahl, "The Passion Narrative," 51–52.

79. Some make an association between the mountain of the final appearance (20:16) with the mountain of the first discourse, the Sermon on the Mount (5:1), and claim this is what the disciples are to teach. See, for example, Hagner, *Matthew*, 2:888; Nolland, *The Gospel of Matthew*, 1270. It is better to look back to all of Jesus' teaching in the Gospel, especially if Jesus' five discourses have some connection with the five books of the Torah. See, for example, Meier, *Matthew*, xii; Meier, *The Vision of Matthew*, 45–51.

80. See especially D. Moody Smith, "When Did the Gospels Become Scripture?" *JBL* 119 (2000): 3–20, esp. 7–18.

81. Luz, *Matthew*, 3:634.

82. As Senior, *Matthew*, 348, puts it: "For Matthew...the Risen Jesus himself is the equivalent to the divine presence within the community as it moves out into history."

83. See Gurtner, *The Torn Veil*, 198: "Matthew asserts that the life-giving death of Jesus inaugurates a new age in which the final, eschatological deliverance from bondage to sin is achieved...For Matthew, Jesus is the true Israel and

the people of God are defined by their relationship to Jesus...Yet the final consummation of the eschatological restoration awaits Jesus' return in glory."

84. Ulrich Luz, *The Theology of the Gospel of Matthew*, trans. J. Bradford Robinson, New Testament Theology (Cambridge: Cambridge University Press, 1995), 5.

85. It has been argued that the warnings and the "woes" directed against the Pharisees found in 23:1–39 may also be directed toward the Matthean Christians who would like to return to their former life and practice in the Synagogue across the road. The Pharisees were not reading or hearing Matt 23, but Christians were. The passage is addressed to crowds and disciples in v. 1. Maybe there was the danger of a lurking "pharisaism" in many of them, as following Jesus was such a radical move from their former life. See, for example, Daniel Patte, *The Gospel according to Matthew: A Structural Commentary on Matthew's Faith* (Philadelphia, PA: Fortress, 1987), 319–20; David E. Garland, *Reading Matthew: A Literary and Theological Commentary* (Macon, GA: Smyth & Helwys, 2001), 232–33; Keener, *Matthew*, 536–37. The most important proponent of this case is Hubert Frankemölle, "Pharisäismus im Judentum und Kirche," in *Gottesverächter und Menschenfeinde?* ed. Horst Goldstein (Düsseldorf: Patmos, 1979), 123–89.

86. Allison, *End of the Age*, 49–50. See Meier, *Law and History in Matthew's Gospel*, 38: "There is much more 'realized eschatology' in Mt.'s theology than is usually admitted."

CHAPTER THREE

The Resurrection of the Messiah according to Luke
Luke 24:1–53

Introduction

It is widely accepted that the author of the Gospel of Luke, like the roughly contemporaneous author of the Gospel of Matthew (about AD 85), used the Gospel of Mark as a source. But Luke is a singularly creative writer, often exercising more originality than Matthew with material from Mark. He also structures his story of Jesus in a way that differs from the other Synoptic Gospels. Luke reports memorable episodes and words from the life of Jesus, found only in Luke.[1] The focus on Mary of Nazareth, the marginalized, the sinners, women, and his remarkable parables (for example, the Good Samaritan [Luke 10:29–37]; the father with two sons [15:11–32]) are but a few indications of Luke's special contribution to the narrative tradition of the earliest Church.

The ongoing story of the Acts of the Apostles, also written by Luke (see Luke 1:1–4; Acts 1:1–2), is important for an appreciation of his understanding of what God did in and through Jesus. The apostles do as they were instructed at the end of the Gospel. They "stay in the city" (see Luke 24:49). After forty days Jesus ascends into heaven, instructing them that they must be his witnesses in Jerusalem, Judea, Samaria, and to the ends of the earth (Acts 1:8). After many journeys, at the end of the book Paul is in Rome, preaching the Gospel unhindered (28:31). In order to give a solid basis to the faith and practice of "Theophilus," to whom the books are dedicated, Luke creatively writes an account that depends on all those who went before him but that bears the sign of a singular creativity (Luke 1:1–4; Acts 1:1–2).[2]

Luke's Passion Story

Luke tells and interprets the well-known events of Jesus' suffering, death, and resurrection in his own way. The essential events that Luke found in Mark, and which no doubt Mark found in the even earlier storytelling tradition of the Church, are still in place: a final meal, Gethsemane, arrest, Jewish trial, Roman trial, crucifixion, death, and burial. As we have seen, Matthew has repeated Mark's account with only minor (but significant) alterations and additions. But Luke is very bold in his creative use of this traditional sequence from its outset. Judas is associated with the plot to kill Jesus from the start. In 4:1–13 Jesus overcame Satan, "and when the devil had ended every temptation, he departed from him until an opportune time" (v. 13). He now reenters the story of Jesus, as he enters into Judas, one of the twelve apostles (22:3).[3] Judas is linked to the chief priests and the scribes who fear the people (v. 2). Luke presents the crowds in a positive fashion. They maintain their sympathy for Jesus (see 23:27–31; 39–43; 48), even though during the passion they are drawn into the condemnation by their leaders (see 23:18).[4] Judas can betray Jesus to them "in the absence of the people" (v. 6).

A strong focus upon the period of the Passover marks the preparation for the meal (22:7–13. See vv. 7, 8, 11, 13).[5] On the day of the unleavened bread, when the Passover lamb was slain, Jesus directs his disciples to prepare for the Passover meal. An improbable series of events leads to the master of the household acquiescing immediately to the request of "the Teacher." Everything takes place exactly as Jesus said it would. He is the master of the situation, despite Judas's joining a plot to kill him. For Luke, all that follows is not a tragic accident of fate.[6]

Throughout his story of Jesus, Luke shows considerable interest in food and meals.[7] The meal section of the Lukan passion narrative is strikingly different from the Markan and Matthean accounts of the final meal.[8] Luke's account of the meal focuses on fragile people who have shared meals with him during the ministry. There is a deep bond between Jesus and the apostles, and he has longed for this meal with them, but it is a final meal before he suffers (v. 15).[9] Luke reports more of the Passover meal, mentioning a first cup (v. 17) and a cup after the supper (v. 20). He associates this first cup with sharing, a symbol of the oneness of the future Kingdom that will be established through Jesus' death and resurrection: the time when Jesus will again drink of the vine. This association of the disciples with Jesus in the initial sharing of the first cup also carries the ominous warning of his oncoming suffering (v. 15) and the promise that the suffering will produce the fruit of the vine in the Kingdom (v. 18).

Only Luke spells out that the bread is a symbol of a body broken for the apostles (v. 19b: "given for you") and that "this cup is poured out for you" (v. 20b). Only Luke adds the words of Jesus: "Do this in remembrance of me" (v. 19c), between the sharing of the bread and the wine.[10] These words may come from early liturgical practice,[11] but poised as they are between Jesus' indication that he is breaking his body and pouring out his blood for the apostles, there is more to it.[12] By the words "do this," they are urged to break their bodies and spill their blood in the future mission. But these privileged and uniquely challenged apostles are marked by weakness and sin. The intimacy of the shared table will be shattered. The account of meal (vv. 14–20) is followed by a long discourse, not found in either Matthew or Mark (vv. 31–38). It begins with Jesus' words: "One who is to betray me is with me on the table." In the light of vv. 3–4, the reader/listener immediately thinks of Judas, but he is not mentioned in vv. 21–23. The apostles question "which of them" would do this (v. 23). In the discourse that follows (vv. 24–38), it becomes clear that Judas is not the only failing disciple; all the apostles are part of the "hand on the table." "Luke's most urgent concern in the Passion story is not with Judas but with the Apostles who remain faithful."[13] Jesus tells all the apostles that they will betray him as they seek ambition and power (vv. 24–30), as they deny and abandon him in fear (vv. 30–34), and in the recourse to arms and violence (vv. 35–38).[14] Even Simon, called upon to "strengthen" his brethren (v. 32), will fail: Peter will deny Jesus three times (v. 34). The discourse addresses the needs and the future of the foundational but fragile apostles of Jesus Christ.[15] They will be granted a kingdom (v. 28), Simon will strengthen them (v. 32), and the two swords are "enough" (v. 38), but the future will not be without its failure.[16]

In the Garden of Olives (not Gethsemane) Luke does not report Jesus' sense of abandonment or the threefold going and coming to Peter, James, and John. He tells the disciples to pray lest they enter into temptation (vv. 39–40), as Satan returns. The time of the "temptation" is at hand, and the disciples are to pray that they not enter into a pact with Satan. Jesus prays that the Father's will be done (vv. 41–42). He rises from his prayer and returns to his disciples, who are so sorrowful that they have fallen asleep. Jesus has never collapsed to the ground (see Mark 14:35), and he does not chide the disciples because they would not watch with him, but his unconditional openness to the will of his Father causes extreme anguish.[17] He again tells them to be constant in prayer that they not enter into temptation (vv. 45–46). Gone is the agony. In its place we have the model of Jesus who shows the disciples what it means to pray to avoid temptation, as the assaults of Satan will soon be unleashed against Jesus and his followers. There will be a struggle, but Jesus shows that openness to the presence of the Father in prayer must accompany this struggle. However, despite his encouragement, the apostles do not join him in prayer.[18]

At his betrayal Jesus remains in control of the situation. Judas, "one of the Twelve," leads the crowd (v. 47). He has fallen to Satan. Even before the betrayal, Jesus says to Judas: "Judas, would you betray the Son of Man with a kiss?" (v. 48). One of those with Jesus asks permission to use the sword, but then strikes the slave of the high priest without receiving that permission (vv. 49–50). Jesus continues to call people to desist from what is wrong and to heal, as the passion begins, recalling Jesus' concerns over the two swords in 22:35–38. The arrest only takes place because Jesus allows it. "The words of Jesus, who understands and controls the situation, are more important than the actions of the adversaries."[19] He permits the arrest because "this is your hour, and the power of darkness" (v. 53). Luke makes no mention of the flight of the disciples (see Mark 14:50; Matt 26:56).

Luke opens the trials by reporting Peter's denials. The reader/listener is able to draw a comparison between the behavior of Jesus and Peter. Jesus has prayed that he might not enter into temptation, but Peter has not.[20] He is sitting among those who arrested Jesus (v. 55) and denies that he knows Jesus (v. 57). Jesus does not fall in the face of temptation; Peter, who has not prayed, does. The crowing of the cock, however, proves that the word of Jesus is the only element of truth in these events. What Jesus said would happen, has happened (v. 60.; see 22:34). By placing Peter's denials *before* the cruelty and injustice done to the innocent Jesus during the trials, Luke is able to dissociate the chief apostle from the violence done to Jesus. It is *before* any of that violence begins that Jesus turns and looks at Peter (v. 61a). The silent look between the unjustly arraigned Jesus and his lying disciple breaks through Peter's frail defenses and reestablishes a union that Peter had broken. Peter remembers the word of Jesus about his denials, and he repents with bitter tears of sorrow (vv. 61b-62).[21] "Luke blends images of the disciples' startling weakness with Jesus' tenacious and ultimately redeeming love for them."[22]

In another sequence unique to the Gospel of Luke, before the trials begin, "the men who were holding Jesus" mock him and beat him. They demand that he prophesy (vv. 64–65). Ironically, Jesus' opponents proclaim the truth. In the programmatic scene in the synagogue at Nazareth (4:16–30) Jesus has announced that "no prophet is acceptable in his own country" (4:24). The passion begins with the trials, but Jesus enters into his passion as the suffering and rejected prophet.[23] The story thus far has made it clear that Jesus is God's Spirit-filled prophet, but that claim is rejected by Israel and its leaders. Luke's version of Jesus' trials is very different from those of Mark and Matthew. He times the Jewish hearing in the morning (22:66–71) and he also has two separate stages in the Roman trial (23:1–5, 13–25), separated by a visit to Herod (vv. 6–12).[24] Across these trials the irony already introduced in the abuse of the true prophet in 22:63–65 is used extensively. In the midst of insult and injury the truth about the prophet Jesus is ironically proclaimed.[25]

In the trial before the Jewish authorities Jesus is asked whether or not he is the Christ (v. 67a). He instructs them on the authority of the Son of Man, which has its beginnings in these Passover events: "From now on…" (v. 69).[26] Since Jesus' other prophecies have come true, so will this promise. As a result of the passion, death, and resurrection of Jesus, he will be enthroned as the Son of Man. But this requires a unique relationship with God. The Jewish authorities understand this and thus ask: "Are you the Son of God then?" (v. 70). Jesus' enigmatic acceptance of their ironic profession of the truth leads them to refuse all his claims. They have indeed heard from his lips that he is the Christ, the Son of Man, and the Son of God, but they reject these truths. There is no formal condemnation of Jesus by the Jewish authorities.[27]

Taken to Pilate, three charges are leveled against him: perverting the nation, forbidding the people to give tribute to Caesar, and claiming to be Christ, a King (23:1–2). Jesus affirms Pilate's query about his being the King of the Jews (v. 3), but this only leads Pilate to tell the chief priests and the multitudes that Jesus is innocent (v. 4). The theme of Jesus' innocence will be stated repeatedly from this point on. Frustrated, the leaders add another accusation: stirring up the people from Galilee to Jerusalem (v. 5). The mention of Galilee enables Pilate to send Jesus to Herod, the ruler of that region. This brief encounter between a vain man who is only interested in Jesus as a miracle worker, and a silent Jesus, may depend upon Isaiah 53:7: "He was oppressed and he was afflicted...yet he opened not his mouth." There is no scourging and dressing as a king in Luke, but Herod dresses Jesus in a royal robe (v. 11) and ironically acts out the truth. Jesus is a king, and is dressed as such, as a corrupt Jewish ruler and a weak Roman governor become friends (v. 12). Like Pilate, Herod is unable to establish any guilt. "Jesus' innocence was so palpable that the two previously irreconcilable rulers in Jewry, one of them a murderous tyrant, came together on this single issue."[28]

Jesus' return to Pilate leads to a twofold insistence that Jesus is innocent (vv. 13–16, 22), but between the frame of these proclamations of innocence Barabbas, whose violent lifestyle is described in detail (vv. 17–19), is preferred to Jesus. A choice of violence over peace, prophecy, Christ, Son of Man, and Son of God has been made. It is a wrong choice. Despite Pilate's repeated insistence that Jesus has done no evil, that he can find no crime in him, that he has done nothing deserving death (vv. 13–16, 22), he responds to the demand: "Away with this man" (v. 18).[29] Barabbas is released, "but Jesus he delivered him up to their will" (v. 25). An innocent person has been mocked and condemned to death by Herod and Pilate. The violent man who has murdered has been given his freedom in the place of Jesus.[30]

Luke tells the traditional sequence of the crucifixion—Jesus carries his cross to the place of execution, he is crucified and utters final words from the cross, and he dies—but the story is told differently. On his way to the place of the skull (see v. 33), Simon of Cyrene is forced to carry the cross of Jesus (see Mark 15:21), but Luke adds that they "laid on him the cross, to carry it behind Jesus" (Luke 23:26). Simon is a model of future Christians who will be called to follow Jesus on this final journey.[31] He is also followed by many people and by the women of Jerusalem who weep and lament over him (v. 27). Jesus warns: if this is happening to me now, as I am slain by the Romans, how much more savage will be the experience of those who are guilty of my death? Readers and hearers of this Gospel, more than a decade after the Roman destruction of the city (AD 70) sense the poignancy of Jesus' telling the women that they will ask the mountains to fall on them and the hills to cover them (vv. 28–31).[32] As Jesus entered the city, he wept over it as he prophesied its destruction (see 19:41–44). As he leaves it, to be crucified outside the city walls, inhabitants of Jerusalem weep over him (23:27).

The innocent Jesus (see vv. 4, 14, 15) is led to the place of the skull and is crucified between two criminals (vv. 32–33). From the cross he offers pardon and forgiveness to the "criminals" who have crucified him: "Father, forgive them, for they know not what they do" (v. 34).[33] The response from the rulers (v. 35) and the soldiers (v. 36) ironically catches up truths proclaimed earlier in the Gospel: "If he is the Christ of God" (v. 35b; see 9:20), "my Chosen one" (v. 35c; see 9:35), "King of the Jews" (v. 36; see 23:3). The rulers scoff, "He saved others, let him save himself" (v. 35a), and the soldiers mock, "Save yourself" (v. 37). Jesus, the innocent crucified One, is Christ of God, Chosen One, King of the Jews, Savior, and Prophet. The theme of the innocence of Jesus is picked up by one of the crucified criminals. Jesus has forgiven all those who have created this "hour of darkness" (v. 34). He asks Jesus to remember him when he comes into his kingdom (v. 42). Following immediately on the charge from the rulers, "He saved others; let him save himself" (v. 35; see v. 37), Jesus makes it clear that his mission is not to save himself but to go on saving others (v. 43).[34]

Signs that indicate the end of an era, and the tearing open of the veil of the Temple indicating the end of God's former ways with Israel, greet the death of Jesus. In Luke's story they *anticipate* the death, while in Mark and Matthew they follow his death. With the turning point of the ages achieved, and the Holy of Holies open to the rest of the world, Jesus dies. His dying words show none of the anguish or terror of Mark and Matthew.[35] He cries out, triumphantly: "Father, into your hands I commend my spirit." The response of the Gentile centurion is "Certainly this man was innocent" (v. 47). Luke, who has never been critical of the ordinary people, reports: "And all the multitudes who assembled to see the sight, when they saw what had taken place, returned home beating their breasts" (v. 48). Repentance begins immediately, as Jesus' death saves: he healed the severed ear of the high priest's slave (22:51), he reconciled Peter with a glance (22:61–62), he extended forgiveness to his executioners (22:34), he invited a repentant criminal to join him in paradise (23:43), and the crowds are moved to repentance at the cross (23:48).

Mark and Matthew had dismissed the disciples from the passion story in Gethsemane (Mark 14:50; see Matt 26:56), but Luke reports: "And all his acquaintances and the women who had followed him from Galilee stood at a distance and saw these things" (Luke 23:49). In Luke's Gospel the disciples do not abandon Jesus, and Jesus does not die alone and forsaken. The earliest Church is gathered at the cross. In the events that have taken place at the cross the disciples have witnessed the forgiveness of sins. They will soon be commissioned to preach repentance and the forgiveness of sins to the ends of the earth (see 24:46–49).[36]

Joseph, from the Judean town of Arimathea, who had not consented to all that had been done, emerges and buries Jesus in a newly preserved tomb. There were many in Israel who were not party to the slaying of Jesus (vv. 50–53). People who had come from Galilee were present at the cross (v. 49), and a man from Judea sees to his burial. Jesus is King of *all* the Jews. It is the day of the Preparation, the eve of the Sabbath. The women know how and where he is buried, and they return to the city to prepare the spices and ointments (vv. 54–56a). "On the Sabbath they rested according to the commandment" (v. 56b). The feverish pace of the passion story slows down, and comes to a stop, as the women rest and wait. This is not the end of Jesus' story. "Bridging Saturday, the Sabbath day, Good Friday and Easter were and remain inseparable."[37]

Luke's Resurrection Story

The Gospels of Mark and Matthew both promise the reconstitution of a disbanded and failed group of disciples "on the other side" of Jesus' death and resurrection. They do this within the context of the Last Supper: "I shall not drink again of the fruit of the vine, until that day when I drink it new in the kingdom of God" (Mark 14:25; see Matt

26:29). Neither Mark nor Matthew report a scene after the resurrection when this promise is fulfilled. It was not needed, as the prophecy points to the celebration of the Eucharist as it was practiced in both the Markan and the Matthean communities.

The Gospel of Luke maintains this tension that looks to a later moment when Jesus will again celebrate a meal with his disciples. Indeed, Jesus makes such a prediction on two occasions: "I shall not eat it until it is fulfilled in the kingdom of God (Luke 22:16), and "I shall not drink of the fruit of the vine until the kingdom of God comes (v. 18). The word *until* rings out across the Gospels and Paul, indicating that the death of Jesus is not the end of the story (see Mark 14:25; Matt 26:29; 1 Cor 11:26). The Gospel of Luke, however, goes further than either Mark or Matthew by reporting two occasions when the risen Jesus shares a meal with his disciples. What Jesus promised at the final meal with his disciples takes place *within the story*. The first of these meal scenes is recorded in Luke 24:13–35, the journey to Emmaus, and the second takes place in Jesus' final appearance to all the disciples (vv. 36–48). This is important for Luke, as he must establish this restored meal fellowship between the risen Jesus and the apostles before he departs in his ascension. These meals form the bridge for the apostles out of the story of their association with Jesus into their mission "to the ends of the earth" (see Acts 1:8). However, before these foundational meal scenes, Luke respects the tradition, and reports the discovery, by women, of the empty tomb (vv. 1–12).

All the episodes of the resurrection account are linked by an insistence that everything took place on the one day. The account opens with the naming of a given day: "On the first day of the week" (v. 1). The reader/listener is next told, "That very same day two of them were going to a village named Emmaus" (v. 13). Toward the end of their journey Jesus' fellow travelers say: "Stay with us for it is toward evening and the day is now far spent" (v. 29). After the breaking of the bread, "they rose that same hour and returned to Jerusalem." They make their report, but "as they were saying this, Jesus himself stood among them" (v. 36). This is the final presence of Jesus to his disciples in the Gospel as, at the end of the day, he leaves them in his ascension into heaven (v. 51). No other "day" has intervened across 24:1–53.[38]

The whole of Luke's Gospel has been directed toward this "day." As Jesus began his journey toward Jerusalem in 9:51, the narrator commented, "When the days drew near for him to be received up, he set his face to go to Jerusalem." That "journey" comes to its close in Jerusalem through "the things that have happened there" (24:18). On this resurrection "day" we sense that we are at the end of a long journey. An important theme of the Gospel of Luke and its companion work, the Acts of the Apostles, is the theme of a journey.[39] Throughout the Gospel a journey leads to Jerusalem, where the paschal events take place. At the beginning of Acts, the early Church is still in Jerusalem. The Spirit is given there, and it is from there that the second journey begins, reaching out to the ends of the earth. The center point of Luke-Acts is the city of Jerusalem. The journey of Jesus leads him there. In Jerusalem the paschal events take place, and he ascends to his Father from that city. Jerusalem is the end of the journey of Jesus, and the journey of the apostles begins there. They are commissioned to go out to all the nations, but they are to "stay in the city" to await the gift of the Spirit (24:49). There they are given the Spirit (Acts 2:1–13), there they first become "Church," one in heart and soul, celebrating the Lord's presence in their meals (2:42–47), just as they celebrated with Jesus throughout his ministry, and especially with the risen Jesus (Luke 24:13–35, 36–48). They eventually set out from Jerusalem, witnesses "in Judea and Samaria and to the ends of the earth" (Acts 1:8; see also 20:7–11; 27:33–36). The city of Jerusalem and the events of that "day" of the resurrection act as a fulcrum around which God's saving history swivels.[40]

Luke 24 is relentless in its focus upon the city of Jerusalem and the "day" of the resurrection. For that reason the structure of 24:1–53 is very simple, united by the city of Jerusalem and the "day."

1. Women find an empty tomb in Jerusalem (vv. 1–12).

2. The journey to Emmaus and the return to Jerusalem (vv. 13–35).

3. The risen Jesus shares a meal, instructs and commissions his disciples in Jerusalem, where they are to stay until they are given the gift of the Spirit (vv. 36–49).

4. The ascension of Jesus from Jerusalem (vv. 50–56).

However much the story that Luke tells has been shaped by the tradition that came to him, even this outline indicates that his resurrection story is different from the accounts of Mark and Matthew. Among the Synoptic Gospels only Luke tells of a journey to Emmaus and an ascension. The meal he shares with the disciples and his commission are not found elsewhere.[41]

The Empty Tomb (vv. 1–12)

The essential elements of an empty tomb account are found in Luke 24:1–12: the women's discovery of an empty tomb on the first day of the week, the appearance of heavenly figures who proclaim the Easter message, and the return of the women to report what has happened (see Mark 16:1–8; Matt 28:1–10; John 20:1–10). Luke, however, has radically reshaped the telling of the story. In the first place, Luke simplifies the complex mix of women who are at the cross, the slightly different group that sees the burial place, and the return to the original group at the cross that is found in Mark 15:40–41, 47; 16:1. Consistent with his intention of continuing the presence of those who played a role during Jesus' ministry, Luke recalls "the women who had come with him from Galilee" (see 8:1–3), as he describes those who "followed" Jesus to his burial in 23:55–56. They have seen to the preparation of the spices in the interval between the burial of Jesus and "the first day of the week" (23:56a; 24:1). Anointing was the motive for the journey of the women to the tomb in Mark 16:1, but it is not mentioned in Matt 28. In Luke it plays only a minor role, perhaps out of respect for the tradition. It also enables Luke to recall the women already mentioned earlier in the story (see 8:1–3).

These are the women who go to the tomb, taking the spices they had prepared (24:1). The narrative is seamless as it moves from the burial of Jesus to the women from Galilee who had followed him to the burial and who had prepared the spices. The discovery of the empty tomb (vv. 2–3) leaves them perplexed, not overwhelmed or amazed (v. 4a; see Mark 16:4–5). Luke wishes to tell his readers and listeners that resurrection faith is not born at an empty tomb. In their perplexity they are confronted with two men, dressed in dazzling apparel (v. 4b). The clothing is a traditional indication that these figures are messengers from heaven, and the response of the women, who bow their faces to the ground in a gesture of reverence and unworthiness, confirms this (v. 5a). They do not wish to face the heavenly figures, thus they turn their faces to the ground.[42] The question the two men pose to the women continues Luke's insistence that faith is not born at an empty tomb. They ask why the women are seeking Jesus in a cemetery. If they wish to find Jesus, they will not find him among the dead: "Why do you seek the living among the dead?" (v. 5b). The men announce the Easter message: "He is not here, but has been raised" (v. 6a),[43] but this has already been anticipated by the indication to the women that they are in the wrong place: the risen Jesus will not be found in a cemetery!

The men now indicate to them that there is a more profound basis for Easter faith than an empty tomb. They may not have found the risen Jesus because the tomb is empty. If they are seeking proof for the Easter message uttered by the men in v. 6b, they are to "remember" Jesus' word to them (v. 6b). They are to recall the message of Jesus, told them during their time with him in Galilee (see 8:1–3). As with all the prophetic utterances of Jesus, what the Son of Man said would take place has happened.[44] The women have journeyed with Jesus from Galilee to Jerusalem, and their presence was first noted in 8:1–3. During that journey they have heard Jesus speak of his forthcoming death and resurrection on three occasions (9:22, 44; 18:31–33). His prophecies come true. What Jesus has promised is the sure basis for hope and belief. He was delivered into the hands of sinful men, and they crucified him. But it is now the third day since he was slain, and the final part of Jesus' prophecy was "and on the third day rise" (v. 7; see 9:22). Jesus' prophecies are repeated, in an abbreviated form in v. 7. Very soon after his first prophecy of his passion and resurrection in 9:22, Jesus had repeated the prophecy, introducing his words with an instruction: "Let these words sink into your ears" (9:44). The men at the tomb now look back to that instruction of 9:44. Jesus had asked his disciples, including the women, to listen carefully to what he was telling them while they traveled with him (see 8:1–3). Their search for Jesus in a graveyard indicates that his earlier words to them are going unheeded. Thus they are commanded: "Remember!" (v. 6).

The women must be regarded as coming to Easter faith. They "remembered his words" (v. 8). In recapturing the words of Jesus, they come to faith, immediately leave the place of the dead (v. 9a), and announce the Easter message to the disciples (v. 9b). In both Mark (16:7) and Matthew (28:7) the women are instructed to tell the disciples that the risen Jesus is going ahead of them into Galilee. This is impossible for Luke, as there can be no going back to Galilee. All the saving events surrounding Jesus' passion, death, and resurrection take place in Jerusalem, and the Acts of the Apostles begins in Jerusalem. As we have seen, the city of Jerusalem is the "fulcrum of salvation history." However, the Galilee tradition is not forgotten; it is preserved in the command to the women to remember what Jesus told them in Galilee (v. 6a).[45]

Only in v. 10 does the storyteller reveal the identity of the women who had traveled with Jesus from Galilee (8:1–3) and had further followed him to his place of burial (23:55–56): "Mary Magdalene, Joanna, Mary the mother of James, and the other women with them." They announce that Jesus' promises of 9:22 and 9:44 (see also 18:31–33, as Jesus approaches Jerusalem) have come true to the eleven remaining apostles and everyone else (v. 10). The group that receives the message of the resurrection is larger than "the disciples and Peter" (see Mark 16:7). But the apostles and everyone else regard such news as an idle tale (v. 11). They are caught in their cultural prejudices, and the evidence of women has no value. "There is a definite air of male superiority in this response."[46] This negative evaluation of women, so contrary to Jesus' attitude to women throughout his Gospel, is evident in the original disciples' decision that the report of the resurrection of Jesus is an "idle tale."[47] Nevertheless, Peter "got up and ran to the tomb." There he finds an empty tomb, with the linen burial clothes now empty. Like the women's initial response, he wonders within himself what all this might mean.[48] As with the women (see v. 4), so also with Peter (v. 12). His visit to the graveyard allows him to see what the women saw: an empty tomb, and the signs of what the Christian reader can recognize as God's victory over death. But this is not enough for those who only see an empty tomb. It only generates wonder about what all this might mean. Easter faith is not born at an empty tomb (vv. 3, 5, 12) but in remembering the words of Jesus (vv. 6–10).

The Journey to Emmaus and the Return to Jerusalem (vv. 13–35)

As Jerusalem is the center of God's history, the opening remarks of the journey to Emmaus are an indication of the wrong choice made by the two disciples. "That very day"—in the midst of the paschal events—two disciples were going to Emmaus, "about sixty stadia away from Jerusalem" (24:13). They are walking *away from Jerusalem* (Greek: *apo Ierousalēm*), the central point of God's story; away from God's journey, making himself known in his Son, from Nazareth (Luke 1—2) to the ends of the earth (Acts 1:8; 28:16–31).[49] Unlike Mark and Matthew, Luke never tells his readers and hearers that the disciples abandoned Jesus. They were even present at the cross, looking on from a distance (see 23:49), and the women who had been with him from his time in Galilee (8:1–3) have followed him to his tomb (23:55–56) and announced the Easter message. But these two disciples have broken that pattern. They walk away from the place and the day of the paschal events. This aspect of the journey to Emmaus is central to Luke's resurrection story.

This impression is further reinforced once the reader/listener notices the details of the account itself. The paschal events are in the forefront of their minds, and the subject of their conversation, as they walk away (v. 14), and as the risen Jesus joins them and "went with them" (v. 15). The use of the personal name "Jesus," followed by "himself" (Greek: *kai autos Iēsous*), makes it clear to the reader/listener (but not to the disciples) that the fellow traveler is certainly Jesus.[50] He has reached out to sinners with pardon, and even offered salvation, on the cross (23:34, 39–43). Now, as the risen One, he "walks with" these two disciples who are abandoning God's saving story. God is also behind this encounter. Luke does not say that they were unable to recognize Jesus, but that "their eyes were kept from recognizing him" (v. 16). There is a mysterious "other" directing the presence of Jesus with the disciples, indicated by the use of the divine passive voice of the verb (Greek: *ekratounto*).[51] God is not mentioned as the subject of the action, but despite the absence of the name, God is responsible. However much they may be abandoning God's story, God is not abandoning them.[52] Jesus opens the conversation by asking them what they were discussing with one another as they walked. They continue to walk away from Jerusalem as they discuss the events that took place there. But at Jesus' question, they stop (v. 16).

A hint of something new has entered the story, but it does not last, as one of them, named Cleopas, responds to Jesus' question.[53] He wonders how Jesus could even ask such a question. Surely, every visitor to Jerusalem would know "the things that have happened there in these days" (v. 18). This is incredible irony, as Cleopas asks Jesus, indeed a visitor to Jerusalem who had journeyed from Galilee to the city, to bring to a climax part of God's saving design. This journey has been under way since 9:51, when Jesus set his face for Jerusalem, "as the days drew near for him to be received up." Cleopas asks the very "visitor," to whom these events happened, why he does not know about them.[54] Jesus, who has been at the center of the events, is also the measure of their significance. But the two disciples know only of the "events," not their ultimate significance. Indeed, "their eyes were kept from recognizing him" (v. 16).

A catechetical-liturgical process begins in v. 19 where, in response to Jesus' further query about the events, they show their extent of their knowledge of "what has happened" in Jerusalem. Crucial to their response to Jesus is their explanation of their expectations of Jesus: "We had hoped that he was the one to redeem Israel" (v. 21). They have not understood the significance of the life, teaching, death, and resurrection of Jesus. They are yet to discover that the resurrection of Jesus is "the resurrection of the Messiah," but "the Messiah of God" (see 9:20), not the Messiah of their expectations. His way of responding to the Father has not fulfilled their hopes for the one who would redeem Israel. But they do know *the facts* of his life, teaching, death, and resurrection.[55]

1. They know of his life, teaching, and miraculous ministry: Jesus of Nazareth, a prophet mighty in word and deed (v. 19).

2. They know of his death: "Our chief priests and rulers delivered him up to be condemned to death, and crucified him" (v. 20).

3. They know of the events at the tomb: "It is now the third day" (v. 21), women have been at the tomb early in the morning, but "they did not find his body" (v. 23).

4. They have even heard the Easter proclamation: There has been a vision of angels who said, "He is alive!" (v. 23).

4. If the witness of the women was not enough, "some of those who were with us" have been to the tomb, and found it empty. "But him they did not see" (v. 24).[56]

The two disciples on the way to Emmaus know everything...but him they did not see (vv. 15–17). Unlike the women, they have not remembered the words of Jesus. Thus they do not understand the *significance* of these *events*, and they continue their walk away from Jerusalem.[57]

The practices of the Lukan Church meet the reader/listener through the subsequent "Liturgy of the Word," as Jesus chides them for their foolishness and opens the word for them, explaining that it was necessary that the Christ should suffer many things to enter his glory (vv. 25–26). He "interpreted to them in all the scriptures the things concerning himself" (v. 27). Jesus journeys with these disciples who have abandoned God's journey, and on the way a "Liturgy of the Word" takes place. He calls to their memory the necessity for the Christ to suffer in order to enter into his glory (v. 26). They should have recalled this, as the women should have recalled it (see vv. 6–7). Not only did Jesus teach these truths (see 9:22, 44; 18:31–33), but it was the true meaning of "all the scriptures," beginning with Moses and the prophets, whose promises Jesus fulfills (24:27).[58] Not only does Luke's use of the divine passive indicate Jesus' role in responding to the design of God, but so does the steady use of the theme of the fulfillment of scripture and Jesus' insistence that it was "necessary" (Greek: *dei*) that these things happen (see vv. 25, 26, 27, 32).

The narrative has now reached a turning point. Initiative must come from the erring disciples themselves. Has the word of Jesus made any impact upon them? The Greek of v. 28 reads: "He pretended (Greek: *prosepoiēsato*) to be going further."[59] Jesus has unfolded God's plan through the explanation of the scriptures. The disciples must now take some initiative in response to Jesus' biblical catechesis.[60] They do so generously: "Stay with us for it is toward evening, and the day is now far spent" (v. 29). As the evening of the Easter "day" draws in, the littleness of faith that led them to leave Jerusalem and the Eleven is being overcome by the presence of the risen Lord (v. 15) and the instruction of his word, asking them to remember (vv. 25–27). A process of repentance and forgiveness is under way, generated by the action of Jesus, who walks with his fragile disciples.

At the meal the disciples recognize him in the breaking of the bread (vv. 30–31).[61] Jesus has set out to follow and to journey with these failing disciples, as they walked away from God's designs for his Messiah (see v. 26). Yet he has accompanied them, made himself known to them, and opened the word of God to them. Finally, he is recognized in the breaking of the bread.[62] The memory of the many meals that Jesus has shared with them, and especially the meal he shared on the night before he died (22:14–38) opens their eyes and anticipates the many meals that will be celebrated in the future.[63] Touched by Jesus' word and presence in their failure, the immediate reaction of the failed disciples is to turn back on their journey: "And they rose that same hour and returned to Jerusalem" (v. 33).[64] The journey "away from Jerusalem" (v. 13: Greek: *apo Ierousalēm*) has been reversed as they turn back "to Jerusalem" (v. 33: Greek: *eis Ierousalēm*). "Jerusalem remains the center of salvation history, the passion and resurrection of Jesus; and the same day, the first day of the week, the first Sunday, remains the favorable time of salvation."[65] Once they arrive back to the place they should never have abandoned and the eleven apostles upon whom the community is founded, before they can even utter a word about their experience, they find that Easter faith is already alive. They are told: "The Lord has risen indeed and has appeared to Simon" (v. 34). Easter faith has already been born in Jerusalem.

The use of the name "Simon" calls for attention. As the Gospel opens, the reader/listener comes to know of a man called "Simon" (4:38). Within the context of a miraculous catch of fish he is called to be a disciple of Jesus, and Jesus introduces a new name for him: "Peter" (see 5:8). The reader/hearer is reminded of this transformation in the Lukan list of the twelve apostles: "Simon, whom he named Peter" (6:14). From that point on, throughout the whole of the Gospel, he is called "Peter" (see 8:45, 51; 9:20, 28, 32–33; 12:41; 18:28). At the Last Supper, where the mingling of the themes of Jesus' sharing his table with the broken and the commissioning of his future apostles is found, he is still "Peter" (22:8, 34, 54, 55, 58, 60–61). Only in foretelling his future denials does Jesus emphatically revert to the name he had before he became a disciple: "Simon, Simon, behold, Satan demanded to have you that he might sift you like wheat" (22:31). The return to "Peter" at the end of Jesus' words is, in itself, a sign that all is not lost (v. 34). Yet, it is to the failed Simon that the risen Lord has appeared, to restore him to his apostolic role (24:34). The name "Simon," without any link with the apostolic name "Peter," appears only before this man's call to be a follower of Jesus (4:18) and at the end of the Emmaus story, when two failing disciples are restored to God's saving story, which is taking place in Jerusalem. There another sinner, Simon, has also been blessed by the presence of the risen Lord (23:34).[66]

The failed disciples have returned to another disciple who had failed his Lord. This return home, however, has happened because the risen Lord reached out to them in their brokenness and made himself known to them in the breaking of the bread:

> Here...we find Jesus eating with outcasts, but this time the outcasts are two of his own disciples who have abandoned their journey of faith, fled Jerusalem, and embarked on their own journey. Jesus crosses the boundaries of disloyalty and breaks the bread of reconciliation with these disciples. Strengthened by the risen Jesus, Cleopas and his companion hasten back to Jerusalem and rejoin the journey of discipleship.[67]

Two disciples with inadequate faith had decided to walk "away from Jerusalem" (v. 13), and the Easter proclamation announced the presence of the risen Lord to the fragile Simon: "The Lord has risen indeed, and has appeared to Simon" (v. 34). This unforgettable story, the subject of imaginative art, poetry, and dramatic representation across the centuries, retains the powerful message that lies at the heart of Luke's Gospel: despite all human sin and frailty, the kingdom of God has been definitively established through the death and resurrection of Jesus.

The Risen Jesus Instructs and Commissions His Disciples (vv. 36–49)

The return of the two disciples from Emmaus to Jerusalem leads into Jesus' final appearance to the apostles. Jesus "stood among them" as they were discussing the events of Simon and the travelers to Emmaus. The traditional Easter greeting of Jesus' peace generates only fear, as they think they are seeing a ghost (vv. 36–37). Consistent with all the Gospels, the appearance of the risen Jesus produces doubt and fear (see Mark 16:8; Matt 28:17; John 20:1–2, 11–17, 24–29). Neither the vision of his hands and feet, nor his request that they touch him, can convince them that he is not a ghost (vv. 39–40).[68] Their fear does not turn into faith but rather unfaith and amazement, mixed with joy (v. 41ab).[69] There is only one way to resolve this unfaith and amazement: to again celebrate a meal, thus continuing the long tradition of the many meals celebrated with the apostles during his life and ministry (vv. 41c–43),[70] and to remind them of his word and the fulfillment of the scriptures

(vv. 44–46). Although commentators almost universally argue that "the scene is intended to stress the identity and the physical reality of the risen Christ who has appeared to his disciples,"[71] more is involved. Jesus is with the apostles from this point on, until he leaves them in the ascension in v. 51. The meal table is the place where he gives them his final instructions, based upon scripture (v. 46), and commissions them to go to "all nations" (v. 47). He leads them to Bethany, blesses them, and is taken up into heaven (vv. 50–51). Only now do the apostles demonstrate their faith. They worship him (v. 52). All fear, doubt, and amazement have disappeared. Read as a single narrative unit, there are close parallels between the experience of the Emmaus disciples and the experience of the eleven apostles.

EMMAUS	JERUSALEM
Talking to one another (v. 14)	Talking to one another (v. 35)
Jesus appears (v. 15)	Jesus appears (v. 36)
He is not recognized (v. 16)	He is not recognized (v. 37)
Jesus asks a rhetorical question (vv. 25–26)	Jesus asks a rhetorical question (vv. 38–40)
Instruction based on scripture (v. 27)	Instruction based on scripture (vv. 44–49)
Revealing actions with bread (vv. 30–31)	Revealing actions with bread and fish (vv. 41–42)
Jesus disappears (v. 31)	Jesus disappears (v. 51)
The disciples return to Jerusalem (v. 33)	The apostles return to Jerusalem (v. 52)

The parallels between 24:13–35 and 36–52 suggest that the postresurrection meals at Emmaus and Jerusalem are carefully constructed to bring to climax the many meals across the Gospel.[72] Fulfilling Jesus' promise at the meal before his death, his sharing the table with his disciples (vv. 13–35) and apostles (vv. 36–49) announces that the kingdom of God has come (see 22:14–23).[73] The use of fish in vv. 42–43 indicates that Jesus is physically present among them, but it also reminds the reader/hearer of an earlier episode. A link has been created across the Gospel between the final commission to the Eleven in 24:36–39 and his initial formation of that same group in 9:10–17, where Jesus had earlier given them bread and fish (9:16).

Jesus drew the disciples who had lost their way at Emmaus back to Jerusalem through a eucharistic table. At another table he commissions his apostles to witness repentance and the forgiveness of sins to all the nations (vv. 44–49). Jesus' suffering and death have interrupted fellowship at table. It has been reestablished by his resurrection, as he promised in 22:16, 18. The apostles have experienced failure, in the person of Peter. But Peter's denials have led him, in sorrow, to repentance (22:54–62). The disciples have experienced failure in the journey of Cleopas and his companion *away from Jerusalem*. But their disappointment with the way God has acted through his Christ, who had to suffer to come to glory, has been overcome by Jesus' journeying with them and opening the scriptures. They experienced the presence of the risen Lord at the table, leading them to the repentance and forgiveness of sins (24:13–35).

As this is the case, a double dynamic is at work in Jesus' commission to the apostles, and both elements will drive their future mission. All that Jesus has said is the fulfillment of God's design, mapped out in the Law of Moses, the prophets, and the psalms. The suffering, crucified, and risen Christ has fulfilled God's design (vv. 44–46). Thus, in the first place, on the basis of their having witnessed the fulfillment of God's design in and through the words and deeds of Jesus, they are to preach repentance and forgiveness of sins to all nations (v. 47).[74] However, as has been made obvious in the two meal encounters in vv. 13–35 and vv. 36–43, on the basis *of their own experience of repentance and forgiveness of sins*, the apostles are commissioned to witness to all the nations (v. 47).[75] They have witnessed the fulfillment of God's design in the words and deeds of Jesus. Luke's story tells of disciples and apostles who have experienced repentance and the forgiveness of sins in their own journeys with the Christ. Even in the presence of the risen Lord they are afraid, doubt, and are amazed (vv. 36–43). The risen Jesus tells them to wait in the city of Jerusalem. There the power from on high will be given to them, and from Jerusalem they will set out to preach repentance and the forgiveness of sins in the name of Jesus (vv. 47–49). As fol-

lowers of Jesus who have themselves sinned, they are eminently quali-
fied to do so![76]

The Ascension of Jesus (vv. 50–53)

The Gospel closes as Jesus leads his disciples out to Bethany. They
are still in the regions of the city of Jerusalem, as they were when he led
them to the Garden of Olives, a place adjacent to Bethany. He says no
words but raises his hands in blessing (v. 50).[77] His journey began in
Nazareth and will conclude in heaven, through the events that have
occurred in the city of Jerusalem. The journey from Galilee to
Jerusalem was mapped out in 9:51—19:44. It comes to an end as he is
carried up into heaven (24:51). But another journey is about to begin,
and the apostles return to Jerusalem, obedient to the command of Jesus
(see v. 49).[78] In the midst of their fear and unfaith, the passion, death,
resurrection, and ascension of Jesus has produced great joy among
these founding figures, who will preach repentance and the forgiveness
of sin, in Jesus' name, to the whole world (v. 52). The Gospel ends where
it began: in the Jerusalem Temple (see 1:5–24), as the apostles are con-
tinually in the courts of the Temple, praising God (v. 53).[79] But so much
has been said and done between the annunciation to Zechariah
(1:5–24) and the continual praise of the apostles in the Temple
(24:52–53). Witnesses of all that has been said and done throughout this
story, the apostles will soon be clothed with the power from on high
(v. 49; see Acts 2:1–4). The journey of the disciples is about to begin,
driven by the Spirit and dominated by the journeys of Paul to the ends
of the earth in Acts 13:1—28:31.

Conclusion

When set side by side with the Gospels of Mark and Matthew, the
Lukan story of Jesus' passion, death, resurrection, and ascension is a
singular literary and theological achievement. Although the passion
narrative has literary links with the earlier Mark, the telling of those
same events is cast in a way that is unique to Luke. The resurrection
narrative is even more original, as only the account of the women's discovery of the empty tomb is common to Mark and Luke. From then on,
Luke has his own unique account: Emmaus, Jesus' meal and commis-

sioning of the apostles, and his ascension.[80] Theological themes that have appeared across the narrative of the Gospel come to a climax as the story of Jesus' life and departure ends. Other themes promise further expansion, as the Lukan story has not reached its conclusion. The passion account is prefaced with episodes that raise the issues of prayer; the role of Satan; and the Eucharist and the eucharistic nature of the lives of disciples, who must now be apostles of Jesus in the long period of time that lies between the departure of Jesus and the return of the Son of Man (see 21:25–36; 22:69). The passion narrative focused strongly upon Jesus as the innocent, suffering Messiah and Son of God who will return as the Son of Man. Even in his moments of greatest insult and injury, Jesus heals, forgives, and promises salvation to fragile and sinful characters in the story, including his disciples and the apostles.

The risen Jesus cannot be found among the dead but generates Easter faith in Jerusalem, journeys with his disciples, forgives the community's foundational members, and commissions them to be his witnesses to the ends of the earth (24:1–53). They have experienced repentance and forgiveness of sin from the Christ who had to suffer in order to fulfill the scriptures. They are sent out to preach what they have experienced. As Jesus returns to his Father, the disciples joyfully return to the focal point of God's saving plan: the city of Jerusalem. There they will wait for the gift of God's power, and from there another journey will begin. They will bear witness to what they have seen and experienced to the ends of the earth (Acts 1:1—28:31).

Notes

1. Luke is so original that scholars once suggested a special source that they called Proto-Luke. It was proposed by Burnett H. Streeter, *The Four Gospels: A Study in Origins* (London: Macmillan, 1924), 233–70. Nowadays the theory is largely abandoned. See Joseph A. Fitzmyer, *The Gospel according to Luke*, 2 vols., AB 28–28A (Garden City, NY: Doubleday, 1981–85), 1:89–91, 104–5.

2. Both books are directed to "Theophilus" (Luke 1:3; Acts 1:1). We cannot be sure whether he is a historical person; his Greek name means "lover of God." He is greeted as "most excellent," a salutation of respect. See François Bovon, *Luke*, trans. Christine M. Thomas and James Crouch, 3 vols., Hermeneia (Minneapolis, MN: Fortress, 2002–13), 1:22–23. Bovon regards

Theophilus as a historical figure, as does I. Howard Marshall, *The Gospel of Luke: A Commentary on the Greek Text*, NIGTC (Exeter: Paternoster Press, 1978), 43; and Christopher F. Evans, *Saint Luke*, TPINTC (London: SCM Press, 1990), 132–34. This is a first hint that the Gospel of Luke is directed largely to a Gentile audience. It is written so that Theophilus will find in the story that follows a "firm basis" (Greek: *asphaleia*) for his Christian beliefs and practices. It is the opposite of making someone fall, thus "a security against falling." See BDAG, 147, s.v. *asphaleia*. On this, see the valuable remarks of Mark Coleridge, *The Birth of the Lukan Narrative: Narrative as Christology in Luke 1–2*, JSNTSup 88 (Sheffield: JSOT Press, 1993), 232–34; and Donald Juel, *Luke-Acts: The Promise of History* (Atlanta: John Knox Press, 1983), 113–23. Juel catches the meaning with the title of his chapter: "So that you may know how well-founded are the things you have been taught." Stuart Moran, *A Friendly Guide to Luke's Gospel* (Mulgrave: Garratt Publishing, 2012), 8, helpfully suggests it means that God can be trusted.

3. Hans Conzelmann, *The Theology of Luke*, trans. Geoffrey Busswell (London: Faber and Faber, 1960), 27–29, 156–57, argued that between 4:13 and 22:3 the story of Jesus' presence is free of Satan. This is not precise, as Satan does appear in 10:18, 11:18, and 13:16. See Bovon, *Luke*, 3:135. Conzelmann is correct, however, insofar as Jesus is never again touched by Satan (NB: "He departed *from him* until an opportune time" [4:13]). See the study of this question by Joseph A. Fitzmyer, *Luke the Theologian: Aspects of His Teaching* (London: Geoffrey Chapman, 1989), 146–74.

4. Robert C. Tannehill, *The Narrative Unity of Luke-Acts: A Literary Interpretation*, 2 vols. (Philadelphia: Fortress, 1986), 1:143–66.

5. See Senior, *The Passion of Jesus in the Gospel of Luke*, The Passion Series 3 (Wilmington, DE: Glazier, 1989), 42–44; Bovon, *Luke*, 3:138.

6. See Bovon, *Luke*, 3:144–45.

7. See, among many, Robert J. Karris, *Luke: Artist and Theologian: Luke's Passion Account as Literature* (New York: Paulist Press, 1985), 47–78. On other earlier indications in the Gospel that prepare for the passion of Jesus, see Senior, *The Passion of Jesus in the Gospel of Luke*, 17–39.

8. On the supper in Luke, see Francis J. Moloney, *A Body Broken for a Broken People: Eucharist in the New Testament*, rev. ed. (Peabody, MA: Hendrickson, 1997), 84–112.

9. I will refer throughout to the Twelve as "apostles." *Only Luke* among the evangelists calls the disciples (Greek: *hoi mathētai*) apostles (*hoi apostoloi*). This is an important indication that the Twelve are chosen to be "sent out" (Greek verb: *apostellō*). Paul, who is similarly in a missionary situation, also uses "apostle." This is especially important in his defense of his own role (see, for example, 2 Cor 11:5–15). See Hans Dieter Betz, "Apostle," *ABD* 1 (1992):

309-11. There are still "disciples" (see, for example, 22:11, 39, 45), but the Twelve are "apostles."

10. The Pauline account of Jesus' last meal (1 Cor 11:23-25) also contains these words. Luke and Paul shared the same tradition about Jesus' final meal. Mark and Matthew have another tradition. John (see John 6:51) has yet another. On this, see Joachim Jeremias, *The Eucharistic Words of Jesus*, trans. Norman Perrin (London: SCM Press, 1966), 160-203; Bovon, *Luke*, 3:153-54.

11. See especially Bovon, *Luke*, 3:158-59, 162-63.

12. See also Senior, *The Passion of Jesus in the Gospel of Luke*, 63-64. Some manuscripts report a shorter version of the words of institution, eliminating everything in vv. 19-20 after the words "this is my body." Nowadays, especially in the light of an ancient papyrus that contains the longer version (the Bodmer Papyrus: P[75]) there is almost universal acceptance of the version that contains: "'Which is given for you. Do this in memory of me.' And likewise the cup after supper, saying 'This cup which is poured out for you is the new covenant in my blood.'" See Jeremias, *The Eucharistic Words of Jesus*, 139-59; Fitzmyer, *The Gospel according to Luke*, 2:1388, and especially the balanced recent discussion in Bovon, *Luke*, 3:154-56.

13. Senior, *The Passion of Jesus in the Gospel of Luke*, 67.

14. On the "two swords," see Charles H. Talbert, *Reading Luke: A Literary and Theological Commentary on the Third Gospel* (New York: Crossroad, 1982), 211.

15. See Brendan Byrne, *The Hospitality of God: A Reading of Luke's Gospel* (Collegeville, MN: The Liturgical Press, 2000), 173-74. Scholars point out that Luke uses the literary form of a "farewell discourse." For further detail, see Moloney, *A Body Broken for a Broken People*, 98-102. But see the modification of this suggestion in Bovon, *Luke*, 3:168-69, and his commentary: "not a farewell speech but a final conversation" (188).

16. See Talbert, *Reading Luke*, 210: "The meal possesses no magical powers. Here is a warning for Luke's community about a danger for which to be alert."

17. Contrary to many commentators, Bovon, *Luke*, 3:197-99, argues cogently for the originality of vv. 43-44: Jesus' angelic support and his perspiration of blood. "One did not need to be docetic to be disconcerted by the episode of Gethsemane and Jesus' all-too-obvious struggle against death" (199; see also 202-4, 211).

18. As Byrne, *The Hospitality of God*, 176, comments: "Behind physical trials and opposition is a malign spiritual power. The only way to emerge victorious is through intense union with God. Otherwise they will 'enter into temptation' in the sense of yielding to the easy way out."

19. Bovon, *Luke*, 3:213.

20. See Bovon, *Luke*, 3:224–25.

21. As Evans, *Saint Luke*, 823–24, comments of Luke's account of Peter's denials: "It is less a paradigm of cowardly discipleship, and more a dramatic account of a crucial moment in the life of Peter, the chief apostle, as an individual, and of his preservation by the Lord for his future work." On the importance of remembering the word of Jesus, see Bovon, *Luke*, 3:233.

22. Senior, *The Passion of Jesus in the Gospel of Luke*, 98. See also E. Earle Ellis, *The Gospel of Luke*, NCB (London: Oliphants, 1974), 260.

23. Luke devotes special attention to Jesus' role as a prophet. This characteristic is not only found in the fact that Jesus' promises and warning come true (as here), but also in the dire warnings that he issues to both his disciples and others across the story, especially in the travel narrative of 9:51—19:44. Luke T. Johnson, *The Gospel of Luke*, SP 3 (Collegeville, MN: The Liturgical Press, 1991), 15–21, draws attention to this feature of Luke-Acts and returns to it across his commentary. See also the survey of scholarship in François Bovon, *Luke the Theologian: Fifty-five Years of Research*, 2nd ed. (Waco, TX: Baylor University Press, 2006), 201–3. David P. Moessner, *Lord of the Banquet: The Literary and Theological Significance of the Lukan Travel Narrative* (Harrisburg, PA: Trinity Press International, 1989), highlights this theme for 9:51—19:44.

24. On the likely sequence of events, see the proposed reconstruction of Raymond E. Brown, *The Death of the Messiah: From Gethsemane to the Grave: A Commentary on the Passion Narratives in the Four Gospels*, 2 vols., ABRL (New York: Doubleday, 1994), 1:610–21.

25. See Bovon, *Luke* 3:237: "Luke 22:54–62 is the story of a conversion. That Jesus himself did not yield at the time of the insults (vv. 63–65) is part of the redemptive action he undertook during his ministry, carried out in his passion, and completed in his resurrection."

26. See, among many, Ellis, *Luke*, 262.

27. See Byrne, *The Hospitality of God*, 178: "Luke communicates the sense that the case against Jesus on the part of the Jerusalem authorities is purely political and false at that."

28. Evans, *Saint Luke*, 853. See also Senior, *The Passion of Jesus in the Gospel of Luke*, 112–16; Bovon, *Luke*, 3:272.

29. Throughout the Gospel "the people" are favorable to Jesus. Now they line up against him (see esp. v. 13). "Abandoned by his own people, Jesus is abandoned by all" (Bovon, *Luke*, 3:275).

30. For the evidence that Luke presents Jesus' death as an idealized martyrdom, see Talbert, *Reading Luke*, 219–25. Parallel to this is the Lukan presentation of Jesus as of no threat to the social order. "The Christian message is on another level" (Bovon, *Luke*, 3:259).

31. Most commentators make this point (e.g., Bovon, *Luke*, 3:299–301), but it is rejected by Evans, *Saint Luke*, 860–61.

32. See Johnson, *The Gospel of Luke*, 373.

33. One again, the textual tradition is not certain, and some see it as an insertion from Stephen's prayer in Acts 7:60. For its authenticity, which I accept, see Tannehill, *Narrative Unity*, 1:272 n. 126; Evans, *Saint Luke*, 867–68; Bovon, *Luke*, 3:306–7. As Ellis, *Luke*, 267–68, rightly points out, Stephen's prayer (Acts 7:60) presupposes the words of the ideal martyr, Jesus.

34. See Fitzmyer, *Luke the Theologian*, 203–33; Senior, *The Passion of Jesus in the Gospel of Luke*, 113–38. Bovon, *Luke*, 3:317, comments upon the use of the verb *save* addressed to the crucified Jesus (vv. 35 [2x], 37, 39): "The actors and the spectators of the drama ironically encourage Jesus to use the power associated with the title [Savior] to escape from the cross. Christ shows that his power exists, but that he uses it differently."

35. However, Bovon, *Luke*, 3:324–25, rightly warns against the elimination of the "rigors of death."

36. See Byrne, *The Hospitality of God*, 184: "They...form a 'point of insertion' into the scene for readers of later generations." See also Senior, *The Passion of Jesus in the Gospel of Luke*, 145–49; Bovon, *Luke*, 3:328–29.

37. Bovon, *Luke*, 3:320.

38. E. Schweizer, *The Good News according to Luke*, trans. David E. Green (London: SPCK, 1984), 369, comments: "It is inconceivable that the scene described in vv. 36–53 took place in the same evening." Surprising it may be, but that is the point Luke wants to make about the unity of the Easter "day" in Jerusalem. See Robert C. Tannehill, *Luke*, ANTC (Nashville, TN: Abingdon, 1996), 348; and the foundational study of Paul Schubert, "The Structure and Significance of Luke 24," in *Neutestamentliche Studien für R. Bultmann*, ed. Walther Eltester, BZNW 21 (Berlin: Töpelmann, 1954), 165–86.

39. There are indications of this "journey" motif in many places in both the Gospel and Acts, but it is most obvious in the journey of Jesus to Jerusalem (Luke 9:51—19:44) and the journeys of Paul that end at the center of the known world, Rome (Acts 13:1—28:31; see the ascending Jesus' commission in Acts 1:8). On Luke 9:51—19:44, see the important study of Moessner, *Lord of the Banquet*. On the same theme in Acts, see 296–307.

40. For more detail, see Richard J. Dillon, *From Eye-Witnesses to Ministers of the Word*, AnBib 82 (Rome: Biblical Institute Press, 1978), 89–91. On Jerusalem as the center of the world, see Mikael C. Parsons, *Luke: Storyteller, Interpreter, Evangelist* (Peabody, MA: Hendrickson, 2007), 83–111. On the unity of Luke 24, generated by these themes, see Evans, *Saint Luke*, 888–89.

41. Although there are very few verbal similarities, a number of these traditions are shared by Luke and John. John also has the risen Jesus share a meal with his disciples (John 21:9–14). Although there is no description of

Jesus' ascending to the Father, he informs Mary Magdalene that although he has not yet ascended, he is about to do so (John 20:17).

42. See Bovon, *Luke*, 3:349–50.

43. As it is missing in some important early manuscripts, the Easter proclamation of Luke 24:6a has long been omitted from translations of the Gospel of Luke. Some translations still do not have it (e.g., RSV and NRSV), while others include it (e.g., JB, NAB). In the past critics thought that it had crept into the Greek text from Mark 6:6. This is no longer judged to be the case, and the words "he is not here, but has been raised" are nowadays judged as belonging to the original text of Luke. They are included in modern editions of the Greek New Testament. For this case, see Fitzmyer, *The Gospel according to Luke*, 2:1442–45. The form of the verb is passive (Greek: *ēgerthē*), indicating that God is the agent, raising Jesus from the dead. On this, see ibid., 2:1545; Bovon, *Luke*, 3:350–51.

44. The theme of "remembering" is important to Luke's Gospel. The disciples are to break bread "in remembrance" of Jesus (22:19), Peter "remembers" (22:61), the women at the tomb "remember" (24:6–8), and the Emmaus disciples "remember" (vv. 30–32). It is part of Luke's presentation of Jesus as a prophet: his words and actions are "remembered." See above, n. 23. See also Bovon, *Luke*, 3:351, and n. 72 on that page.

45. See Johnson, *The Gospel of Luke*, 391, on Luke's handling of the Galilee tradition. See also Tannehill, *Luke*, 351.

46. Johnson, *The Gospel of Luke*, 388.

47. Evans, *Saint Luke*, 898, rightly adds: "The empty tomb, even when interpreted by heavenly messengers, was not regarded as a proof of resurrection."

48. The tradition about Peter recorded in v. 12 is not found in a major textual tradition, and is textually insecure. It is very close to John 20:6–7 (especially the reference to the burial clothes, found nowhere else in the Synoptic tradition). This passage may have been imported into Luke 24 from John 20 by early scribes. It is omitted by the RSV but included in the NRSV, JB, and NAB. For this position, see Evans, *Saint Luke*, 899–900. However, it is consistent with Luke's general picture of the apostle Peter, and it helps explain the report of the two disciples in the next episode: "Some of those who were with us went to the tomb, and found it just as the women had said; but him they did not see" (v. 24). If v. 12 is not part of the original text, it is hard to find a point of earlier reference for v. 24. Although not certain on text-critical grounds, I tend to accept v. 12 as authentic. See the more detailed discussion supporting its inclusion in Fitzmyer, *The Gospel according to Luke*, 2:1542, 1547. See also Schweizer, *Luke*, 365; Johnson, *The Gospel of Luke*, 388; Bovon, *Luke*, 3:353–54.

49. See also Moran, *A Friendly Guide to Luke's Gospel*, 45–47. Remarkably, major commentators do not see the importance of Luke's indication that the two disciples were walking "away from Jerusalem" (Greek: *apo Ierousalēm*). See, for example, Marshall, *Luke*, 892–893; Schweizer, *Luke*, 370. Johnson, *The Gospel of Luke*, 393, Fitzmyer, *The Gospel according to Luke*, 2:1562, and Bovon, *Luke*, 3:371, suggest that Emmaus is mentioned because it is "in the vicinity of Jerusalem" (Fitzmyer), and thus there is no journey away from Jerusalem. Similarly, see Dillon, *From Eye-Witnesses to Ministers of the Word*, 85–86. They see the importance of Jerusalem but do not wish to compromise Luke's "desire to locate the appearance of the Risen One in the holy city or its surroundings" (Bovon).

50. See Johnson, *The Gospel of Luke*, 393. This is the last time in the direct narrative that the name appears.

51. See Bovon, *Luke*, 3:372. We have already seen this use of the divine passive in the Markan and the Matthean resurrection stories. It will appear again in the Johannine story. It is a way of indicating the action of God without mentioning the name, and is very widely used in biblical literature.

52. Tannehill, *Luke*, 352, rightly points out that the disciples are not without guilt in their inability to recognize Jesus: "This concealment reflects their unreadiness to deal with Jesus' death. This is a culpable failure that must be overcome." See also Tannehill, *Narrative Unity*, 1:227.

53. See Moran, *A Friendly Guide to Luke's Gospel*, 45. Bovon, *Luke*, 3:373, points out that Cleopas's question is "not without a touch of aggressiveness." For speculations about the identity of Cleopas and the other disciple, see Evans, *Saint Luke*, 906–7; Bovon, *Luke*, 3:373.

54. See Byrne, *The Hospitality of God*, 187. This is missed by many who regard Jesus as "another traveler," like the disciples (see, e.g., Schweizer, *Luke*, 372).

55. Their knowledge of the "brute facts" of the resurrection story is widely recognized. As Bovon, *Luke*, 3:373, remarks: "Every word of this summary is found in chaps. 22–23." For suggestive analyses of what this means for Lukan thought, see Dillon, *From Eye-Witnesses to Ministers of the Word*, 55–56, 110–11; Johnson, *The Gospel of Luke*, 393–94.

56. This remark from the disciples looks back to the textually doubtful v. 12.

57. For an excellent study of the inherent, but misunderstood, Lukan Christology involved in the disciples' words to Jesus, see Dillon, *From Eye-Witnesses to Ministers of the Word*, 111–45; Bovon, *Luke*, 3:374.

58. Jesus' interpretation of all the scriptures to show what must happen to the Christ in vv. 25–27 and vv. 45–46 shows Luke's conviction that he is writing an account of "the resurrection of the Messiah."

59. See BDAG, 884, s.v. *prospoieomai*: "make/act as though, pretend." See also Bovon, *Luke*, 3:374–75.

60. This shift in the initiative is more than "a narrative device meant to bring loveliness and humanity to the story" (Johnson, *The Gospel of Luke*, 396), although it also does that.

61. The nature of this "recognition" has been the subject of much discussion. As they walked, they now recall, their hearts were burning (v. 32). In the breaking of the bread "their eyes were opened" (v. 31). This is a Lukan version of the important New Testament tradition of the "sight" of the risen Jesus, communicated in different ways across the Gospels (and Paul). There is a sameness between the sight of the pre-Easter and the post-Easter Jesus (as they "remember" the earlier meals). But there is also an important difference (see v. 16: "their eyes were kept from recognizing him"). God and God's design is important in the non-recognition of v. 16 (passive: "their eyes were kept") and the recognition in v. 31. The same Greek verb is found in both places. Sight of the risen Jesus is a gift of God, the result of the action of the risen Jesus who has manifested himself to them. Again the passive verb is important in v. 31: "Their eyes were opened and they recognized him." See Bovon, *Luke*, 3:375.

62. On the eucharistic character of 24:30, see J. Dupont, "The Meal at Emmaus," in J. Delorme et al., *The Eucharist in the New Testament* (London: Geoffrey Chapman, 1965), 115–121; Dillon, *From Eye-Witnesses to Ministers of the Word*, 149–155. Dillon has further pointed out that in both Luke and Acts "breaking of the bread" is associated with instruction concerning Jesus' person and mission. See also Bovon, *Luke*, 3:375.

63. See Byrne, *The Hospitality of God*, 190: "In the exposition of the word and in the eucharistic celebration (Word and Sacrament) he will be present to them throughout the remainder of the 'day,' the day of the Church, whose preaching in his name and in his Spirit will extend the 'day' of salvation (cf. 4:16–20) to the end of time." See also Johnson, *The Gospel of Luke*, 396, 399.

64. The fact that they "return to Jerusalem" in v. 33 further enhances the importance of their traveling "away from Jerusalem" in v. 13. Many scholars have seen the theological importance of this "return." For detail of this scholarship, see Dillon, *From Eye-Witnesses to Ministers of the Word*, 92–94.

65. Bovon, *Luke*, 3:376. This fine summary statement hardly fits with Bovon's earlier agreement with Fitzmyer and Johnson that a journey *away from* Jerusalem is not intended (371).

66. Most scholars see this return to "Simon" as an indication of the traditional nature of 24:34, reflecting Easter confessions that are much older than Luke's Gospel (see 1 Cor 15:4). See, for example, Fitzmyer, *The Gospel according to Luke*, 2:1569: "a stereotyped formula for appearances." See also Marshall,

Luke, 899–900. I am suggesting that there is a more subtle Lukan point at stake. For a similar suggestion, see Dillon, *From Eye-Witnesses to Ministers of the Word*, 100 n. 88. See also Tannehill, *Narrative Unity*, 1:292–93.

67. Robert J. Karris, "God's Boundary-Breaking Mercy," *BT* 24 (1986): 27–28. For a good study of the defects of the disciples in the Gospel of Luke, especially as they emerge over the passion narrative, see Tannehill, *Narrative Unity*, 1:153–74.

68. On the Johannine parallels with the "touching" and "eating," see Bovon, *Luke*, 3:388–89. Far from early Christian apologetic, Bovon suggests that: "It is therefore possible…that the flesh and the bones of the Risen One permit one not only to recognize the historical Jesus, the Christ of the past, but also to imagine the Christ of the future, the triumphant risen one" (391–92).

69. The presence of "joy" in what is otherwise described as lack of faith is puzzling. Johnson, *The Gospel of Luke*, 402, helpfully suggests that v. 41 indicates a purely emotional experience that is too powerful for true belief, and a restatement of the basic Lukan truth that resurrection faith requires the interpretative word (see vv. 44–46). See also Tannehill, *Luke*, 359–60. Marshall, *Luke*, 902, suggests: "It was too good to be true." More theologically, Bovon, *Luke*, 3:392, describes the emotion as "the psychological, physical and existential disruption caused by contact with the divine, more specifically, as the result of God's intervention, that is, Christ's resurrection." See also: "Christ was always the same, even though he had passed through death and reached the divine glory" (401).

70. The importance of the table-fellowship in this passage has been shown by Demetrius R. Dumm, "Luke 24:44–49 and Hospitality," in *Sin, Salvation, and the Spirit: Commemorating the Fiftieth Year of the Liturgical Press*, ed. Daniel Durkin (Collegeville, MN: The Liturgical Press, 1979), 230–39. See also Tannehill, *Luke*, 357–58.

71. Fitzmyer, *The Gospel according to Luke*, 2:1575. See also Talbert, *Reading Luke*, 238–39. For some helpful reflections on the need for this point of view in the Lukan community, see Ellis, *Luke*, 274–76.

72. See Bovon, *Luke*, 392–93; Tannehill, *Narrative Unity*, 1:289–93.

73. See Senior, *The Passion of Jesus in the Gospel of Luke*, 56–58.

74. See Bovon, *Luke*, 3:395–96, on the extension of what has already been said to the disciples into the Christian mission.

75. On this, see Dillon, *From Eye-Witnesses to Ministers of the Word*, 197–203. See also Dillon, "Easter Revelation and Mission Program in Luke 24:46–48," in Durkin, *Sin, Salvation, and the Spirit*, 240–70. For the ongoing importance of this commission in Acts, see Johnson, *The Gospel of Luke*, 402–3.

76. On the Easter appearances as a restoration of failed discipleship, see Tannehill, *Narrative Unity*, 1:277–301. As he writes: "What was closed can be reopened" (299). It must be, as the apostles are the main protagonists in the Acts of the Apostles. See also Bovon, *Luke*, 3:396, 413; Francis J. Moloney, "Luke 24: To Be Witnesses of the Forgiveness and Compassion of Jesus," in *Apostolic Passion: "Give Me Souls,"* ed. Rafael Vicent and Corrado Pastore (Bangalore: Kristu Jyoti Publications, 2010), 183–95.

77. On the blessing as putting the apostles "under the protection of God," see Talbert, *Reading Luke*, 232–33. See also Evans, *Saint Luke*, 928; Johnson, *The Gospel of Luke*, 403–4; Tannehill, *Luke*, 363–64; Bovon, *Luke*, 3:410–11.

78. On the two "journeys," that of Jesus and that of the disciples, see Bovon, *Luke*, 3:404–5.

79. See Bovon, *Luke*, 3:413.

80. The uniqueness of the Lukan passion and resurrection narratives led a number of older scholars to suggest that Luke was no longer dependent upon Mark for this part of his story. Nowadays almost all scholars accept that Luke continued to have Mark before him as he wrote, but that he exercises his theological and literary creativity in Luke 22—24. Especially helpful in this respect are the introductory source analyses to the various sections of the passion and resurrection narratives in Bovon, *Luke*, 3:132–421. He shows convincingly that Luke alternates between a creative use of Mark and an equally creative use of his own source. He does not identify or reconstruct that source. See also François Bovon, "The Lukan Story of the Passion of Jesus (Luke 22–23)," in *Studies in Early Christianity*, WUNT 161 (Tübingen: Mohr Siebeck, 2003), 74–105.

CHAPTER FOUR

The Resurrection of the Messiah according to John

John 20:1–31; 21:1–25

Introduction

The secret to unlocking the meaning of the Gospel of John is to accept what the author says in the Prologue (John 1:1–18). The reader/listener is asked to accept that the Word, who preexisted all creation and is so close to God that what one is the other is (vv. 1–2), became flesh and dwelt among us (v. 14). Jesus Christ, who is always turned toward the Father, tells God's story (vv. 17–18). On the basis of these Johannine truths one can penetrate the mystery of the Johannine Jesus and begin to understand the authority and the exalted nature of his revelation of God to us. An acceptance of what Jesus makes known brings light and life. However, one also can reject Jesus' origins, the purpose of his life, teaching, death, and resurrection. This leaves people in darkness and sin (see 3:18–21, 31–36; 8:12; 9:1–39; 11:9–10; 12:35–36, 44–50; 20:30–31). John tolerates no "in-between" position; a God who so loved the world that he gave his only Son that the world might be saved (3:16–17) offers no other options. The presentation of Jesus across the gospel narrative is determined by this unique Christology.[1] It continues into the passion narrative (18:1—19:42). Based upon the same tradition of an arrest, a Jewish and a Roman hearing, crucifixion, and burial, the Johannine passion narrative is most unlike the presentation of the suffering and crucified Jesus of the Synoptic Gospels. On the cross God's love is revealed and by means of the cross Jesus is glorified. John's presentation of the revelation of the glory of God and the glorification of Jesus reaches its culmination in the two resurrection stories that bring this Gospel to a close (20:1–31; 21:1–25).

The two resurrection stories call for a brief explanation. Most (but not all) scholars accept that the original literary shape of the Gospel was 1:1—20:31. The original Gospel came to an end with the resurrection narrative of 20:1–31, closing fittingly with the words of the author: "Jesus did many other signs in the presence of the disciples that are not written in this book. But these have been written so that you may believe that Jesus is the Christ, the Son of God, and that believing you might have life in his name" (vv. 30–31). However, in every early manuscript that we have of the Gospel of John, this passage is followed by John 21:1–25, that also closes solemnly: "There are many other things that Jesus did. If every one of them were written, I suppose that the whole world would not have room for all the books that would be written" (21:25).

The chapter on the resurrection narratives of the Gospel of Mark also reflected upon two endings to that Gospel. However, it is clear from the ancient manuscripts that Mark originally ended with 16:8.[2] It was more than a century later that scribes added vv. 9–20. *This is not the case with John 21:1–25.* There is no indication in the earliest manuscripts we have that the Gospel ever circulated publicly without the second resurrection narrative. An original Gospel ended with 20:30–31. But there were problems generated by that story, and subsequently within the community for whom it was written, that remained unresolved. Thus, when the Gospel of John finally saw the light of day in its entirety, it ran from 1:1—21:25.[3] As that is the case, this chapter provides a narrative commentary to *both* endings of the Gospel of John.[4]

John's Passion Story

The single most obvious feature of the Johannine story of Jesus' passion and death is the careful and impressive elimination of descriptions of insult and excruciating suffering from the passion tradition.[5] This tendency of the Johannine passion story is driven by its Christology, sketched above. John 18:1—19:42 is a systematic presentation of Jesus as king, "lifted up" on the throne of the cross in a consummate revelation of love in self-gift, the perfection of all that he has been sent to achieve. Because of the Johannine Christology, the cross is the time and the place, the "hour" of the revelation of God's love, and the means by which the Son is glorified (see 11:4; 12:28; 13:1, 18; 17:1). However, it is not only christological. It is the foundational moment of a "new family" on which he bestows the gifts of the Spirit (19:30), baptism, and Eucharist, symbolized by the water and blood that flow from his pierced side (vv. 31–37).

This does not detract from the fact that in John 18:1—19:42 Jesus is arrested, interrogated by both Jewish and Roman authorities, crucified unto death, and buried.[6] The traditional story remains at the heart of its Johannine version, a further indication that the earliest Christian response to the scandal of the crucifixion of the Messiah was to tell the story of Jesus' death and resurrection as its longest coherent narrative.[7] Early Christians could not sidestep the historical fact that Jesus of Nazareth, whom they now regarded as their Messiah, and even as the Son of God, had been done to death by crucifixion. In John the account of the passion events has been boldly reimagined.

Jesus' so-called arrest *in a garden* (18:1–11) is not an arrest. Jesus is in total command of the situation, laying his opponents low with his self-revelation (v. 5: "I am he" [Greek: *egō eimi*]), and insisting that his purpose to found a community through his disciples not be thwarted (vv. 5–7). There is no "hour of darkness" (see, in contrast, Mark 14:43–50; Matt 26:47–56; Luke 22:47–53), and the episode with the sword is transformed; Jesus must drink the cup the Father has given him (v. 11). He is the master of the situation, and the passion story can begin because Jesus permits it. "Jesus' cause is not furthered by violence. He has chosen a very different route in obedience to the will of the Father."[8] Jesus is taken and led to Annas in vv. 12–13, while Peter follows and waits "outside." Jesus is not "tried" by Annas in vv. 19–24.[9] He is questioned about his disciples and his teaching (v. 19). He reduces his opponents to a frustrated slap in v. 22 after he has pointed out that his teaching is well known, but that his time of making it known is over (see 12:36b). The slap is one of two found in the story (see also 19:3); both take place as the truth has been proclaimed but rejected by this gesture.[10] The teaching of Jesus has now been entrusted to his disciples, those who have heard him (18:21). Jesus points away from himself to the future existence of a community that will be the bearer of his word. But as Jesus is making this clear, one of its leading members, Peter, is denying Jesus (vv. 17, 25), as Jesus had said he would, before the cock crowed (vv. 15–18, 25–27; see 13:38). Jesus has entrusted his word to a community of fragile disciples (see also 13:18–20). Enigmatically, the Jewish hearing points the reader/listener to "those who have heard him," the post-Easter Church. That is where they will find the teaching of Jesus that has been "spoken openly to the world" (v. 20).[11] There is no violent rejection of Jesus' status, no condemnation to death (see, by way of contrast, Mark 14:61–64; Matt 26:63–66; Luke 22:67–70).

The trial before Pilate lies at the heart of the passion story, preceded by an episode in a garden (18:1–11) and Jesus' indication that his revelation is to be found with fragile disciples who are, nevertheless, "those who have heard him" (vv. 12–27). After the introduction (v. 28), Pilate presents Jesus as their innocent King to "the Jews" *outside* (18:29–32; 38b–40; 19:4–7; 8–12) and discusses Jesus, his kingship, and his origins *inside* (18:33–38a; 19:8–12), after which he hands Jesus over to be crucified (19:16a).[12] There is only one episode in this long report that is not introduced by a verb that indicates a change of place from outside to inside, or vice-versa: 19:1–3. It lies at the very center of the narrative, the fifth of nine scenes. Only in this scene is Jesus treated violently; he is scourged, crowned with thorns, and struck. But these gestures are symbolic and mean more than might be assumed in a first reading of the passage. The soldiers scourge Jesus, crown him with thorns, and dress him with a purple robe (vv. 1–2). Ironically, the suffering Jesus is dressed as a king, and the soldiers proclaim the truth as they say: "Hail, the king of the Jews!"[13] As in 18:22, the slap indicates a rejection of the truth that they have just proclaimed: Jesus is the suffering king, crowned and dressed as such. There is no mention of his being stripped of his clothing, there is no kneeling before him, there is no mocking, no spitting, no striking his head with a rod. Most important, in contrast to Mark and Matthew, the royal signs of the crown and the purple robe are not taken from Jesus at the end of the mockery (see Mark 15:16–20; Matt 27:27–31). Jesus goes to the cross dressed and crowned as a king. Suffering is present, as it must be in the story of the crucifixion, but it is muted and totally subordinated to John's christological and theological agenda. Jesus is innocent, but he must be "lifted up" (18:29–32). He is born to be king (vv. 33–38a), an innocent king

(38b-40), crowned and dressed as king (19:1-3), "the man" whom "the Jews" insist must be "lifted up" in crucifixion, the Son of God (vv. 4-7), authorized and empowered by heaven (vv. 8-11), the rejected king, as "the Jews" now have no king but Caesar (vv. 12-15). The king is handed over to be lifted up (v. 16a).[14]

The description of the crucifixion is heavy with significance. The physical "lifting up" is described briefly (v. 18). But once Jesus is enthroned, he is universally proclaimed as a king, a claim rejected by "the Jews" (vv. 17-18). The unity of his precious inner garment, which cannot be torn apart by the attending soldiers (vv. 19-24), is a symbol of the community that he will found in the central scene as he consigns Mother to Disciple and Disciple to Mother, and "because of that hour" they become one family (vv. 25-27). His death marks his end, the perfection of the scriptures, and the consummation of the task that the Father had given him, and in death he pours down the Spirit upon his "new family" (vv. 28-30). Only in the Gospel of John does the narrator report Jesus' final words, "It has been brought to its completion," and his final action, "He bowed his head and handed down the Spirit" (v. 30). From his side flow the waters of baptism and the blood of Eucharist that will nourish the members of the newly founded community (vv. 31-34). Because of this death they will gaze upon the pierced one, their perfect paschal sacrifice, to behold Jesus' final demonstration of his words in 15:13: "No one has greater love than this" (see vv. 35-37). There is no cry of dereliction, no mocking, no ironic request that he come down from the cross, no questioning of his ability to save himself as he saved others, no questioning of his trust in God, no abuse from the crucified criminals, no accompanying apocalyptic signs (earthquakes, darkening of the day, the tearing of the curtain, the rising from the grave of the saints), no recognition that a great wrong has been done (cf. Mark 15:22-32; Matt 27:33-44; and Luke 23:33-43 [crucifixion]; and Mark 15:33-41; Matt 27:45-56; and Luke 23:44-49 [the death of Jesus and subsequent events]). If the events that preceded the trial before Pilate (18:12-27: Peter's and Jesus' interrogation by Annas) were concerned with the Church, however fragile, the events that immediately follow the Roman trial (19:16b-37: Jesus' crucifixion and death) return to a Johannine theology of the Church. As Raymond Brown has correctly remarked, "The Johannine crucifixion scene is, in a certain way, less concerned with the fate of Jesus than with the significance of that fate for his followers."[15]

Jesus' burial *in a garden* follows immediately.[16] Unlike the Synoptic tradition (see Mark 15:42–43; Matt 27:57–61; Luke 23:50–56), Jesus' body is bravely requested by two former "secret disciples," Joseph of Arimathea (v. 38) and Nicodemus (v. 39; see 3:1–2).[17] Jesus has been "lifted up" and draws everyone to himself, as these earlier fear-ridden men come out of the darkness into the light and anoint Jesus with a hundred pounds of a mixture of precious myrrh and aloes. The Church moves into action as it anoints the body of Jesus in a way that parallels a royal burial and places it in a new tomb. It is the Jewish day of Preparation, and the Christian reader/listener waits expectantly, knowing that this burial is not the end of Jesus' story (vv. 38–42).

John's Original Resurrection Story (20:1–31)

It has been claimed that so much happens in the Johannine passion account that there is little need for a story of the resurrection. Jesus has been exalted as universal king by means of his being "lifted up" (see especially 18:28—19:16a), the community has been founded (18:1–11; 18:12–27; 19:25–27), the scriptures have been fulfilled as Jesus has perfected his task and poured down the Spirit (19:28–30). The ongoing presence of the crucified Jesus in baptism and Eucharist has been granted so that later generations might also believe, even in his absence (19:31–37). The nascent community emerges bravely from its former obscurity (19:38–42), and all who accept the revelation of a God of love in this man who laid down his life because of his love for his friends will gaze upon the pierced One (19:37; see 15:13). As Jesus stated in his final prayer: "This is eternal life, that they know you, the one true God, and Jesus Christ whom you have sent" (17:3). Bringing to perfection the promise of the Prologue (see 1:18), the crucified Jesus Christ has made God known. What more is needed?[18]

The readers and hearers of the Gospel of John would have been well aware of the tradition that Jesus had been raised from the dead, and they wanted to hear that ending. But there is more to John 20—21 than the continuation of the resurrection tradition. As with Mark, Matthew, and Luke, John tells the resurrection story *for his own purposes.*

Essential elements of Jesus' life and teaching in his public ministry (1:19—12:50), and his instructions to his disciples during his final evening with them (13:1—17:26) remain unresolved. John has indicated that the disciples did not understand what Jesus was saying and doing, but that this would be transformed after he had been raised from the dead, when he was glorified (see 2:22; 12:16). Jesus has promised the gift of the Paraclete (14:15-17, 25-26; 15:26-27; 16:7-11, 12-15). He has commanded his disciples to love one another as he had loved them (13:13, 34-35; 15:12, 17; 17:21-26). But there are also christological issues yet to be resolved. Jesus has indicated earlier that even though he will willingly lose his life, he will take it up again (10:17-18). He has described his situation as "no longer in the world" but coming to the Father (17:11, 13). These promises are yet to be fulfilled. Part of his "hour" will be his glorification in his return to his Father, to the glory that was his before the world was made (1:1-2; 17:4-5, 24). His departure from this world, and what that might mean for his disciples, is a central theme in 14:1-31 and 16:4-33; his request to return to the glory that was his before the world was made opens and closes his final prayer (17:5, 24). There are thus two major elements in the Johannine resurrection narratives: the consequences of the completion of the "hour" *for Jesus*, and the consequences of his death, resurrection, and ascension *for believers of all times*.[19]

The final chapter of the original gospel narrative (20:1-31) faces both of these issues. The epilogue (21:1-25) is concerned mainly with the latter: the challenges that must be faced by Johannine disciples of all ages and, most important, the apostolic foundations of subsequent discipleship.

The resurrection of Jesus from death, fulfilling his earlier promises, is stated with simplicity and assuredness. Indeed, it is almost understated; by this stage of the development of the Christian tradition it is taken for granted. There is no need for proof. The action of God in the raising of Jesus is indicated by the discovery of an empty tomb by Mary Magdalene and the use of the passive verb indicating that the stone *"had been taken away"* (v. 2). This point of view is supported by Mary Magdalene's enduring conviction that someone had taken away the body and placed it elsewhere (see 20:1, 2, 13, 15). She may have been wrong in understanding who was responsible, but she was correct in suggesting that someone other than Jesus had entered the story. This is further reinforced by the description of the empty tomb and the location of the burial clothes in vv. 5–7. The description of the state and the location of the linen cloths and the napkin are in the passive voice (vv. 5–7: "placed" and "folded"). Someone had entered the story of the crucified One and seen to it that all the signs of death have been removed from his crucified body, folded and laid aside. Recalling the episode of Lazarus, who emerged from his tomb still wrapped in the clothing of death and will finally die, Jesus' death clothing has been emptied once and for all.[20] John uses the divine passive, continuing the widespread practice of the Gospels, and indeed the rest of the New Testament, to indicate that Jesus was raised by God (see, for example, 1 Cor 15:3–7, 12–14, 17; Rom 1:3–4; Mark 16:6; Matt 28:7; Luke 24:7; Acts 2:24, 32; 13:33; Col 2:12). It is true that earlier in the Gospel Jesus had indicated that he would lay down his life and that he has power to take it up again (10:17–18), but God is behind everything that Jesus does, and everything that is done to Jesus. Jesus has been raised by God.[21]

John has a literary tendency to "frame" episodes. A number of examples of this practice can be found across the Gospel. The oneness between God and the *Logos* in 1:1 and the oneness between the Father and the Son in 1:18 opens and closes 1:1–18; the Mosaic Law is used by "the Jews" to put Jesus on trial in 5:16–18, and at the end of his discourse that runs from 5:16–47, Jesus claims that Moses accuses (5:45–47); a miracle happens at Cana in 2:1–12, and Cana is again the location for a miracle in 4:46–54; the passion narrative begins with a scene in a garden in 18:1–11, and closes with another in 19:37–42. The same feature appears at a macro level across the Gospel; the most well-known "frame" is created by the often-identified parallels between 1:1–18 and 20:30–31.[22]

A feature of the Cana-to-Cana section of the Gospel, which traced a series of responses to the word of Jesus from the Mother of Jesus, "the Jews," Nicodemus, John the Baptist, the Samaritan woman, the Samaritan villagers, and the royal official (2:1—4:54), has been the presentation of *differing* responses to Jesus by a number of characters in the story. Reading these successive episodes leads the reader/listener through a catechesis on true faith by means of examples of the non-faith of those who rejected Jesus ("the Jews" and the Samaritan woman in a first instance), partial faith from those who accepted him on their terms (Nicodemus and the Samaritan woman in a second moment), and true faith from those who unconditionally accept Jesus and his word, cost what it may (the Mother of Jesus, John the Baptist, the Samaritan villagers, and the royal official).[23] As this "journey of faith" *began the story* (2:1—4:54; after the Prologue and the call of the first disciples [1:1–51]), a parallel "journey of faith" *closes the story* (20:1–29).[24] At the end of the story, however, a well-schooled reader/listener finds that the journey of faith is not made by *different* characters, but by the *same* characters, and each character involved is a foundational figure for the Johannine Church: the Beloved Disciple, Peter (20:2–10), Mary Magdalene (vv. 1–2, 11–18), and Thomas (vv. 24–29). Apart from Jesus, the only other characters who appear in John 20 are the disciples assembled in a locked room (vv. 19–23). They receive Jesus' gifts of peace and joy, the Spirit, and their commission from the risen Jesus. The Easter message has already been proclaimed to them by Mary Magdalene. As she saw "the Lord" (v. 18), so they have also seen "the Lord" (v. 20). The focus of the narrative upon three foundational characters who will bridge the gap between the story of Jesus and subsequent generations of Johannine disciples (vv. 2–10; 11–18; 24–29), represented by the gathering in the upper room (vv. 19–23), leads directly to Jesus' final words: the blessing of future disciples who will believe without seeing (v. 29). Only then can John state why he has written this "scripture" (vv. 30–31).[25]

The Beloved Disciple (vv. 2–10)

The Beloved Disciple is with Peter when Mary Magdalene brings the bad news of the empty tomb along with the claim that the body has been stolen (v. 2). He is explicitly named as "the other disciple whom Jesus loved" (v. 2), even though throughout the remainder of this episode he is spoken of as "the other disciple" (vv. 4, 8). The storyteller has singled out this figure for major roles at crucial moments earlier in the narrative: at the supper (13:23), and at the cross (19:25–27). Unique to this disciple is the love that he shares with Jesus. As we will see, this fact is a key to understanding the blessing of all future disciples in 20:29.

Both Peter and the Beloved Disciple return to the tomb that Mary Magdalene has just left. She ran away from the tomb, but they run back there. Nothing is said about their acceptance or rejection of the message; they are going to see for themselves (v. 3). However, even though Peter initially leads the way, the other disciple outruns him and arrives first. There is something special about the other disciple, but there is still no indication of faith, even though he looks into the tomb and sees the clothes of death empty and waits for the arrival of Peter (vv. 4–5). Peter arrives and sees the linen cloths and the further sign of the head cloth rolled up and put in a separate place. The empty cloths ("folded" and "placed") are a sign of the presence of God, who has entered Jesus' story and raised him from death. The clothing of death has been emptied. However, we are told nothing of Peter's response to this sight (vv. 6–7). Only now does the other disciple enter the tomb, see the signs of victory of God over death, and the narrator announces: "He saw and he believed" (v. 8). This is an important moment. The other disciple, described in v. 2 as "the disciple whom Jesus loved" *did not see the person of Jesus*; he saw the signs of the victory of God and believed.[26] The episode closes with an acknowledgment that the two disciples *as yet* did not know the scripture, that he must rise from the dead (v. 9). The Beloved Disciple comes to belief without seeing Jesus and without the scripture. The scripture that they did not know is the scripture (Greek: *hē graphē*) of the Johannine story, as we will see below.[27] It was impossible for characters *in the story* to be readers/hearers *of the story*. Thus the "scripture" of the Gospel of John is not available to the Beloved Disciple. But he has been presented as the first disciple to come to belief in the risen Jesus, *even though he does not see Jesus*; nor does he know the "scripture" of the Gospel of John. Both disciples are dismissed from the scene as they return home and do not appear again in 20:1–31.[28] The response of the other two foundational disciples, one a woman and the other a man, is strikingly different from that of the Beloved Disciple.

Mary Magdalene (vv. 1–2, 11–18)

Mary Magdalene is oblivious of any possibility of resurrection; she insists that the body has been stolen when she discovers an empty tomb (vv. 1–2). She is so inconsolable that not even the two angels seated in the tomb generate any of the fear or amazement that is normally found in the empty tomb stories (see Mark 16:6, 8; Matt 28:5; Luke 24:5). When they ask why she is weeping, she simply restates her concerns about the stolen body and the fact that she does not know where the body has been placed (vv. 11–13). The same disposition of unfaith continues when Jesus appears. Jesus is described as "standing," indicating the presence of the risen One, but she did not recognize him. There is no suggestion from Mary Magdalene of the possibility of resurrection.

Jesus repeats the question of the angels about her weeping, but she thinks he is the gardener, and again asks about the removal of the body and its current location (vv. 14–15). However, once Jesus identifies her by name, she greets him as her rabbi and wishes to cling to him, to restore the bodily relationship she had with him during his ministry. There is no recognition of Jesus' teaching on the "hour" of his glorification through death and resurrection and his promised return to his Father (vv. 16–17a).[29] Her attachment to Jesus is very *physical,* and Jesus asks her to abandon that form of conditioned faith and announce the completion of the "hour" to his brethren. She finally confesses that she has seen the risen Lord (v. 18).[30] She has made her journey of faith, but she has been called to abandon all attachment to the *physical reality* of the body of Jesus, as he is ascending to God. In doing so, she becomes "the apostle to the apostles."

Disciples behind Closed Doors (vv. 19–23)

Jesus' words of explanation to Mary Magdalene indicate that the departure by means of ascension is imminent (v. 17), but before it takes place, he commissions his disciples in vv. 19–23. Prepared by the Easter message from Mary Magdalene (v. 18), when the crucified and risen Jesus appears among them, instead of the usual doubt and puzzlement, they are full of joy (vv. 19–20). They receive his peace and are told that as the Father had sent Jesus, so Jesus is now sending them (see also 13:18–20; 17:18–19). Given the importance of Jesus' promise in the discourse to give the disciples his "peace" (see 14:27 [twice]; 16:33), the peace greeting of Jesus in 20:19, 21, 26 must be seen as a fulfillment of that promise, also taking place as the "hour" concludes.[31] The same process of fulfillment is also indicated by the joy of the disciples "when they saw the Lord" (v. 22). Throughout his discourse, and also in his prayer, he has told them of the joy that will flow from his departure from them (15:11; 16:20, 21, 22 [verb *rejoice* and noun *joy*], 24; 17:13).[32] The association between the departure of Jesus and the gift of joy is explicit in 16:20 ("Your sorrow will be turned into joy") and 17:13 ("Now I am coming to you; and these things I speak in the world, that they may have my joy fulfilled in themselves"). The joy of the disciples at the sight of the risen Lord fulfills Jesus' promises. However fragile, they are to be his sent ones, the bearers of his word (see 18:21), full of the peace and joy generated by the "hour," and whoever receives them

will receive Jesus and the one who sent him (13:20). As Sandra
Schneiders argues:

> *How are post-paschal disciples to encounter the risen Lord?*
> The negative answer from the first two scenes is that it is not
> through physical sight or touch of his earthly body, that is,
> not in the flesh, but somehow in his disciples. Scene three
> [vv. 19–23] narratively explores this cryptic answer.[33]

The commission of the disciples is further defined by a second
gift of the Spirit and the command that they continue his critical presence in the world as they forgive and retain sin (vv. 22–23). The importance of this second gift is indicated by Jesus' breathing upon them,
recalling the moment of creation in LXX Genesis 2:7 (see also LXX
Ezek 37:9–10; Wis 15:11). The disciples who have received the command to love as Jesus loved them continue to be gifted by his life-giving
love. They receive his peace that produces joy (vv. 19–20); they are commissioned as sent ones of Jesus, just as he was the sent one of the Father
(v. 21); and they receive the second gift of the Spirit as they are commissioned to repeat Jesus' judging presence in the world during his
absence (vv. 22–23).

The first gift of the Spirit is given from the cross to the symbolic
infant Church, the Mother and the Disciple (19:30). Not all interpreters
recognize this. Most translations avoid a direct rendering of the Greek
of 19:30 as "he handed down the Spirit" in his moment of death. They
prefer to repeat a euphemism for death (RSV: "gave up his spirit") parallel to the Synoptic Gospels (see Mark 15:37; Matt 27:50; Luke 23:46).
Most translators and commentators cannot accept that the Spirit is
given at the cross because it is given in 20:22, and it is not possible that
the Spirit be given twice.[34] Recognition of the fact that both 19:30 and
20:22 form part of Jesus' "hour" makes the question of "two gifts of the
Spirit" irrelevant. The gift of the Spirit, promised across the Gospel, and
especially in the Paraclete sayings in the discourse of 14:1—16:33, cannot be limited to 20:22, which is closely tied to the authority of the disciples to forgive and retain sin (v. 23). The Spirit/Paraclete offers more
to the disciples of Jesus than their role, gifted by the Spirit, as the ongoing presence of Jesus' light in a dark world (see 9:4).[35] There is more to
the Spirit-filled Church than this: "another Paraclete," continuing the

revealing presence of Jesus (14:16–17), teaching all things, calling to their remembrance what Jesus has said (14:26), witnessing Jesus' presence to them as they witness (15:26–27), guiding into all truth, and glorifying the absent Jesus by taking what was of Jesus and declaring it to the disciples (16:13–14).[36] "The community and all its members is Jesus at work in the world and his work is to take away sins by giving life in all its fullness."[37] At the cross the Spirit is poured down upon the community of faith and love in a *foundational* moment within the context of the "hour." In his final appearance to the disciples, equally part of the "hour," Jesus gives the disciples their *mission* to continue his critical presence in the world during the time of his absence. Both moments are needed for the fulfillment of Jesus' promise of the Paraclete.[38]

> The oneness of the hour and all that is achieved by and through it is nowhere clearer to the reader than in these two episodes that take place at the hour: the founding gift of the Spirit (19:30; see 14:16–17) and the commissioning of the disciples who have been with him from the beginning to be his witnesses empowered by the Spirit (20:22; see 15:26–27).[39]

Jesus has now brought the "hour" to a close. He has made visible the love of God on the cross, and by means of the cross and resurrection he will be glorified by returning to the Father and the glory that was his before the foundation of the world (11:4; 12:23, 27–28; 13:1; 17:1–5). He has loved and founded a Spirit-filled community of disciples, and he has commissioned them (19:30; 20:22–23).[40]

Thomas (vv. 24–29)

Thomas goes through a faith journey parallel to that of Mary Magdalene.[41] Initially, he is not present when Jesus appears to the disciples and commissions them (v. 24). On hearing that Jesus is risen and has been with them, he will not believe, *unless* Jesus fulfills certain *physical* conditions. Thomas must be able to see and touch the body of the risen Jesus. Only under those conditions will Thomas believe (v. 25). Finally, Jesus comes again, and Thomas is there. He asks Thomas to do exactly as he required for proof but commands him to abandon his situation of "no faith" (vv. 26–27).[42] There is no indication that Thomas responded to Jesus' invitation. Overcome, he makes his confession of faith: "My Lord and my God." (v. 28). Thomas has made a striking journey from absence (v. 24) to faith (v. 28), through a conditioned faith that insisted upon the *physical reality* of the body of Jesus (v. 25). But he is privileged in a way that all subsequent generations of disciples cannot be:

> Through his death, Jesus gives himself completely in love for others, and this love gives them life. Through his resurrection Jesus shows that this love has a future. To see the love and the life that the crucified and risen Jesus gives is to see who God is. Therefore, when shown the wounds of the living Christ, Thomas can say, "Here I see God."[43]

Mary Magdalene has come to love, life, and faith because she saw Jesus, and the same must be said of Thomas. But what of later generations of disciples who will never be "shown the wounds of the living Christ," those who are reading and hearing this story of Jesus? They too are summoned to a future determined by the love and the life of the crucified and risen Jesus. It is at this point that Jesus says his final words, blessing future generations: "Have you believed because you have seen me? Blessed are those who have not seen and yet believe" (v. 29). Wherein lies that blessedness?

Disciples Who See (vv. 1–29)

The disciples, both female and male, are confused and lacking belief. Mary Magdalene does not even imagine resurrection as the explanation of an empty tomb (20:1–2, 11–15), Peter and the Beloved Disciple run to the tomb in puzzlement and perhaps hope (vv. 3–7), while Thomas will believe only if he is granted a physical experience of Jesus' crucified and risen body (vv. 24–29). Mary Magdalene is led to belief in the risen Lord by means of an appearance, a desire to touch, and a commission (vv. 16–18); Thomas believes in Jesus as Lord and God by means of an appearance, a desire to touch, and a challenge (vv. 26–29); while the Beloved Disciple *sees and believes*, but he does not *see* the risen Jesus, nor does he seek physical confirmation of a risen body (v. 8).

The disciples, gathered in a room with the doors tightly closed for fear of "the Jews," are full of joy when they see the risen Jesus among them, bearing the signs of his crucifixion in his hands and his side; they see, but they do not seek to touch the risen body of the Lord or the marks of crucifixion (20:18–20). These disciples are the only characters in 20:1–29 who have no hesitation in accepting that God has raised Jesus from the dead. But they have been prepared for their encounter. They have already heard of the resurrection and of Jesus' proximate return to his Father and God, who is now their Father and God, from Mary Magdalene. She has done as the risen Jesus instructed her. She has returned to the new family of God (v. 17: "go to my brethren...I am ascending to my Father and your Father, to my God and your God") and informed them that the transforming moment of his return to the Father is at hand (vv. 17–18). As across the gospel resurrection narratives, also in John, resurrection produces confusion and puzzlement (see Mark 16:8; Matt 28:17; Luke 24:1–11, 13–35).

Despite the fact that there is no description of a resurrection moment (cf. Matt 28:1–3), the Gospel of John joins the unified chorus of all New Testament witnesses: Jesus has been raised from the dead, as he promised. But the "hour" of Jesus is driven by Jesus' love for his disciples (see 13:1) and God's design to give life to the world through him (3:16–17). Future disciples are to love as he has loved (13:15, 34–35; 15:1, 17; 17:21–26). John's original resurrection story (20:1–31) closes with Jesus' demonstrating his concern for all future disciples. Thus, turning away from Thomas to speak to generations of readers and hearers, those who have not seen Jesus but still believe (v. 29), John closes his book by telling those readers and hearers why he wrote it (vv. 30–31). It is to those subsequent generations that we must now turn, as they are the recipients of Jesus' love command. They too are to love as he has loved (13:34–35; 15:12, 17).

Disciples Who Do Not See Jesus Yet Believe (vv. 29–31)

Looking back across the faith journeys recorded in the episodes of the Beloved Disciple, Mary Magdalene, and Thomas, there is an important link between Jesus' final blessing of those who do not see and yet believe, and the experience of the Beloved Disciple, who did not see and yet believed (v. 8). This is what it means to be a beloved disciple. The author, in fact, suggests that later generations, those who do not see and yet believe (v. 29), have an advantage. They have been be provided with a "scripture" (Greek: *hē graphē*) that the Beloved Disciple did not have (v. 9). Jesus did many signs, but they have not been *written* (Greek:

gegrammena) in this book (v. 30). There is a purpose behind the selection. What has been *written* (*gegraptai*) was "so that *you* [later generations of disciples who have not seen, but have this Gospel, this "writing" (*graphē*)] may believe that Jesus is the Christ, the Son of God, and that believing you may have life in his name" (v. 31). This was *not yet* available for the Beloved Disciple (v. 9), but it is in the hands of those who are reading John's story of Jesus and in the ears and hearts of those who are hearing it. The Beloved Disciple *believed without seeing Jesus,* and he did not yet have the scripture (vv. 8–9). All subsequent disciples are to become *beloved disciples,* also believing without seeing, but having the scripture of the Gospel of John in hand.[44] "The rhetorical purpose of this Gospel is to bring the narrative tradition of the Bible to a culmination in Jesus."[45] But the crucial issue is that these disciples, like the first Beloved Disciple to believe without seeing, are also *beloved disciples* who do not see. It is only through loving disciples that the love and the life of the crucified and risen Jesus Christ will be made visible, experienced by those who hear of Jesus through their word (see 17:20–23). As Dorothy Lee puts it:

> The whole narrative of John 20 functions to reassure the reader that the incarnation is still palpable, even if in a different way, through the life-giving presence of the Spirit-Paraclete activating the eucharistic life, love and mission of the community.[46]

Originally, the Gospel came to an end with this strong recommendation that all subsequent disciples be "beloved disciples." The love theme is never far from the surface of the narrative that tells of Jesus' "hour." The command to love has been directed to the disciples through the story (13:34–35; 15:12, 17). But only one disciple has been expressly identified as the disciple whom Jesus loved (13:23; 19:25–27; 20:2–10). He has played a crucial role at the supper (13:23), at the cross (19:25–27), and at the resurrection (20:2–10). He is the model disciple, and the characteristic of his discipleship is that he is loved. Jesus has asked, however, that disciples love as he has loved (13:34–35; 15:12, 17). Only in this way will others recognize them as Jesus' disciples (13:34–35); only in this way will they make known to the world that the Father sent Jesus to give love and life to the world (3:16–17; 17:21, 23).

For this reason, later in the history of the development of the Johannine storytelling tradition, a further resurrection chapter is added to an original that ended in 20:30–31. The theme of love is one of several issues left unresolved by John 1:1—20:31 and responded to in 21:1–25, especially in the narrative presentation of the relationship between Peter and the Beloved Disciple. They are to provide the foundational experience for further disciples who are to make known the love of Jesus and the love of God (3:16–17; 13:1–38; 17:1–26). Whether or not subsequent "Johannine communities" will bear fruit depends upon their responding to Jesus' command to love (15:12–17).

John's Additional Resurrection Story (21:1–25)

The story of Jesus told in 1:1—20:31 left some crucial issues unresolved, especially concerning the nature of the ongoing life of the community of faith and love founded at the cross (19:25–27). Who could belong to this community? Who were its authorities, and what was the nature of their authority? During the Gospel, Jesus has only issued two commandments: believe and love (see 13:34; 14:1, 11, 15, 21; 15:10; 12; 16:27, 31). They are both essential to Christianity, but a Christian community needs more than belief and love to exist—both in itself, and in its relationships with the world around it. Most likely, some time later in the life of that community, in a period closer to the writing of the Letters of John, which also show the internal tensions of communities trying to live according to the Jesus of the Gospel, John 21 was added to the original Gospel. But it has always been part of the Fourth Gospel that has been read and heard in the Christian Church for almost two thousand years. Another of the tensions that emerged from the Gospel was the relationship between the Beloved Disciple and Peter. What was their role, and how was their authority to be exercised?[47] This second resurrection story, therefore, is more concerned with the inner workings and responsibilities in the post-Easter community than about the Christology of the risen Jesus.

The narrative of John 21:1–25 unfolds in three sections, determined by the characters and the action in each section. Many commentators read vv. 24–25 as the conclusion to the chapter and the end of the final edition of the Gospel.[48] However, given the importance of

Peter and the other disciple, foundational leaders of future disciples commanded to love as Jesus has loved, v. 24 closes vv. 15–24. A traditional final statement is found in v. 25, matching the original ending of 20:30–31.[49] The following literary structure respects the attempt of the storyteller to trace the establishment of roles in the community.[50]

1. *Verses 1–14*: Jesus' appearance to his disciples at the side of the Sea of Tiberias leads to a miraculous catch of fishes and a meal by the lake, during which both the Beloved Disciple (v. 7) and Peter (vv. 7, 11) play important cameo roles.

2. *Verses 15–24*: A discussion between Jesus and Peter clarifies the role of Peter the shepherd (vv. 15–19), and a question from Peter to Jesus concerning the Beloved Disciple establishes his role as the one who has written this story. One is shepherd, the other is witness, and love is crucial to both ministries.

3. *Verse 25*: Conclusion.

Jesus' Appearance to the Disciples on a Galilean Fishing Trip (vv. 1–14)

The account opens with a laconic statement from the narrator that the Lord revealed himself. The verb used (Greek: *phaneroō*) has never been used in John 20 (or elsewhere in the New Testament) to speak of resurrection appearances. Its use is extremely rare in the Synoptic tradition (Mark 4:22; 16:12, 14), but it has been used regularly in the Fourth Gospel to speak of the revelation that takes place in Jesus (see 1:31; 2:11; 3:21; 7:4; 9:3; 17:6). What is about to be reported is something more than a physical appearance. "The whole verse makes the effect of the announcement of a theme."[51] The characters are introduced, and a decision is made to set out on a fishing trip. Among the seven disciples introduced there are some surprises. Simon Peter is named first, as one would expect (see 6:67–69; 13:6–9; 20:2–7), and the identification of Thomas as "the twin" looks back to 20:24. But only here is Nathanael described as "the man from Cana of Galilee," and the sons of Zebedee appear in the Johannine story for the first time. The two remaining unnamed disciples leave open the possibility of the presence of the Beloved Disciple, but given his importance in v. 7 and vv. 20–24 it is strange that he is not listed. This omission, however, adds to the drama when he first appears from nowhere as an active character in v. 7. Peter's decision to go fishing, the other disciples' decision to join him, and the information that their night in the boat produced no catch has been the source of much scholarly speculation that can be noted, but need not be resolved here.[52] Peter and the disciples decide to return to their every-day activities and interests. It is as if their experience with Jesus was a thing of the past, as they return to their former world. It is an essential part of the setting for the appearance that follows, despite its uncomfortable narrative sequence from 20:1–31. Jesus will shortly ask Simon Peter what he loves most, "these things" or Jesus (see vv.15-17).

At a time that links Mary Magdalene's unbelieving visit to the empty tomb in the darkness of very early morning (see the Greek of 20:1: *prōi*), Jesus stands on the beach "just as day was breaking" (see the Greek of 21:4: *prōias*).[53] Another traditional resurrection motif emerges as they are unable to recognize him. He initiates contact as he addresses them as "children" (Greek: *paidia*). This form of address, not found elsewhere in the Fourth Gospel (but see 1 John 2:14, 18; 3:7), indicates an intimate authority.[54] Jesus commands them to cast the net on the right side of the boat, promising that they will find fish (v. 6a). The obedient response of the disciples to Jesus' command bears fruit. On several occasions during his ministry Jesus exercises authority over nature (see 2:1–11; 6:1–15; 16–21), and the miracle that results from the disciples' wordless performance of his commands does not come as a surprise (v. 6b).

In the recognition of Jesus and the response to the miracle, the two disciples who played such an important role at the empty tomb, Peter and the Beloved Disciple (cf. 20:3–10), assume leading roles. The Beloved Disciple recognizes the risen Jesus and tells Peter, but not the other disciples: "It is the Lord" (v. 8).[55] The Beloved Disciple and Peter are "paired," as in the rest of the Gospel (see 13:23–24; 18:15–16; 20:2–10). Paralleling events reported in John 20, the response of these same two disciples at the empty tomb is recalled (see 20:4–10): the Beloved Disciple is the one who confesses his faith in Jesus as the risen Lord, while Peter responds to his indications, just as he had "followed" him in 20:6. He adjusts his scant clothing and leaps into the water.[56] The other disciples bring the boat to land, dragging the net with them (v. 8). The reader/listener is not told of Peter's belief, only of his energetic response to the Beloved Disciple's confession. The other disciples serve merely to round off this part of the story, bringing the boat (presumably along with the Beloved Disciple) and the fish to join Peter and Jesus on the shore.

The account of the miracle and the Easter meal are skillfully joined. On arrival at the shore, the disciples see that a meal has been prepared: a charcoal fire with fish lying on it, and bread (v. 9). Peter's restoration is under way. He had earlier joined those who had gone out to arrest Jesus with lanterns and torches by a charcoal fire (see the Greek of 18:3, 18: *anthrakian*). He is now invited to join Jesus at a meal prepared on another charcoal fire (Greek of 21:9: *anthrakian*).[57] Peter's presence links the miraculous haul of fish with the meal. He responds to Jesus' instruction to bring some of the fish that were caught (vv. 10–11) by hauling the net ashore. The detail of the great catch of 153 large fish that, miraculously, did not tear the net, has teased the minds of readers of this Gospel for centuries. It is impossible to summarize the many suggestions that have been made over the centuries to explain the use of 153 large fish.[58] No doubt the author had good reason for choosing the number 153, for either symbolic meanings or as the result of a mysterious combination of possible numbers, or even because he had it on good tradition that there were exactly 153 fish in the net![59] The never-ending proposals for its meaning probably indicate that, whatever its meaning, it is lost to us now. What is important for the reader/listener is that the risen Jesus has worked a miracle, the result of which is a large number of fish that *should have* torn the net. The seamless garment that could not be torn apart is in the mind of the author (see 19:23–24).[60] The universality of the Christian community, the result of the initiative of Jesus (see v. 6), the leadership of the Beloved Disciple and Simon Peter (see vv. 7, 10–11), and the participation of the disciples in the mission (see 4:34–38; 13:18–20; 17:18; 20:22) is the main point of the story.[61] No matter what the extent of the "catch" that will eventually form the post-Easter community, it will not be torn apart.

Jesus continues to determine the action as he commands them to eat the first meal of the day. There is a transformation of the disciples from v. 4, where they did not recognize Jesus. Guided by the faith of the Beloved Disciple and the actions of Simon Peter, they no longer dare query the identity of Jesus. They now recognize that the risen Lord is present, as the Beloved Disciple had announced to Peter in v. 7 (v. 12).

In v. 9 fish and bread were already prepared for a meal, and these elements recall the miracle of 6:1–15, where both bread and fish were multiplied to feed a multitude at Passover time. There were hints of early Christian eucharistic celebrations there, and they are also present in this passage, particularly in the indications that Jesus "took the bread and gave it to them, and so with the fish" (v. 13; see 6:11). Within an overall message of a universal community, gathered as the result of the initiative of the risen Christ, recognized as "the Lord" by the Beloved Disciple (v. 7) and under the leadership of Simon Peter (vv. 8–9), the eucharistic hints indicate the presence of one of the central acts of worship of the Johannine community (see 6:1–15, 51–58; 13:21–38; 19:35).[62] This episode closes with the announcement from the narrator that this was the third time that the risen Jesus was revealed (v. 14) to the disciples, looking back to the use of the same Greek verb in v. 1 (*phaneroō*).

Peter, the Shepherd, and the Beloved Disciple, the Witness (vv. 15–25)

The rest of the chapter is dedicated to Simon Peter, the Beloved Disciple (vv. 15–24), and the author's conclusion (v. 25). Continuing the previous narrative, "When they had finished breakfast" (v. 15a), the author focuses upon the figure of Simon Peter. Jesus' thrice-repeated question asks Simon Peter to commit himself to love Jesus more than everything that has determined his life to this point: boats, nets, the catch, or anything else that might be self-serving (see v. 3: "Simon Peter told them, 'I am going fishing.'").[63] Peter responds unconditionally, further confessing that his love for Jesus is known by the all-knowing risen Lord. On the basis of this response to his question, Jesus commands Peter to pasture his sheep. A relationship between the role of Peter and the role of Jesus the Good Shepherd in 10:1–18, especially in 10:14–18, is established. What is surprising, however, is that this same question, answer, and imperative is repeated three times (vv. 15–17). There may be precedents for a threefold declaration in front of witnesses before contracting oneself to a binding situation, and there are subtle changes in the words of both Jesus and Peter that have long generated discussion among interpreters.[64]

But the major reason for Jesus' demanding a threefold confession of love is Peter's threefold denial of Jesus at the outset of the passion narrative (cf. 18:15–18, 25–27).[65] However fragile, Peter has been close to

Jesus throughout the ministry (cf. 1:40–42; 6:67–69; 13:6–10, 36–38; 18:15), a closeness dramatically destroyed by the disciple's threefold denial and the subsequent events of the crucifixion of Jesus. The royal lifting up of Jesus on the cross, the foundation of a new family of God, and the gift of the Spirit (19:17–37) have been marked by the presence of the Beloved Disciple (cf. 19:25–27)—and the absence of Simon Peter! The denials must be overcome, and an element in the rhythmic repetition of the same question is the hint of an accusation: "You once denied me…Are you sure of your relationship to me now?" Essential to that relationship is love for Jesus (see 8:42; 14:21, 23–24 [framed positively and negatively], 28; 16:27). In the dynamism of love within the Fourth Gospel, the disciple must love the Son, as the Son loves the Father and the Father loves the Son. Only when that dynamism of love is in place is Jesus' request of the Father possible: that his disciples be swept up into the love that exists between the Father and the Son (17:24–26).[66] It is a relationship of love that must be established, and Peter's embarrassed but honest protestations of love lead to the establishment of a new relationship: Jesus appoints Peter as the one who shepherds his sheep. As Rekha Chennattu rightly remarks: "The threefold profession of love and commitment on the part of Peter therefore reinforces the idea that Peter's unconditional love for Jesus is the foundation and source of his mission as the shepherd of the new covenant community."[67]

The pastoral role that Peter is called to fill associates him with the Good Shepherd. He is charged to "shepherd" and "feed" the "lambs" and "sheep" of Jesus. Discussions of the Petrine office in the Roman tradition of Christianity are out of place in any reading of this passage.[68] Peter's love for Jesus (vv. 15c, 16b, 17b) must be shown in his preparedness to make his own the words of Jesus, the Good Shepherd (vv. 15d, 16c, 17c): "I came that they may have life, and have it more abundantly" (10:10); "I know my own and my own know me" (10:14); "I lay down my life for my sheep" (10:15; see vv. 11, 17, 18); "I have other sheep, that are not of this fold…There shall be one flock, one shepherd" (10:16). Although Peter does not yet know it, this will cost him no less than everything (vv. 18–19).

Introduced by the Johannine double "amen," Jesus reminds Peter of a time in the past, during the ministry of Jesus, when Peter showed a great deal of good will (especially 6:67–69) but ultimately went into denial.[69] That was the time when Peter was young, when he girded himself and went where he would (v. 18a). He has now overcome the scandal of his rejection of Jesus and has unconditionally committed himself to the way of the Good Shepherd (vv. 15–17). The time will come, "when you are old," when Peter will lay down his life for the sheep of Jesus that have been entrusted to his care. Another will gird him and carry him where he would prefer not to go. Despite scholarly squabbles over the exact nature of the way this might be applied to crucifixion, there can be little doubt that by the time this episode was written Peter had already stretched out his hands, an executioner had girded him with a cross, and he had laid down his life for the flock of Jesus.[70]

Simon Peter's commitment to the way of the Good Shepherd associates him with the meaning of the death of Jesus. Death did not fall upon Jesus as a terrible end to a self-sacrificed life. His unconditional acceptance of the will of the Father (see 4:34; 5:36; 17:4) revealed the love of God for the world (3:16). Through this Jesus was glorified (cf. 11:4; 12:23; 13:31–32; 17:1–5), and Jesus gave glory to God (cf. 11:4, 40; 12:28; 13:31–32; 17:1–5). Peter's unconditional acceptance of the role as shepherd of the sheep of Jesus (vv. 15–17) will also lead to the glorification of God in his self-gift in love unto death (v. 19a). The link between Peter and Jesus reaches beyond the pasturing task of the Good Shepherd; Peter is also to glorify God by his death, as Jesus did by his death (v. 19a; see 11:4; 12:27–28; 13:31–32).[71] Having explained all the implications of being the shepherd of his flock (vv. 15–19a), there is little else for Jesus to do but invite Peter to follow him down this way (v. 19b). This "following" has a physical meaning, as Peter walks behind Jesus (see v. 20a), but it also means an "undeviating discipleship all the rest of his days,"[72] which follows Jesus' revelation of the love of God by loving his sheep as Jesus has loved him (13:34–35; 15:12, 17).

Responding to the call to "follow" Jesus in v. 20, Peter does what Jesus had commanded in v. 19. However, as he follows, he turns and sees the Beloved Disciple, described as the one who had lain close to Jesus' breast and had been asked for the identity of the betrayer (see 13:23–25). He is also "following" (v. 20). These two figures, one whose love for Jesus has just been reestablished (vv. 15–17) and the other whose love has never been in question (13:23–25; 19:25–27; 20:2–9), are again paired as "followers" of Jesus, with all that this entails (see vv. 18–19). Peter poses a question that will be answered first by Jesus in v. 22 and then by the narrator in vv. 23–24: "Lord, what about this man?" (v. 21). The question of the relative roles of these two disciples is raised and answered. A post-Easter Johannine community of "followers," aware that they have all been commanded to love as Jesus has loved, look back upon these two foundational figures and ask about the relative significance of their roles in the ongoing life of love to which they have been called.

Peter has been firmly established as a disciple and a pastor as a result of his loving commitment to Jesus (vv. 15–17), but questions remain related to his relationship with the figure of the Beloved Disciple. The paths of these two characters have been entwined across the latter part of the Gospel, at the last meal (13:23–25), in the court of the high priest (18:15–16), and at the empty tomb (see 20:3–10). On those earlier occasions, despite Peter's obvious importance, the Beloved Disciple held pride of place (13:23; 18:15–16; 20:4, 8). Peter denied his association with Jesus (18:17–18), while the Beloved Disciple was with the Mother of Jesus at the cross, and "because of that hour" took her to his own home (19:25–27). He was the only one reported to have come to faith at the empty tomb (20:8). As his role at the final meal, the cross and the empty tomb indicates, the community whose Jesus story is found in the Gospel of John regarded the Beloved Disciple as the founding figure of the community (see 19:25–27).[73] However, if the story has reported that Peter was appointed disciple and pastor of the community as a result of his love for Jesus (vv. 15–17), not only Peter *in the story* but also *the readers and hearers of the Gospel* might ask: "What about this man?" (v. 21). Has the epilogue relegated the Beloved Disciple to a role of lesser significance than the one that he assumed in the earlier parts of the Gospel, especially as the son of the Mother of Jesus in 19:25–27?

Jesus' response addresses an issue that must have been part of the community's wondering. It has in its recorded memory of Jesus' words a promise that the Beloved Disciple would not die before Jesus' return, but this memory needs correction. The exact words of Jesus were: "If it is my will that he remain until I come, what is that to you? Follow me!" (v. 22). Jesus challenges Peter to maintain his role as a follower of Jesus, and he is not to worry about the destiny of the Beloved Disciple. His own destiny has been made clear to him in vv. 18–19. But the community's memory of these words seems to have focused upon the wrong issue. What is central to Jesus' words, comments the narrator, is the conditional: "*If it is my will.*" Jesus did not say that the Beloved Disciple would not die before the coming of Jesus, but that his future would be determined by the will of Jesus. The death of the Beloved Disciple is the problem behind this clarification of what exactly Jesus had said. "The saying spread abroad...that this disciple was not to die" (v. 23a), but "this saying," this expression of popular opinion, was based on a faulty understanding of Jesus' earlier words. The Beloved Disciple is no longer alive, and the community should not wonder at his death.[74] Whatever has happened to the Beloved Disciple is but the fulfillment of the will of Jesus for him. Both Peter (cf. vv. 18–19) and the Beloved Disciple (vv. 22–23) have died, but they *both* have been established by Jesus as foundational figures of a future community of disciples commanded to love as Jesus loved (13:34–35; 15:12, 17)—because of their love for Jesus (21:7, 15–17, 20).

The community that received this Gospel lived in a time after the death and departure of Jesus, and the deaths of Simon Peter and the Beloved Disciple. The narrator, therefore, has more to say about the Beloved Disciple. Matching Jesus' establishment of Peter as pastor and disciple, whose love for Jesus will lead him to death (vv. 15–19), the final words from the narrator clarify the significance of the Beloved Disciple. The mutual consigning of Mother and Disciple at the cross and the gift of the Holy Spirit to this nucleus of the new family of God (cf. 19:25–30) point unambiguously to subsequent disciples' esteem for the Beloved Disciple as the founding figure of the Christian community to which they belong. But he has done more than this. The Beloved Disciple is also the author of the community's story of the life and teaching, death and resurrection of Jesus (v. 24). The narrator's words are close to the earlier intervention of the narrator in 19:35: "we know that his testimony is true."[75]

Living in the in-between-time, between the death and departure of Jesus and the deaths of Peter and the Beloved Disciple, the community has a link between the events of the past and the experience of the present provided by the Beloved Disciple's witness. He was a disciple of Jesus who both witnessed "these things" and then became the author of a record that transmitted "these things." The witnessing of what was written is still present (the Greek *ho marturōn* is a nominal use of a present participle) because of the action of the Beloved Disciple (*ho grapsas* is a nominal use of an aorist participle indicating a task completed in the past).[76] On the basis of this recorded witness, alive despite the death of the Beloved Disciple, the community can be confident of the truth of its Jesus story and its commitment to love as Jesus has loved.

In John 21 a very significant Christian tradition has its formal beginnings. Peter is the appointed shepherd of the flock, called to love to the point of death (cf. vv. 15–19), while the Beloved Disciple is the bearer of the authentic Jesus tradition (v. 24).[77] Both are crucial to a community of disciples called to love as Jesus loved (13:15, 34–35; 15:12, 17). As Bradford Blaine has remarked: "Peter is described as *one who loves Jesus* while BD is described as *one who is loved by Jesus*. This is further evidence that we are to think of the two disciples as composite halves of the ideal Johannine Christian."[78] But the two ministries must be distinguished. Considering the story of the entire Gospel, there can be little doubt about the identity of the most significant disciple. He is the one whom Jesus loved. However, Peter is also called to service and death on the basis of a restoration of his love. The ministry of the Beloved Disciple has been to witness to Jesus in a way that goes on generating life and love because of what was written. The ministry of Peter is to shepherd the flock. The former is the more charismatic role of witnessing, while the latter is the difficult task of governing and caring for the flock. Both are essential, as the Johannine community was discovering, but both ministries are founded on love. The love shown in the witnessing of the Beloved Disciple and the love shown in the service unto death of Simon Peter are the bedrock upon which all subsequent Johannine disciples might attempt to respond to the commandment of Jesus: "A new commandment I give to you, that you love one another; even as I have loved you, that you also love one another. By this everyone will know that you are my disciples, if you have love for one another" (13:34–35).[79]

Conclusion

Despite the splendor of the Johannine passion narrative, in which Jesus makes known God's love for the world (see 3:16–17), glorifies God, and is himself glorified by means of the cross (see 11:4; 12:28; 13:31–32; 17:1–5), bringing to perfection the task given him by the Father (see 4:34; 17:4), the resurrection story plays an essential role in the Fourth Gospel. By means of the use of the divine passive in 20:1, 7, and Mary Magdalene's correct intuition that someone has entered the tomb in vv. 2, 13, 15, John continues the traditional proclamation that God has entered the story of the crucified Jesus. He has been raised. It now remains for Jesus to return to the Father, to the place where he was before the world was made (1:1–2; 17:5). His departure, so strongly affirmed to the disciples in 14:1–31 and 16:4–33, is now imminent, and he asks Mary Magdalene to abandon her hopes for the restoration of the Jesus she once knew. He is ascending to his Father and God (20:17). The departure of the risen Jesus is necessary; it establishes a new situation. The Father and God of Jesus is now the Father and God of the disciples, Jesus' brethren (v. 17). The post-Easter Church, filled with the gift of the Holy Spirit (19:30; 20:22), will continue Jesus' mission and his revealing presence in the midst of light and darkness (vv. 21–23).

In a unique fashion the Johannine story also continues the tradition of the struggle of the earliest Church to recognize and accept the action of God in the risen Jesus. Mary Magdalene (vv. 1–2, 10–15), Peter and the Beloved Disciple (vv. 2–7), and Thomas (vv. 24–27) must make a journey from doubt and incredulity. Mary Magdalene and Thomas eventually make their confession of faith, but only after an encounter with the risen Lord: they *see* Jesus, and thus come to faith (vv. 16–18, 28–29). Only the Beloved Disciple does not see Jesus. He sees the signs of God's victory over death, and believes (v. 8). John 20 closes with Jesus' blessing on all believers in the post-Easter Church who will also believe *without seeing* the now absent Jesus (v. 29). John has written a Gospel for those who do not see Jesus. They have the scripture, written that they might believe that Jesus is the Christ and the Son of God. They will be granted life in his name (vv. 30–31). The traditional proclamation of what God did for Jesus, and what the risen Jesus does for believers, continues to be central to the Johannine resurrection story, as it is told in 20:1–31.

John 21 focuses more intensely upon the post-Easter Church. The theme of the inability of the disciples to recognize the risen Jesus continues (see 21:4), but it only plays a minor role. The miraculous catch of fish, the result of obedience to Jesus' command, indicates that the community must be open to all and it will not be torn apart (vv. 6–7). The leadership of the community is established. Simon, son of John, must three times confess his love for Jesus. Unconditionally committed to Jesus, he is appointed the shepherd of the flock, who will eventually lay down his life for them, thus glorifying God, as the death of Jesus had glorified God (vv. 15–18). Tensions between the roles of Peter and the Beloved Disciple are resolved. They have both left the community through death (vv. 18–19, 21–23), but they are the foundational disciples without whom there would be no post-Easter community. As Peter is the founding shepherd, the Beloved Disciple is the one who witnesses to Jesus in the Johannine story (v. 24), now the "scripture" where the post-Easter community comes to faith in Jesus as the Christ, the Son of God, and has life in his name (20:30–31). In its own inimitable fashion the Fourth Gospel has continued and developed the profound intuitions and belief of the earliest Church, founded in the experience of the risen Messiah. God has acted in the resurrection of the Messiah, and the risen Jesus has established a Spirit-filled community that will continue his mission, despite ongoing doubts, lack of faith, and human frailty.

Notes

1. For a summary of Johannine Christology, see Francis J. Moloney, "Johannine Theology," *NJBC*, 1417–26.

2. It is also possible, but not probable, that the original autograph of the Gospel of Mark lost its ending, but it was not noticed, or seen as important. See above, 6–7.

3. For a more detailed study of this question, indicating the dissimilarity and the continuity, between John 1—20 and 21:1–25, see Francis J. Moloney, "John 21 and the Johannine Story," in *Anatomies of Narrative Criticism: The Past, Present, and Futures of the Fourth Gospel as Literature*, ed. Tom Thatcher and Stephen D. Moore, SBL Resources for Biblical Study 55 (Atlanta: Scholars Press, 2008), 237–51.

4. For much of what follows I am drawing upon Francis J. Moloney, *Love in the Gospel of John: An Exegetical, Theological, and Literary Study* (Grand Rapids, MI: Baker Academic, 2014), 135–89.

5. See the comparative list in C. H. Dodd, *The Interpretation of the Fourth Gospel* (Cambridge: Cambridge University Press, 1963), 425–31.

6. For the suffering elements in John's passion narrative, see Craig R. Koester, *The Word of Life: A Theology of John's Gospel* (Grand Rapids, MI: Eerdmans, 2008), 70–72.

7. See Martin Dibelius, *From Tradition to Gospel*, trans. Bertram Lee Wolf, The Library of Theological Translations (Cambridge and London: James

Clark, 1971), 178–81. For Dibelius, the evidence points to this long narrative existing before Mark.

8. Andrew T. Lincoln, *The Gospel according to Saint John*, BNTC (London: Continuum, 2005), 446.

9. On this, see Andrew T. Lincoln, *Truth on Trial: The Lawsuit Motif in the Fourth Gospel* (Peabody: MA: Hendrickson, 2000), 21–29. "The Jews" have already tried him during his public ministry. They have come to their verdict (11:47–53), and Jesus has accepted their verdict of death (12:27–33).

10. See Ignace de la Potterie, *The Hour of Jesus: The Passion and Resurrection of Jesus according to John: Text and Spirit* (Slough, UK: St. Paul Publications, 1989), 72–74; Raymond E. Brown, *The Death of the Messiah: From Gethsemane to the Grave: A Commentary on the Passion Narratives in the Four Gospels*, 2 vols., ABRL (New York: Doubleday, 1994), 1:413.

11. On the "ecclesial" nature of 18:12–27, see Francis J. Moloney, *The Gospel of John*, SP 4 (Collegeville, MN: The Liturgical Press, 1998), 486–92.

12. On 18:28—19:16a as an ironic "trial in reverse," see Lincoln, *Truth on Trial*, 123–38. Against the background of Second Isaiah, Lincoln concludes: "He can be seen as confuting every tongue that rises against him in judgment (cf. Isa 54:17) and even, though on trial, as the judge who executes justice (cf. Isa 42:1, 2, 4)," 138.

13. Only in John 19:3 is Jesus hailed as "*the* King of the Jews," with the definite article. In the parallel Mark 15:18 and Matt 27:19 no article appears. Luke does not report this detail.

14. On the tragic irony of the cry that they have no king but Caesar, see Lincoln, *The Gospel according to Saint John*, 470–71.

15. Raymond E. Brown, *The Gospel according to John*, 2 vols., AB 29–29A (Garden City, NY: Doubleday, 1966–70), 2:912.

16. The Johannine use of garden scenes to open (18:1–11) and close (19:38–42) the passion story is sometimes seen as a reference to the garden theme in Genesis. See Mary Coloe, "Theological Reflections on Creation in the Gospel of John," *Pacifica* 24 (2011): 1–12.

17. Lincoln, *The Gospel according to Saint John*, 484, helpfully suggests that the description of Joseph looks back to the leaders of "the Jews" described in 12:42 who believed in him but would not confess it for fear that they might be put out of the synagogue. See Barnabas Lindars, *The Gospel of John*, NCB (London: Oliphants, 1973), 592: "These secret believers now come out into the open, carrying forward the idea of confession of faith latent in the piercing episode."

18. See, for example, Rudolf Bultmann, *Theology of the New Testament*, trans. Kendrick Grobel, 2 vols. (London: SCM Press, 1955), 2:56: "If Jesus' death on the cross is already his exaltation and glorification, *his resurrection*

cannot be an event of special significance. No resurrection is needed to destroy the triumph which death might be supposed to have gained in the crucifixion" (italics in original).

19. On the claims of this paragraph, see the remarkable essay of Sandra M. Schneiders, "The Resurrection (of the Body) in the Fourth Gospel: A Key to Johannine Spirituality," in *Life in Abundance: Studies in John's Gospel in Tribute to Raymond E. Brown*, ed. John R. Donahue (Collegeville, MN: The Liturgical Press, 2005), 168–98.

20. For the relationship between the cloths of Lazarus (11:44) and the cloths in the tomb of Jesus (20:7) see, among many, Brendan Byrne, *Lazarus: A Contemporary Reading of John 11:1–46*, Zacchaeus Studies: New Testament (Collegeville, MN: The Liturgical Press, 1991), 64–65.

21. See Moloney, *The Gospel of John*, 519–20, 522–23.

22. See especially the work of George Mlakhuzhyil, *The Christocentric Literary Structure of the Fourth Gospel*, 2nd ed., AnBib 117 (Rome: Gregorian and Biblical Press, 2011).

23. See Francis J. Moloney, *Belief in the Word: Reading John 1–4* (Minneapolis, MN: Fortress, 1993), 192–99.

24. For a more detailed presentation of what follows, see Francis J. Moloney, *Glory Not Dishonor: Reading John 13—21* (Minneapolis, MN: Fortress, 1998), 153–81; Moloney, *John*, 515–45.

25. As Lindars, *The Gospel of John*, 595, says of John 20: "All that remains now is to explain more clearly the nature of the act of faith by which the life in Christ may be appropriated."

26. Some claim that the Beloved Disciple does not come to resurrection faith. For the discussion, and strong support for the position taken above, see Lincoln, *The Gospel according to Saint John*, 490–91.

27. For a detailed argument that the author of the Fourth Gospel regarded what he was writing as "scripture," indeed, the completion of scripture, see: Francis J. Moloney, "The Gospel of John as Scripture," *CBQ* 67 (2005): 454–68; Moloney, "The Gospel of John: The 'End' of Scripture," *Int* 63 (2009): 356–66.

28. They return as major players in 21:1–25. It could be assumed that they were at the gathering in 20:19–23. However, v. 10 states that they returned to their homes (plural), not to the disciples locked in the room for fear of "the Jews" in v. 19.

29. As Schneiders, "The Resurrection," 183, puts it: "She voices the position of one who has not grasped the meaning of 'the hour,' Jesus' transition from the dispensation of the flesh to the dispensation of glory. She is seeking 'the Lord' whom she equates with his corpse." See also Lincoln, *The Gospel according to Saint John*, 496: "His resurrection becomes part of the overall theo-

logical point the evangelist makes about Jesus—he is the unique revelation of God, the one who has come from God and is going to God."

30. See the important remarks of Rekha M Chennattu, *Johannine Discipleship as a Covenant Relationship* (Peabody, MA: Hendrickson, 2006), 150–55, that suggestively point to Mary's role as a "reclaiming of the covenant relationship." Her journey from non-faith to active faith is complete.

31. The greeting "peace be with you" can be read as simple Semitic greeting, just as modern Jews greet one another with the word *shalōm* and the Arabic-speaking people with the expression *salām*. The context makes this possibility most unlikely.

32. The steady use of the Greek verb *to rejoice* and the noun *joy* across the promises and the prayer of 15:11, 16:20, 21, 22, 23, 24, and 17:13, and the appearance of the verb *to be glad* in v. 20, "when they saw the Lord," are clear cases of a fulfillment that takes place at the "hour" of Jesus' death, resurrection, and ascension.

33. Schneiders, "The Resurrection," 184 (italics in original). See also Chennattu, *Johannine Discipleship as a Covenant Relationship*, 159–61.

34. See, among many, Gary M. Burge, *The Anointed Community: The Holy Spirit in the Johannine Tradition* (Grand Rapids, MI: Eerdmans, 1987), 133–35, and the desire of Koester, *Word of Life*, 146, to have it both ways, with 19:30 foreshadowing the gift of 20:22. See also Lindars, *The Gospel of John*, 582–83. For Lincoln, *The Gospel according to Saint John*, 498–99: the Spirit is "available" at 19:30, and in 20:22 Jesus "confers" it on his disciples.

35. This sentence succinctly suggests my interpretation of v. 23. What exactly is meant by "If you forgive the sins of any, they are forgiven; if you retain the sins of any, they are retained" is a notorious problem for Johannine interpretation. It has been further complicated by the Roman Catholic identification of this passage as a biblical basis for the sacrament of penance. The interpretation suggested above is that after Jesus' return to the Father, his critical presence in the world, bringing a light into darkness that is sometimes accepted and sometimes rejected, will continue in the experience of the disciples. Put positively, they will continue to embody the *critical presence* of the revelation of God in the world, thus forgiving and retaining. Raymond E. Brown, *The Gospel according to John*, 2:1044, puts it well: "The power to isolate, repel and negate evil and sin, a power given to Jesus by the Father and given in turn by Jesus through the Spirit to those whom he commissions." The critical exposing of right and wrong that results from the gift of the Paraclete is found in 16:7–11. See Moloney, *John*, 440–41, 445–47.

36. For a rich summary of the Johannine promise of the gift of the Spirit/Paraclete, see Koester, *Word of Life*, 147–60.

37. Schneiders, "The Resurrection," 187.

38. See Chennattu, *Johannine Discipleship as a Covenant Relationship*, 161–63. Jean Zumstein, "Jesus' Resurrection in the Farewell Discourses," in *The Resurrection of Jesus in the Gospel of John*, ed. Craig R. Koester and Reimund Bieringer, WUNT 222 (Tübingen: Mohr Siebeck, 2008), 103–26, rightly points to the importance of Jesus' resurrection appearances as fulfillment of the promises of Jesus' departure in 14:18–19 and 16:16–22. The same must be argued for the gift of the Spirit in *both* 19:30 and 20:23 for the fulfillment of the Paraclete promises of 14:1—16:33.

39. Moloney, *Glory Not Dishonor*, 172. There is no point in comparing the Lukan Pentecost and the Johannine gift of the Spirit at the "hour." See Xavier Léon-Dufour, *Resurrection and the Message of Easter* (London: Geoffrey Chapman, 1974), 173: "John sets forth an essential dimension of the Easter mystery which Luke has deliberately extended in time."

40. See the insightful remark about "the disciples" in vv. 19–23 in Schneiders, "The Resurrection," 186: "He comes to 'the disciples,' which in John is an inclusive group of men and women, itinerants and householders, Jews, Samaritans and Gentiles. Believers, the Church as community and not as hierarchical institution, is the foundational symbolic expression of the risen Jesus. The Church is his body." For a further rich study of 20:19–23 as a commissioning of the disciples to continue the presence of Jesus, see Sandra M. Schneiders, "The Raising of the New Temple: John 20.19–23 and Johannine Ecclesiology," *NTS* 52 (2006): 337–55.

41. The parallel search for a physical experience of touching the risen Jesus links Mary Magdalene and Thomas, and distinguishes their responses to the resurrection from that of the Beloved Disciple. See Dorothy A. Lee, "Partnership in Easter Faith: The Role of Mary Magdalene and Thomas in John 20," *JSNT* 58 (1995): 37–49. See also Sandra M. Schneiders, "Touching the Risen Jesus: Mary Magdalene and Thomas the Twin in John 20," in Koester and Bieringer, eds., *The Resurrection of Jesus in the Gospel of John*, WUNT 222 (Tübingen: Mohr Siebeck, 2008), 153–76.

42. The use of the Greek word for *unfaith* (*apistos*) is found only here in the Gospel of John. It is a strong way of saying "no faith." It is best known from its use in the Synoptic tradition to describe a "faithless generation" (see Matt 17:17; Mark 9:9; Luke 9:41).

43. Koester, *Word of Life*, 107.

44. On this, see Brendan Byrne, "The Faith of the Beloved Disciple and the Community in John 20," *JSNT* 23 (1985): 83–97. See also Lindars, *The Gospel of John*, 602: "He (the author) is concerned that *the reader* should believe, and sets the Beloved Disciple before him as the first example for him

to follow. *His* kind of faith will be commended by the risen Jesus himself in verse 29."

45. Sherri Brown, *Gift upon Gift: Covenant through Word in the Gospel of John*, PTMS (Eugene, OR: Wipf and Stock, 2010), 225. See also Lindars, *The Gospel of John*, 616; Udo Schnelle, *The Human Condition: Anthropology in the Teachings of Jesus, Paul, and John*, trans. O. C. Dean, Jr. (Minneapolis, MN: Fortress, 1996), 121.

46. Dorothy A. Lee, *Flesh and Glory: Symbolism, Gender, and Theology in the Gospel of John* (New York: Crossroad, 2002), 48.

47. This question is well answered by Brad B. Blaine, *Peter in the Gospel of John: The Making of an Authentic Disciple*, Academia Biblica 27 (Atlanta: SBL, 2007), 149–54 (on Peter and the Beloved Disciple in vv. 7–8) and 161–95 (on Peter and the Beloved Disciple in vv. 15–25).

48. See, for example, Raymond E. Brown, *The Gospel according to John*, 2:1065; George R. Beasley-Murray, *John*, WBC 51 (Waco, TX: Word, 1987), 396.

49. For a detailed discussion of 21:25, see Moloney, *John*, 562–66; Craig S. Keener, *The Gospel of John: A Commentary*, 2 vols. (Peabody, MA: Hendrickson, 2003), 1240–42.

50. See Raymond E. Brown, "John 21 and the First Appearances of the Risen Jesus to Peter," in *Resurrexit: Actes du Symposium International sur la Résurrection de Jésus*, ed. Eduard Dhanis (Rome: Editrice Libreria Vaticana, 1974), 434–35.

51. Rudolf Schnackenburg, *The Gospel according to St. John*, trans. Kevin Smyth et al., 3 vols. (London: Burns and Oates; New York: Crossroad, 1968–82), 3:352.

52. What is the tradition history of 21:1–14, especially in the light of Luke 5:1–11 (see Moloney, *John*, 552–53)? In a unified story, how is it possible that the disciples, after 20:19–23, could so easily give themselves to their every-day activity? Solutions range from speculations about the mental state of the post-Easter disciples (Beasley-Murray, *John*, 399–400), to Peter's symbolic leading the mission as "fishers" of people (C. Kingsley Barrett, *The Gospel according to St. John* [London: SPCK 1978], 579), to aimless disorientation (Raymond E. Brown, *The Gospel according to John*, 2:1096), to apostasy (Edwyn C. Hoskyns, *The Fourth Gospel*, ed. Francis N. Davey [London: Faber and Faber, 1947], 552).

53. This Greek word used for "early in the morning" in 20:1 and 21:4 is only found in an indeclinable form (see also 18:28) in John 18:1—20:31. This is one of many indications of the close linguistic connections that exist between John 1—20 and John 21. For further indication, see Moloney, *John*, 551–52, 558. They indicate what I have called "continuity and discontinuity" between the Gospel and its epilogue. They were written separately but are to be read

together. There are a number of places where the use of Greek words is evidence of this continuity and discontinuity. I will note several of them.

54. See BDAG, 749, s.v. *paidion*: "one who is treasured in the way a parent treasures a child." The regular presence of the expression to address believers in 1 John may indicate a chronological proximity between John 21 and 1 John.

55. The confession of the Beloved Disciple that Jesus is "the Lord" matches the resurrection confession of Mary Magdalene in 20:18.

56. My paraphrase, "adjusts his scant clothing," renders a strange indication that before Peter leapt into the water, he dressed himself. Normally, one would do the opposite. Raymond E. Brown, *The Gospel according to John*, 2:1072, helpfully explains that while fishing Peter was only lightly clad in a single garment. To remove that would have left him naked, so "he tucked in his outer garment, for he was otherwise naked." The Greek verb for *to gird* (*diazōnnymi*) is only found here and in 13:4–5, where Jesus girds himself with a towel, in the whole of the New Testament. This is another striking case of continuity in discontinuity. For a suggested interpretation of a link between the two "girdings," see Moloney, "John 21," 224. See also, Keener, *John*, 1227–28.

57. The use of this word in John 18 and 21 is another example of dissimilarity and continuity.

58. For a good survey of the suggestions, see Beasley-Murray, *John*, 401–4; Thomas L. Brodie, *The Gospel according to John: A Literary and Theological Commentary* (New York: Oxford University Press, 1993), 586–88. Lincoln, *The Gospel according to Saint John*, 513, is no doubt correct when he suggests that "the specificity given to the number of the fish does suggest that symbolism is likely to be involved." Brodie, *The Gospel according to John*, 588, rightly remarks: "If the reader cannot figure out the 153, the text still has meaning." See also, Lindars, *The Gospel of John*, 629. For the suggestion that there were, in fact, 153 fish, see Keener, *John*, 2:1233. It is not helpful to claim that "a correct interpretation depends upon a correct interpretation of the significance of the number 153," as does Hoskyns, *Fourth Gospel*, 553.

59. But 153 fish is not a particularly large catch in a net.

60. The same Greek verb (*schizō*) is used in 19:24 and 21:11.

61. On this, see Raymond E. Brown, *The Gospel according to John*, 2:1075; Chennattu, *Johannine Discipleship as a Covenant Relationship*, 171–73.

62. See Brodie, *The Gospel according to John*, 585–86.

63. I am grateful to my former student Dr. Sherri Brown for this observation. As she commented to me in her critical reading of this text: "Part of the purpose of John 21 is to make sure that Peter does not do it again (old life [i.e., deny Jesus]), but rather fulfills his mission to begin to tend the sheep (new life). Jesus' question begins that process which ultimately reconstitutes Peter."

64. Here, more than anywhere else in the Gospel, the debate over the Johannine use of the two Greek verbs for *love* (*agapaō* and *phileō*) is most intense. For some, Jesus tries twice to have Peter confess that his love is unconditional (vv. 15 and 16, using *agapaō*), but on both occasions Peter responds that he has "friendship love" for Jesus (vv. 15 and 16, using *phileō*). On the third occasion Jesus gives in and asks Peter for his "friendship love," and Peter is happy to remain there (in v. 17 both Jesus and Peter use *phileō*). This is attractive, as Peter's journey with Jesus lies ahead of him (see vv. 18–19). However, there is a similar variety of different Greek words used in these few verses for *lambs* (v. 15) and *sheep* (vv. 16–17), *feed* (vv. 15, 17) and *tend* (v. 16). This has led the majority of scholars to regard the three questions and their answers as using different words for stylistic reasons. They all say the same thing, despite the different Greek words used. See the excellent summaries of Barrett, *St. John*, 584–85, and Keener, *John*, 2:1235–36. For an impressive differing opinion, see David Shepherd, "'Do You Love Me?' A Narrative-Critical Reappraisal of *agapaō* and *phileō* in John 21:15–17," *JBL* 129 (2010): 777–92.

65. See Lincoln, *The Gospel according to Saint John*, 517–18; Brodie, *The Gospel according to John*, 590–91.

66. The point of comparison "more than these" focuses upon Peter's leaving everything associated with former ways to embrace unconditional love for Jesus. For an extensive use of Jewish material to provide possible background and meaning to this narrative, see Roger David Aus, *Simon Peter's Denial and Jesus' commissioning of Him as His Successor in John 21:15-19: Studies in Their Judaic Background*, Studies in Judaism (Lanham, MD: University Press of America, 2013), 179–269.

67. Chennattu, *Johannine Discipleship as a Covenant Relationship*, 178. Augustine's splendidly concise exegesis (only five Latin words) of Jesus' insistence upon Peter's threefold commitment to love supports this interpretation: "He makes sure of love so as firmly to establish unity" (*Serm.* 46, 30: "*Confirmat caritatem ut consolidet unitatem*" [CCSL 41:556]). Blaine, *Peter in the Gospel of John*, 169–70, disagrees. He suggests that the threefold confession leads to Peter's threefold appointment as "feeding lambs, tending sheep, and feeding sheep."

68. See the wise detailed discussion in Raymond E. Brown, *The Gospel according to John*, 2:1112–17.

69. The typically Johannine use of a double "amen" (found only in John) is another example of continuity in discontinuity.

70. See Raymond E. Brown, *The Gospel according to John*, 2:1118; Ernst Haenchen, *John 1—2*, trans. Robert W. Funk, 2 vols., Hermeneia (Philadelphia:

Fortress, 1984), 2:226–27. For early Christian references to Peter's death, see Schnackenburg, *St. John*, 3:482 n. 76.

71. The reader/listener also recalls earlier use of exactly the same Greek words by the narrator in v. 18: "This he said to show by what death he was to glorify God." They repeat what was said earlier in the story of Jesus' death: "This he said to show by what death he was to die" (12:33; 18:32). See also Blaine, *Peter in the Gospel of John*, 172–75. The dissimilarity and continuity between John 1—20 and 21 is again found in the repetition of this sentence across John 12, 18, and 21.

72. Beasley-Murray, *John*, 409. For a very positive assessment of the role of Peter in John's Gospel, including John 21, see Blaine, *Peter in the Gospel of John*. See also R. Alan Culpepper, "Peter as Exemplary Disciple in John 21:15–19," *Perspectives in Religious Studies* 37 (2010): 165–78.

73. This is not the place to discuss the person of the Beloved Disciple and his relationship to John, the Son of Zebedee. For further information on these and related matters, see R. Alan Culpepper, *John, the Son of Zebedee: The Life of a Legend,* Studies on Personalities of the New Testament (Columbia, SC; University of South Carolina Press, 1994).

74. On the death of the Beloved Disciple, see Raymond E. Brown, *The Gospel according to John*, 2:1118–20; Schnackenburg, *St. John*, 3:368–71.

75. See Lincoln, *Truth on Trial*, 152–58.

76. On the Beloved Disciple as the "writer" of the text as we have it today, see Moloney, *John*, 561–62, and the discussion documented there.

77. It could be said that Peter represents the pastoral ministry while the Beloved Disciple represents the prophetic ministry. But while Peter and the Beloved Disciple are powerful symbols, they are more than that. They were part of the living memory of the original Johannine experience that inspired a later generation that had not seen Jesus (20:29). See Sherri Brown, *Gift upon Gift*, 235–36; Moloney, *John*, 523.

78. Blaine, *Peter in the Gospel of John*, 182.

79. See Chennattu, *Johannine Discipleship as a Covenant Relationship*, 173–76.

CHAPTER FIVE

The Resurrection of the Messiah

Historical and Theological Reflections

We are all essentially story people. However familiar or unfamiliar we are with the four Gospels, details from the events described in Mark 16, Matthew 28, Luke 24, and John 20—21 form part of our Christian culture. We have heard it all before, and we gladly hear it again and again, as these stories are an essential part of the Christian story.[1] Reading and listening to these stories of the death and resurrection of Jesus have enriched the understanding of the centrality of the resurrection of Jesus in the Christian story and have made an inestimable impact upon Christian belief and behavior for centuries. As contemporary believers, however, we necessarily want to ask further questions of these stories. Given the significant differences in detail among the four narratives, what really happened?

Living at the beginning of the third millennium, we are often described as "post-Enlightenment" Christians. This technical term means that we live in a world strongly determined by reason, especially in that part of the world dominated by European traditions. In the eighteenth and nineteenth centuries, with the development of scientific knowledge and the improvements in so many educational and social situations as the breadth and depth of knowledge exploded, the search for the "truth" was often reduced to an insistence that only what could be factually or scientifically proven could claim to be true.

This, of course, has never been all-determining in the human search for meaning, as so much that is important to us cannot be proven in that way. How does one test the objective truthfulness of one person's love for another? Genuine human relationships can exist only when we surrender the need to be all-knowing and controlling, when we live with the mystery of the other person. Are there objective proofs for the quality of art, literature, and music? Some of the fundamental aspects of human society—the challenge to live peacefully together, to serve the suffering and the underprivileged, to educate the young, to care for the aged and the dying—cannot be explained entirely on the basis of human reason. Is it only right reason that inspires the remarkable work of *Doctors without Borders*? The Enlightenment, accompanied by so much exciting scientific, cultural, and geographical discovery, has produced a remarkable leap forward for people in many (but not all) parts of the world. But the rigid application of a principle of reason alone has severe limitations.[2] There are elements in the Christian tradition that defy a rigid application of reason and a search for facts that can establish their scientifically controlled truthfulness. Perhaps the most confronting of them are the gospel stories of a virgin birth and the bodily resurrection of Jesus.[3]

The Resurrection of the Messiah: What Happened?

It is inevitable that the question "what actually happened?" be asked of the Christian Easter proclamation that the crucified Jesus of Nazareth was raised from the dead and that his body was no longer in the place where those who had slain him had laid it (see Mark 16:6). Paul's words to the Corinthians, written about AD 54, have remained true for Christians across almost two thousand years:

> Now if Christ is preached as raised from the dead, how can some of you say that there is no resurrection of the dead? But if there is no resurrection of the dead, then Christ has not been raised; if Christ has not been raised, then our preaching is in vain and your faith is in vain. (1 Cor 15:12–14)

There is ample proof, even from non-Christian sources, that Jesus of Nazareth was crucified.[4] The Christians believed that his death and burial were not the end, even if that meant ridicule from the world around them (see 1 Cor 1:22–25). They told stories in their preaching to affirm *the fact that he had been raised*. By means of these stories they instructed and encouraged later generations with *the message of what the resurrection meant* to them. Notice that Paul states that Christ is *preached* as raised from the dead (15:12). Already in the first decades of the existence of Christian communities the "preachers" told the story of the resurrection of Jesus. Indeed, writing to the Corinthian community in AD 54, Paul tells its members that he is passing on to them what he had received from those who went before him (15:1–2). From the very beginnings the resurrection accounts have been part of the Church's "proclamation." They were never an attempt to found the Church upon scientifically controlled historical data. Those questions belong to our era.

As with all the Jesus stories in the four Gospels, the resurrection narratives show the usual signs of the creative presence of later writing, reading, and listening communities. This creativity was generated by the different uses of sources, literary skills, pastoral needs, as well as the situation of each community for which the story was originally written.[5] The preaching of God's saving intervention into the life and death of Jesus by raising him from the dead was probably first put into writing in about AD 54 by Paul in 1 Corinthians 15. Confessional formulas based upon Jesus' death and resurrection can be found in various forms across very early traditions in the New Testament.[6] The Gospel of Mark, the first to tell the story of the third day, the empty tomb, the presence of the young man, the Easter proclamation, and the commission to go to Galilee to see the risen Jesus, as he had promised, appeared about AD 70. To the best of our knowledge, it was not until the Gospel of Mark appeared that a coherent "story" was told of the resurrection of Jesus and the events that accompanied and followed it. It is more than likely that there were earlier storytelling traditions of this crucial event for the Christian communities, but we have no evidence of them.[7] The first part of this final chapter reflects upon what we can establish from the gospel resurrection narratives about what actually happened. Only then can we close our study of the resurrection of the Messiah, asking what the Gospels tell us the about the meaning of the resurrection for the foundational belief and experience of Christianity—and for subsequent Christian belief and experience.

A comparative study of the four Gospels shows that the following elements form the core of each gospel story, no matter how differently they were shaped in the fourfold storytelling traditions of the Gospels of Mark, Matthew, Luke, and John:

1. On the third day women (in John only one woman: Mary Magdalene) discovered an empty tomb.

2. A young man (Mark), an angel (Matthew [John: two angels]), or two men (Luke) at the tomb proclaimed to the women (in Mark, Matthew, and Luke) that Jesus had been raised by God.

3. The risen Jesus appeared to a number of people. This element is missing in Mark, but the tradition is presupposed by the instruction given to the women in Mark 16:7 that they are to tell the disciples and Peter that Jesus is going ahead of them into Galilee, where they will see him.

4. The risen Jesus commissions the disciples for their future task, in different ways promising that he (Matthew and John 21 [?]) or his Spirit (Luke and John [the Paraclete]) will be with them always.

From this list of elements that are common to all the Gospels, there is only one that can be subjected to objective historical investigation: an empty tomb.

There are no documented incidences of the resurrection from the tomb of a person who was certainly dead.[8] There are no scientifically controllable criteria to judge with absolute certainty what was said to the women at the tomb in the Easter proclamations. These proclamations differ markedly from Gospel to Gospel. Mark (16:6-7) and Matthew (28:6-7) are very similar, although not identical, but Luke (24:5-6) and John (20:17, 21-23; 21:15-17) are unique. These irreconcilable differences put them outside certain historical reconstruction. The same must be said for the various appearances of Jesus. He appears to the women in Matthew (28:8-10), to Mary Magdalene in John (20:11-18), to the disciples on the road to Emmaus in Luke (24:13-35), to the disciples gathered in Jerusalem in Luke (24:36-48) and John (20:19-23), to the disciples before his ascension at Bethany in Luke (24:50-53). The final commissions also differ radically across the four traditions and are clearly determined by the missionary situations of

Matthew (28:16–20) and Luke (24:44–48), and by the intracommunity needs of John (20:19–23; 21:1–25). We can decide to *believe* that the witness of the early Church about the Easter proclamation, the various appearances, and the commissions are true, but we cannot *prove* that they are true in a scientific and objective fashion.[9] We return to the appearances and the commission below, but it might be possible to trace solid evidence that one fact was not be shaped by the storytellers: Jesus was crucified and was laid in a tomb. After three days that tomb was found empty (Mark 16:1–5; Matt 28:1–6; Luke 24:1–3; John 20:1–2).

Apart from a few exceptions that never became mainstream, for the greater part of the past two thousand years scholars, preachers, and the Christian faithful did not question the existence of an empty tomb and the historicity of Jesus' appearances and founding commissioning of the disciples.[10] Debates around the interpretation of what might have happened as God raised a dead body, the differences in the reports of appearances, and the various commissions were common. But that they took place in observable history was rarely questioned. This situation changed with the advent of critical scholarship in the middle of the nineteenth century, but the questions were largely marginal to the faith and practice of the Christian Churches. Indeed, they were regarded by most, church leadership and faithful alike, as a dangerous threat to the very existence of Christianity.[11] They also tended to arise among scholarly circles in Germany. Mainstream scholarship continued as always, but there was a breach emerging in the wall, and it could be claimed that the radicals in Germany, especially at the University of Tübingen, were the fathers of critical New Testament scholarship.[12] At the turn of the century Brook Foss Westcott, one of the great British scholars of the nineteenth century, was able to claim: "If resurrection not be true, the basis of Christian morality, no less than the basis of Christian theology, is gone."[13] His historical investigation concludes that "it is not too much to say that there is no single historic incident better or more variously supported than the Resurrection of Christ."[14] The strength of these statements is an indication that a growing number of European scholars were claiming the opposite!

As interpreters of the Gospels began to scrutinize the evangelists' ability to take various pieces of material from traditions that came to them, and to shape other material, using the forms that were common in the literature of that time, the discipline of form criticism emerged.[15]

For many decades (from the 1920s till the 1950s) the Gospels were seen as the final product of a process that edited received material and created other stories. Historical research was limited to determining what came to the writer from Jesus himself and what had been determined by the life of the Church. In that scholarly atmosphere an increasing number of scholars suggested that the resurrection accounts, including the story of the empty tomb, had been produced in the life of the early Church. This was not necessarily a denial of resurrection *faith*. The earliest Christians were convinced that the crucified Jesus was alive again and that his presence gave life and a future to the community. But this did not necessarily call for the existence of an empty tomb or historical/physical appearances of Jesus.[16]

The next wave of scholarly reading of the Gospels accepted the work of the form critics but pointed to the theological agenda that ran across the whole utterance of each Gospel. The evangelists certainly received and used material that was prior to them or that was shaped in the community. But the juxtapositioning of those various elements formed a deliberately constructed *theological whole*. This methodological approach, called redaction criticism, did not replace form criticism but developed it into a more theological discipline.[17] It has been at the center of gospel studies from the 1950s till the present time. Skepticism about the historicity of the empty tomb is also found among many redaction critics. Contemporary readings of the Gospels focus more and more on the reader and the listener, and fewer questions are asked about the events and the world that formed the Gospels. What is most important to most contemporary interpreters is the impact a narrative makes upon the world *in front of the text*, reading or hearing the story. Whether the *facts* of the narrative are true is not a major concern.[18]

The form critics, the redaction critics, and the exponents of the numerous contemporary literary interpretations of the gospel stories do not (generally) deny the creative and foundational experience of resurrection faith.[19] Paradigmatically, Rudolf Bultmann will not admit that faith can be based on a historical event, as it must be an act of pure faith accepting the proclamation of God's saving intervention without human and thus historical support.[20] For Bultmann, Jesus only rises in the proclamation of the risen One: "The faith of Easter is just this—faith in the word of preaching."[21] As one of the significant recent scholars who deny the historicity of the physical resurrection, Willi Marxsen, has famously said: "*All the evangelists want to show that the activity of Jesus goes on*"[22] [italics mine]. Everyone—those who deny the historicity of the empty tomb, and those who defend it—would agree: the activity of Jesus goes on, despite his apparent defeat on the cross. As far as the earliest Christians were concerned, it is claimed, Jesus was alive, and they did not concern themselves with an empty tomb.

In none of the Gospels is Easter faith generated by an empty tomb. Empty tombs generate fear, wonder, and even flight (Mark 16:8; see also Matt 28:1–5; Luke 24:1–3; John 20:11–17). As is widely known, Charlie Chaplin died on Christmas Day in 1977. He was buried shortly after in the village cemetery at Corsier-sur-Veve, near Lausanne, Switzerland. Two months later his grave was found empty. There was no outcry from Switzerland that the famous Charlie Chaplin had risen from the dead. His body had been stolen, and eventually the perpetrators were found, and the body restored to a more secure grave. The women at the tomb are sent away from the cemetery, as Jesus will not be found among the dead (especially Luke 24:5–6; but also Mark 16:7; Matthew 28:7; John 28:17). Already late in the first century there were stories about disciples stealing the body (Matt 28:11–15), or a gardener who had removed it (John 20:14–15). Empty tombs are not "good news"; they are bad news, as someone has tampered with the remains of the beloved one who was placed there. These sentiments lie behind all the gospel accounts of the women's sad but loving journey to the tomb, heightened in Mark and Luke with the motivation for their visit: they want to anoint his hastily buried body with reverence (Mark 16:1; Luke 23:55–24:1).

This is not the place to rehearse the many theories that have been put forward to explain how an empty tomb story may have come into existence. Dale Allison has surveyed the discussions in a masterly fashion.[23] Only a few recent suggestions will be mentioned here. The only gospel account that matters is Mark 16:1–8. Matthew and Luke have received the tradition from him. I suspect that there may have also been a pre-Johannine tradition with roots in solid historical memory (the woman at the tomb in John 20:1–2, whose announcement brings Peter to the tomb [vv. 3–8]) that also played into the Synoptic Gospels (for example, Luke 24:12, 24). For some scholars the tradition about an empty tomb existed prior to Mark but did not go back to a historical discovery on "the third day." It had been born in association with the practice of Christian visits and liturgies at a tomb. Mark did not invent it, but his narrative is based on a prior non-historical tradition that had religious and theological motivations. For others, Mark invented the story, and from there it passed into all subsequent tradition from his creative storytelling.[24] There are more subtle explanations. A recent suggestion, accepted by some significant Catholic scholars, looks back to the disciples' remembrance of Jesus' presence and teaching during his ministry. He spoke of himself as the Son of Man, and he was understood as the expected eschatological prophet. Within Judaism these figures were expected eventually to be victorious over death. The earliest disciples experienced the presence of the living Jesus after his death. They recalled the teaching of the pre-Easter Jesus, regarded him as the eschatological prophet, and thus insisted that he had been raised from the dead. Belief in the resurrection of Jesus had grown from a seed sown among the disciples before Jesus' passion and death. In this understanding, Easter faith is already born in the preaching of the pre-Easter Jesus. The story of the empty tomb became part of that understanding of the living presence of the risen Jesus, fulfilling the expectations that surrounded the eschatological prophet.[25]

For various reasons it is widely accepted by other scholars that skepticism is warranted. There are many possible causes for an empty tomb. Within the gospel stories themselves one hears hints that some suggested at the time the stories were composed that someone (disciples [see Matt 28:15] or the gardener [see John 20:14–15]) had removed the body. The response to that anti-Christian apologetic is that Jesus was raised from the dead. We are dealing with late-first-century anti-Christian polemic and Christian apologetic that can prove nothing about a physical empty tomb, but these tales suggest that from the beginning some suggestion of "trickery" was present and that bodily resurrection is not the only explanation for an empty tomb.[26] There could be other explanations, coming from religious speculation of the time: apotheosis, or exaltation by God into heaven.[27]

None of these explanations is found in the texts, despite the brilliant scholarship that unearths them. An evaluation of the evidence that defends the historicity of an empty tomb remains very strong, and it could be said without fear of contradiction that most Christian scholars, from across the many forms of Christianity, adhere to this view.[28] Although this study is devoted to the Gospels, earlier pre-gospel witnesses knew about a tomb. Although it is an argument from silence, the fact that Paul explicitly states in 1 Corinthians 15:4 that after execution Jesus was buried, and then later describes a series of appearances, suggests that an empty tomb tradition was "in the air" before him.[29] The story of a death, a tomb, and subsequent appearances was not born with the Gospel of Mark (see 1 Cor 15:3–8).

Fundamental to the Christian story is the unhelpful fact that the empty tomb was found by women. Most likely, the Johannine account of Mary Magdalene at the tomb early on the Sunday morning reflects the oldest tradition.[30] Within the Jewish world (and indeed elsewhere at the time), the witness of women was valueless, but the witness of only one woman was even worse. Thus, from a tradition that reported a single woman finding an empty tomb (John 20:1–2), a more elaborate tradition developed, telling of the presence of three women (Mark, Matthew, Luke)—better three witnesses than one![31] The further visit to the tomb by Peter, indicated by John 20:3–8 and perhaps Luke, depending on the authenticity of Luke 24:12 but supported by Luke 24:24, does nothing to alter the original experience of an empty tomb; that discovery did nothing for anyone, except to generate amazement, fear, and puzzlement.[32] The theological reason for this is provided by Luke 24:24, "but him they did not see." There can be no sidestepping the fact that the founding narrative of the discovery of an empty tomb in Mark 16:1–8 is extremely low key. As Allison asks: "Why were there no witnesses to the resurrection itself? Why were the only witnesses to the empty tomb biased and not so wholly credible? Why were there no spectacular or miraculous demonstrations?" He points out that, when compared with Mark 16:1–8, the other Gospels and the non-canonical Gospel of Peter "are more theological and more apologetically conscious."[33] The empty tomb of Jesus, like the empty tomb of Charlie Chaplin, is not "good news." Precisely because this is the case, it appears likely that there was an empty tomb. Despite subsequent scholarly speculation, and the strong evidence of the interest that Christians showed in the tombs of holy men and women, and especially martyrs, there is little trace of any devotion to the tomb of Jesus.[34] Is that because it had become irrelevant (see Luke 24:5: "Why do you look for the living among the dead?")?

To affirm the historicity of an empty tomb does nothing for Easter faith. The earliest Christians did not come to faith because of an empty tomb. Christians who nowadays base their faith in Jesus and the religion of his followers miss the point of the gospel's proclamation of the good news of Easter.[35] An empty tomb is bad news! However, the *fact* of an empty tomb throws light upon the appearances.[36] This is the crucial issue. In several places in the Gospels, as we have seen, the risen Jesus establishes, in encounters with his disciples, that the Jesus whom they now acclaim as Lord is the same as the Jesus they knew during his life and ministry. This is the point of the resumed meals in the Lukan and the Johannine tradition (see Luke 24:28–31; 41–43; John 21:9–14), and the presentation of his wounded body to his disciples in Luke (24:39–40) and to Thomas in John (20:24–29).[37] But while it has been possible to investigate the historical evidence for an empty tomb, we cannot do this for the appearances.

Recently, in a valuable survey of contemporary thinking on the resurrection, Gerald O'Collins reprimands Dale Allison's inability to prove the historicity of the appearances, and his recourse to parallel "visions" that may serve to help us understand what might have happened to the disciples.[38] O'Collins writes: "This one-sided privileging of the disciples' experience and activity runs dead contrary to the primacy of the divine initiative that pervasively shapes the Easter narratives and theology of Paul and the evangelists."[39] His claim for the primacy of God's initiative is sound, as we will see in our closing reflections on the meaning of the gospel narratives. But this is to misunderstand what Allison is trying to do. One cannot be a "historian" and document in a scientific fashion "the primacy of the divine initiative." It is only possible to try to recover the experience of the disciples. Most people who give their lives in service of a religious cause lay claim to "the divine initiative." But can they show that this "initiative" was "historically verifiable"? The tragic cases of many of our contemporaries who have betrayed the Christian mission and its message by the subsequent abuse of their "ecclesiastical privileges" are a strong hint that God may not have always been the whole reason for their self-gift for the sake of the Christian mission. But we can never *prove* that. O'Collins has drawn a fundamentally important *theological* issue into Allison's attempt to work as a *historian*. They both have their place. I agree with O'Collins that the theological is by far the more important, as does Dale Allison,[40] but we must not confuse these issues in an attempt to respond to the contemporary question about what really happened, a question that was of no concern to those who passed on the earliest witnesses.

What happened in the post-Easter appearances? It is impossible to describe "what happened" in any concrete sense.[41] We simply have no parameters within which we can judge what might have happened when someone who was crucified and buried appeared to women (all the Gospels), to two disciples on the road to Emmaus (Luke 24:13–35), to Peter (1 Cor 15:5; Luke 24:34), to a variety of gatherings of the disciples (Matt 16:16–20; Luke 24:35–53; John 20:19–23; 21:4–23), to the Twelve, to the more than five hundred, to James, to all the apostles, and to Paul (1 Cor 15:5–9).[42] How can we decide whether or not Jesus suddenly appeared in locked rooms (see Luke 24:36; John 20:19, 26), or describe what sort of "risen body" the women and the disciples actually "saw"? We can only speculate, but we cannot extend anything from measurable human experience to affirm historically certain answers to these questions.[43] In the end these modern questions take us nowhere. They lead to speculations that can either be affirmed or denied, depending upon the circumstances of the person making the judgments. One thing is certain: the witness of the earliest Church that Jesus "appeared" is firm.[44] We are not in a situation to describe the *physical* experience of these encounters, but that they took place should not be questioned.[45] *What* took place is hard to determine, but *that* these encounters took place is affirmed across many traditions (Paul, Mark, Matthew, Luke, John, and other New Testament witnesses). Brown rightly asserts that they cannot be regarded as "purely internal" experiences.[46] What must be noticed is the use of the passive mood in so many of the verbal descriptions of these encounters, part of the use of the so-called divine passive across the resurrection accounts. As we have seen so regularly across the Gospels, the earliest narrative witnesses, depending upon traditions that they received, had no hesitation in affirming "the primacy of the divine initiative."[47] But once this is accepted, we are moving away from the realm of controllable human experience to the realm of the inbreaking of the divine into the human. We are invited to understand what the New Testament narratives wanted to say about what God has done in and through the death and resurrection of the Son. Raymond Brown correctly identifies the resurrection of Jesus as something that God did for Jesus as an *eschatological* event, and what Jesus did for humankind as "the interaction between the eschatological and the historical."[48] These events took place, and the witness of the Christian Church and its subsequent traditions exist because of them. As believing Christians, receiving that witness within the same context of faith in the God of Israel and of Jesus Christ that generated the Christian community, directed by the ongoing presence of the risen Lord (Matt 28:20; John 21:1–25) in and through his Spirit/Paraclete (Luke 24:49; Acts 2:1–4; John 14:15–17, 25–26; 15:26–27; 16:7–11, 12–16; 19:30), we accept these faith-filled witnesses of the action of God. There is no "knock-down" objective historical proof for the resurrection events reported in the gospel narratives.[49] But there is objective evidence that the earliest Church came into existence because of the encounter with the risen Jesus—whatever that means.[50] As Ed Sanders puts it: "That Jesus' followers (and later Paul) had resurrection experiences is, in my judgment, a fact. What the reality was that gave rise to the experiences I do not know."[51] Equally clear is the fact that the Jesus of history was now their risen Lord. Early Christians told stories containing that confession of faith. Some of them became part of the Christian scriptures (see Luke 24:34; John 20:18, 20, 25, 28; Mark 16:19–20).[52]

The Resurrection of the Messiah: What Does it Mean?

On the basis of the genuine human, but indescribable, experience of the encounter between the risen Jesus and the earliest witnesses, resurrection faith was born. The fact that God's action for humankind in and through Jesus could be perceived and received *only in faith* does not minimize the importance of this experience. As, among others, Roger Haight has convincingly shown, "faith" is not something that belongs to a specially gifted group, or perhaps (in a more negative judgment) among the ignorant and naïve.[53] It is a "universal human phenomenon,"[54] as freedom is of the essence of the human condition, and there is no real freedom unless it passes into action. All human action, however, is not aimed at nothingness, but "when one searches the horizon of finite existence for that which bestows salvation (in a broad human, and not specifically Christian, sense), it cannot be found...It is this non-availability which determines faith as a constitutive dimension of human life."[55] This search leads to the acceptance of values that reach beyond what is immediately available, and thus transcend what can be controlled and measured by human criteria. The object of faith may not be a significant part of one's day-to-day life and relationships and may, in fact, be rated rather low in a person's scale of things that matter. Nevertheless, as Haight points out:

> The ultimate issue in the question of faith does not deal with yes or no, faith or unfaith. Rather the point at issue is which faith to choose: Which faith makes most sense? This is one of the positive and constructive themes of historical consciousness that has considerable practical value. The pluralism of the objects of faith shows that faith is not demonstrable knowing, and that it is universal and inescapable.[56]

It is into this sphere of human experience that God's action in the resurrection of Jesus addressed the earliest Christians. As Haight would say, faith in Jesus as the risen Lord made "most sense" to them; thus they chose to confess that faith, and eventually to write stories to share and communicate that faith.[57] In this way they expressed their beliefs in a way that played a central and crucial role as the driving force of "the sum total of their decisions."[58]

We can now return to our narrative commentaries on the Gospels of Mark, Matthew, Luke, and John, by way of conclusion, to gather how Christianity's earliest storytellers articulated their beliefs, confident that they expressed the "one faith" generated by the resurrection of the Messiah. In these stories we have the beginnings of the narrative articulation of a theology of the resurrection. The earliest Christian writers were most concerned about what the resurrection of Jesus meant. While some aspects of each narrative are unique, variations of the same theological message are communicated in a different way across the four gospel traditions. What follows will gather issues that can be associated with the central theological themes—what God did for Jesus, and what the risen Jesus did for his followers—that emerge from our narrative-critical commentaries on Mark 16:1–8, Matthew 28, Luke 24, and John 20—21.[59]

What God Did for Jesus

Resurrection Is the Result of the Initiative of God

The indication that the action of God lies behind the resurrection of Jesus is found across all four Gospels. This is dramatically true in

Mark and Matthew, when the resurrection narratives are read as the continuation of the passion narratives. In Mark 15:34 the crucified Jesus cries out in anguish from the cross, asking why God has abandoned him. The reader/listener is aware of the relationship that exists between Jesus as the "beloved Son" of God from the prologue of 1:1–13, the voice from heaven at the transfiguration, again declaring Jesus as God's Son, to whom all must listen in 9:7, and in the final confession of the Roman centurion in 15:39: "Truly, this man was the Son of God." Exactly the same impression is created for the reader/listener by Matthew's story, as the crucified Jesus asks why God has abandoned him in 27:46. Jesus' sonship has been shown by means of the infancy story in Matthew 1— 2 (see especially 1:20–23), the testing of God's Son in the temptations in 4:1–11, the voice from heaven at the transfiguration in 17:5, and the confession of the Roman centurion, and all who were there with him in 27:54: "Truly, this was the Son of God." The passion narratives of Mark and Matthew close with a question hanging over the story: Has God abandoned his Son? The reader/listener asks: Is this the way God shows his pleasure in his beloved Son (see Mark 1:11; 9:7; Matt 17:5)?

The resounding response to the question is found in the series of passive verbs, indications of the action of God, in the resurrection narratives. The stone *has been rolled back* (Mark 16:4), or *was rolled back* by an angel of the Lord (Matt 28:2). The Easter message to the women announces: "He *has been raised* [by God]" (Mark 16:6; Matt 28:6). The beloved Son has not been abandoned by God; his unconditional acceptance of all that has been asked of him by the God whom he called "Father" (see Mark 14:36; Matt 26:39) has been accepted as his Father enters the realms of death and raises his Son to life. Jesus' unconditional "yes" to God is now responded to by God's unconditional "yes" to Jesus. This message is primarily about what God has done for Jesus, but there is an associated message for all who follow Jesus. As God has given life to his Son, so God will also give life to those who follow him. Jesus has thus instructed his disciples during his ministry (see, for example, Mark 8:34–35; Matt 16:24–25). The action of God in the resurrection sets God's seal upon that instruction. Associated with the use of the divine passive is the use of the Greek expression *dei* ("must") to indicate that what took place was part of God's design. Beyond its use in the passion prediction during Jesus' ministry ("The Son of Man *must* go up to Jerusalem"), this theme is present in the death and resurrection stories in Mark (14:21), Matthew (26:54), and especially in Luke (22:7, 37; 24:7, 26, 44) and John (12:34; 20:9).

As well as sharing Mark's presentation of the resurrection as God's response to Jesus' unconditional self-gift, Matthew introduces a spectacular presentation of the death and resurrection of Jesus as the "turning point of the ages." As Jesus begins his ministry, the reader/listener is directed forward to some future time when heaven and earth will pass away and everything will be accomplished (Matt 5:18). The ministry of Jesus and the disciples is limited to "the lost sheep of Israel" (10:5–6; 15:24). This is transformed by the action of God in Jesus' death and resurrection. By accompanying Jesus' death (27:51–54) and resurrection (28:1–4) with motifs from Jewish apocalyptic expectation that describe how God will *finally* enter the human story, Matthew *anticipates* that eschatological moment. God has acted decisively at the moment of Jesus' death and resurrection. Poised between God's action in and through the death and resurrection of Jesus, the Christian Church listens to God's word, now communicated through the teaching of Jesus, until the end of the ages, awaiting a future moment when God will come again (28:16–20).

The resurrection account of Luke 24 is strikingly different. It proclaims the initiative of God more subtly but with equal force. The Gospel of Luke reaches a climax on the "day" of the resurrection. Only at the resurrection does the reader/listener discover that everything has been pointing to this "day" in the city of Jerusalem as the fulcrum of God's saving plan for humankind. It began as Jesus was born on a journey (see Luke 2:1–7). It gathered pace as Jesus set his face toward Jerusalem, the place from which he would depart (9:51), but not until he had been slain there, an innocent savior (23:46–47); be raised from the dead there (24:6); draw his fragile disciples who are walking away from Jerusalem back there (vv. 13–35); and insist that his apostles remain there until he sent them the power of the most high (vv. 48–49). From Jerusalem, as he leaves them, the Spirit-directed apostles are directed to reach out to the ends of the earth (Acts 1:8; 28:31).[60] The resurrection and ascension of Jesus is the culmination of *God's design* for Jesus, and the beginning of *God's design* for the apostles. Into this overall Lukan presentation of God's initiative, the traditional indication of God's action in the use of the divine passive to describe Jesus' having been raised is still present (24:6).

But Luke's singular contribution to a theology of God's initiative in the resurrection is found in his strong insistence that everything that has taken place had to take place *to fulfill the scriptures.* The Christ *must* suffer these things, and thus enter into his glory (vv. 26–27). The risen Jesus opens the scriptures to his wondering disciples (v. 32), and he instructs his future witnesses that everything written in the Law of Moses, the prophets and the psalms *must* be fulfilled. The Christ *must* suffer and, on the third day, rise again (vv. 44–46). The use of the Greek expression *must* (*dei*) is universally used in the Gospels, and especially in the passion predictions, to indicate that God's will *must* be done. But not only is the scripture fulfilled in Jesus' death and resurrection. The women are told at the empty tomb that they *must* remember what Jesus told them while he was with them in Galilee, "that the Son of Man *must* [*dei*] be delivered into the hands of sinful men, and be crucified, and on the third day rise" (vv. 6b–7). The words of Jesus during his ministry match the promises of the scriptures. Indeed, Jesus' teaching is elevated to become a "scripture" that *must* be "remembered" (see v. 8). Because of God's initiative, entering the realms of death (v. 6a), bringing to fulfillment everything that had been promised by the scriptures, there is no point in seeking Jesus among the dead (v. 5).

The Johannine understanding of Jesus as the incarnate Logos of God (John 1:1–18) leads the author into another approach to the presentation of God's initiative in the resurrection of Jesus, but for the Fourth Gospel, the story is more about what the risen Jesus does for the disciples than what God has done for Jesus. Indeed, earlier in the story, in a way unlike anything in the Synoptic Gospels, Jesus has said that he alone has the authority to lay down his life for his sheep and to take it up again (10:17–18). Despite that claim, and the narrative's interest in what the risen Lord does for the disciples, John maintains the traditional use of divine passives to show that someone other than Jesus has entered the story. The stone *had been taken away* from the tomb (20:1); the linen cloths *had been placed* and *had been folded* (vv. 5–7). The Beloved Disciple does not see the risen Jesus at the empty tomb. He sees these signs of the action of God, and he "saw and believed" (v. 8). He comes to belief, even though he as yet does not know the scripture of this Jesus story, that he *must* (Greek: *dei*) be raised from the dead (v. 9). Also seeing as the divine passives, Mary Magdalene correctly insists in her unfaith that someone has taken away the body of Jesus (vv. 2, 13,

15). She is wrongly searching for a corpse, but she is correct in her suggestion that someone has entered the realms of death and "taken away" Jesus from the tomb. But the "taking away" is not by stealth but by resurrection.

The Crucified One Is Alive

The central message of all four gospel accounts lies in the proclamation that the Jesus of Nazareth who was crucified is no longer among the dead. This is said across the Synoptic Gospels by means of the Easter proclamation to the women at the tomb. Mark begins the tradition as the young man announces: "You seek Jesus of Nazareth, who was crucified. He has been raised, he is not here; see the place where they laid him" (Mark 16:6). The women knew the Jesus who came from Nazareth, and they had seen him crucified and buried (see 15:40–41, 47). They are now invited to look at the place where those who had done him to death in a cruel execution had laid him; he is not there. He has been raised. Matthew rewrites this Easter message in a more elegant Greek sentence associating the message more closely with the angel and with Jesus' predictions.[61] But the message is the same: "I know that you seek Jesus who was crucified. He is not here; for he has been raised, as he said. Come, see the place where he lay" (Matt 27:6).

Luke continues the tradition of an Easter proclamation with the traditional expression: "He has been raised" (24:6a).[62] But Luke goes to greater lengths to insist upon the fact that the crucified Jesus is now alive. Not only is God's intervention announced in v. 6a, but the two men ask the women why they are looking for Jesus in the wrong place: "Why do you seek the living among the dead?" (v. 5). They develop the Matthean addition to Mark's proclamation (Matt 28:6: "as he said"), asking the women to "remember" what he had told them in his words to them in Galilee: "that the Son of Man must be delivered into the hands of sinful men, and be crucified, and on the third day be raised" (Luke 24:7). The scriptures have been fulfilled, and the promise of Jesus has been fulfilled. Thus they are able to remember that Jesus was not to remain among the dead, and they announce the Easter message to the "Eleven and all the rest" (v. 9). Luke adds Jesus' showing his hands and his side to show that he is not a ghost but the Jesus that they had known during his ministry (vv. 39–40). Finally, as throughout the Gospel, he sits at table with the Emmaus disciples and the disciples in Jerusalem.

In breaking bread and fish he resumes the practice of sharing meals that has marked his presence with them across the Gospel of Luke.[63]

The Johannine accounts of the resurrection continue an insistence upon the physical presence of Jesus. Mary Magdalene wants to cling to the risen Jesus but is asked to desist (John 20:17). Thomas insists that he will only believe if he can put his finger into the mark of the nails and his hand into the pierced side. The risen Jesus offers him that opportunity, if that is what he requires for true belief (vv. 24–27). As Jesus joins the disciples behind closed doors, where they hid for fear of the Jews (v. 19), he also shows them his hands and his side (v. 20). In a similar fashion, in John 21, Jesus' appearance by the side of the lake caused such fear that no one would dare ask who he was (21:12). In order to overcome their fear and to show that the risen Jesus was the man they knew, he invites them to "come and have breakfast," and he shared bread and fish with them (vv. 12–13).[64] There is no Easter proclamation at an empty tomb. It is transferred to the words of Mary Magdalene, who, doing as she was instructed by the risen Jesus, announces to the disciples: "I have seen the Lord" (20:18).

The Risen Jesus Is Constituted Messiah and Lord

Continuing the tradition that began with Raymond Brown's classic studies, *The Birth of the Messiah* and *The Death of the Messiah*, this volume has the title: *The Resurrection of the Messiah*. There is some inaccuracy in associating the term *Messiah* with the all resurrection narratives. It is appropriate for Luke and John, but it can only be said of Mark in an applied sense that Jesus is constituted Messiah and Lord at the resurrection.[65] Matthew, who in many ways continues the Markan tradition concerning Jesus' messiahship, focuses especially upon the lordship of the risen Jesus in 28:16–20.

In the Markan Christology, Jesus is established as Messiah by his suffering and death. Throughout the Gospel of Mark Jesus avoids any public acclamation as the Christ, preferring to direct his disciples to recognize him as the Son of Man (see especially Mark 8:27–31).[66] It is not until the passion is under way that he accepts the charge of the high priest, "Are you the Christ, the Son of the Blessed?" with his response, "I am" (14:61–62). The same process takes place when he is interrogated by Pilate, "Are you the King of the Jews?" He responds, "You have said so" (15:2).[67] The climax of the Markan presentation of Jesus is *on the cross*. In a moment of supreme irony, the chief priests and the scribes mock the crucified Jesus: "Let the Christ, the King of Israel, come down now from the cross, that we may see and believe" (15:31–32). The reader/hearer knows that it is *on the cross* that Jesus is the Christ, the King of Israel. If he were to "come down from the cross," he would no longer be the Christ.[68] But the association of Jesus' messiahship with the resurrection can be made through Jesus' own self-revelation as the Son of Man. Jesus will not accept a messianic acclamation that is not clarified by his own description of his role as the Son of Man who must suffer, die, and be raised on the third day (see 8:31; 9:31; 10:32–34). In his acceptance of a messiahship in his suffering (14:61–62; 15:2) and on the cross (15:31–32), he is living out his God-given destiny as the Son of Man who must suffer, die, be raised, and eventually come as judge in glory (see 14:62).[69] It can be claimed that:

> Mark was able to focus initially on a Christ who is a suffering Son of Man (8:29–31), but whose suffering led to the vindication of the resurrection and in his ultimate return in glory and with authority. Thus "the Son of Man" emerged as his major expression to communicate his interpretation of Jesus of Nazareth—slain, vindicated, and the apocalyptic judge.[70]

The brief resurrection narrative in Mark 16:1–8 never explicitly proclaims the risen Jesus as the Messiah, but there is much in the Christology of the story as a whole that points in that direction.[71]

In a way similar to Mark there is no immediate association with messianic claims in Matthew's resurrection narrative. For both Mark and Matthew Jesus is pronounced Messiah and Son of God on the cross (Mark 15:32; Matt 27:42) and at his death (Mark 15:39; Matt 27:54). But Matthew's final scene with the Eleven on the appointed mountain in Galilee presents the risen Jesus as the Lord of heaven and earth: "All authority in heaven and on earth has been given to me" (28:18). It is as Lord that the risen Jesus can demand from his Eleven, and all subsequent disciples, a mission that breaks through the established Mosaic laws that limited God's people to Israel, an initiation rite to circumcision, and the teaching of the Torah (vv. 19–20). It is as Lord that the risen Jesus will be with his followers to the close of the age (v. 20).

The Lukan resurrection story concentrates upon the necessity of Jesus' death *and resurrection*. Initially this necessity is announced at the tomb, as the angels ask the women to recall the words Jesus had spoken to them while he was with them in Galilee: he would suffer, be crucified, "and on the third day be raised" (Luke 24:7). This theme is then repeated three times in the subsequent episodes in the story. On the walk to Emmaus the risen Jesus accuses the disciples of being foolish and slow of heart: "'Was it not necessary that *the Christ* should suffer these things and enter into his glory?' And beginning with Moses and all the prophets, he interpreted to them all the scriptures concerning himself" (vv. 25–27). After they have recognized Jesus at the breaking of the bread, they acknowledge this moment of revelation in their words to one another: "Did not our hearts burn within us while he talked to us on the road, while he opened to us the scriptures?" (v. 32). It is as "the Christ of God" that Jesus must suffer *and rise* (see 9:20–22). At his final meal with his disciples, both of the elements mentioned return: Jesus' own words, and the teaching of the scriptures. He said to them:

> "These are my words which I spoke to you while I was still with you [see 24:7], that everything written about me in the law of Moses and the prophets and the psalms must be fulfilled." Then he opened their minds to understand the scriptures and said to them, "Thus it is written, that *the Christ* should suffer and on the third day rise from the dead." (24:44–46; see vv. 26–27)

For the Gospel of Luke, Jesus' messianic status is established by means of Jesus' death and resurrection. They fulfill Jesus' promises and bring to completion the definite plan and foreknowledge of God, revealed in the scriptures.[72]

From the first page of the Gospel of John, Jesus is called "the Christ" (1:17). Strangely, however, in a way similar to Mark, during his ministry Jesus sidesteps any attempts on the part of others to proclaim him as the Christ. The narrator makes it clear that they misunderstand him when they raise the messianic question (4:25–26, 29; 7:26–31, 41–42; 9:22; 10:24; 11:27; 12:34). A similar narrative technique is used in those few places where some wish to make Jesus a king (1:49; 6:15; 12:13).[73] It is only in and through his "hour" that Jesus will be established as the Messiah (17:3), as it is only in his "hour" that he is acclaimed and proclaimed King (18:28—19:16a; 19:17-22, 38-42). In a way typical of the Christology of the Fourth Gospel, Jesus' messianic status must be determined by his relationship with God as the incarnate Logos (1:14), the only begotten Son (1:18). For this reason, at no stage during his ministry is it appropriate that he be regarded as the Messiah. Only by means of Jesus' perfect fulfillment of the task that he has been given by the Father (see 4:34; 17:4; 19:30) is he established as "the Christ." He is proclaimed Christ in 1:17, and again described as the Christ in Jesus' prayer to the Father, accepting that it has been his mission, as the Christ, to provide eternal life by making God known in the accomplishment of his task (17:2-4).[74] Only at the very end of his Gospel does John inform his readers and listeners that he has told them a story of Jesus so that they too may believe in the name of Jesus, the Christ, the Son of God, and thus have life in his name (20:30-31). It is as the crucified, risen, and glorified Christ that Jesus gives eternal life.[75] It is against this background that one can best understand the steady use of the expression *Lord* in John 20—21 (see 20:2, 13, 15, 18, 20, 25, 28; 21:7 [twice], 12, 15, 16, 17, 20, 21).[76] The resurrection of Jesus, the Christ, the Son of God, also establishes him as Lord.

Jesus' Earthly Mission Ends: The Ascension

The early Church had to face the historical fact that Jesus of Nazareth, crucified and risen, was no longer present with his followers. Mark 16:1-8 devotes no attention to this problem, and Matthew sidesteps it by indicating that the risen Jesus will be with his followers till the end of the ages (Matt 28:20). What that means is difficult to grasp, unless one looks at the Lukan and Johannine presentation of Jesus' ascension and the subsequent gift of the Spirit/Paraclete.

Whatever we make of the descriptive details of the ascension of Jesus, both Luke and John affirm that he leaves the first disciples in his return to his Father by means of ascension.[77] Luke's resurrection narrative closes with a simple statement: "He parted from them and was carried up to heaven" (Luke 24:51). This departure is not met by sorrow, but by great joy, and a constant presence in the Temple in Jerusalem, blessing God (vv. 52-53). There has been a remote preparation for this association of Jesus' departure with his resurrection. In 9:51, as Jesus set out on his journey to Jerusalem, the reader/listener was told: "When the days drew near for him to be received up, he set his face to go to Jerusalem." The final action of Jesus in Jerusalem is promised by this initial indication of the central role that Jerusalem will play in the paschal events. It points to the way Jesus' presence will conclude, "when he was to be taken up into heaven."[78] Jesus leaves the city of Jerusalem and the apostles to return to his Father. In the meantime the apostles are to stay in the city. He will send the promise of his Father upon them. They will preach repentance and the forgiveness of sins in the name of the crucified and risen Christ to all nations, beginning from Jerusalem (24:47–49).

For the Gospel of John, the departure of Jesus is a central theme across his final discourse with his disciples on the night before he died (John 14–16). This is especially the case in 14:1–31 and 16:4–44, two discourses that are parallel in many ways.[79] The fact and the necessity of his departure are stated and restated in 14:12, 19, 27–28; 16:5–7, 10, 16, 28. There are several reasons why Jesus *must* go away, but the most important is that he returns to the Father so that he might send the Spirit/Paraclete, who will be with them in his absence (see 14:15–17, 26; 16:7–11, 13–15). The gift of the Spirit is also associated with Jesus' glorification. At the Feast of Tabernacles in Jerusalem he spoke of the gift of living water, clarified as the Spirit that those who believed in him were to receive. At that stage of the story the gift was not yet available, "because Jesus was not yet glorified" (7:37–39). The story thus looks forward to a future gift of the Spirit that will be associated with Jesus' glorification, and his departure. These two moments coalesce in his "hour" of death and resurrection. As he dies, he pours down the Spirit (19:30), and as risen Lord he breathes upon them and gives them the Spirit that, as his sent ones, they may continue his critical and judging presence (20:22–23). This is also the moment of his departure. Mary Magdalene is told that she must not cling to him (20:17a), "for I have not yet ascended to the Father; but go and say to them, I am ascending to my Father and your Father, to my God and your God" (20:17bc). Jesus' departure by means of ascension is necessary for the establishment of the post-Easter situation of the Johannine community.[80] In Jesus' absence the Father and God of Jesus will become the Father and God of the disciples. Thus they will continue Jesus' presence as his sent ones (see 17:18; 20:21), strengthened, guided, taught, and reminded of all that he has taught by the Spirit/Paraclete. It is necessary for them that he depart through his ascension (16:7). The time of Jesus is at an end; the time of the Spirit-filled Johannine community has come.

What the Risen Jesus Did for His Followers

Resurrection Is the Fulfillment of Jesus' Promises

Throughout the ministry of Jesus he spoke of his need to go to Jerusalem, to suffer and die there. On the third day he would rise. These predictions of Jesus' passion, death, and resurrection have their narrative origins in the Gospel of Mark (see 8:31; 9:31; 10:32–34), and they are repeated in the Gospel of Matthew (16:21; 17:22–23; 20:17–19) and the Gospel of Luke (9:22, 44; 18:31–33). However, Matthew adds a further prediction, as he opens his passion narrative, unique to Matthew: "When Jesus had finished all these sayings, he said to his disciples, 'You know that after two days the Passover is coming, and the Son of Man will be delivered up to be crucified'" (26:1–2). Unlike any other of Jesus' predictions of his suffering in the Gospels, the Matthean Jesus' introduction to his passion makes no mention of the resurrection. This abbreviated passion prediction, in the light of the earlier predictions of the death *and resurrection* (see 16:21; 17:22–23; 20:17–19), generates a tension in the narrative. Is what had been promised during Jesus' ministry now abandoned? This matter is taken up in the Easter proclamation at the empty tomb. The angels remind the women that the crucified One they are now seeking cannot be among the dead, for "he has been raised, as he said" (28:5). What was absent in 26:1–2 returns in 28:5.

Luke also adds a further prediction of Jesus' death and resurrection but locates it at the heart of the Easter message, as the two men instruct the women who have been with Jesus since Galilee (see 8:1–3) that they are to "remember" what Jesus had said to them, "that the Son of Man must be delivered into the hands of sinful men, and be crucified and on the third day be raised" (24:7). As we have seen, the promises of Jesus have now become more than promises. They are the words of Jesus that must be "remembered." They have become part of the scriptures that must form the faith and lifestyle of his followers.

The Gospel of John continues this tradition but in his own way. For John, the crucifixion of Jesus is the time and place where he makes known the love of God, by showing that God so loved the world that he gave his only Son so that the world might not perish but have life (John 3:16–17). No one has greater love than to lay down his life for his friends. Those who live by his commandments are his friends (15:13–14). Thus, for John, the cross cannot be the lowest moment in Jesus' career that has to be overcome by God's action in raising him from the dead. The cross is the high point in Jesus' revelation of God's love (see 13:1, 15, 18, 34–35; 15:12, 17).[81] It is there that he reveals God's glory, and by means of the cross he returns to the glory that was his before the creation of the world (see 11:4; 17:5). The cross, along with the resurrection and ascension, forms part of "the hour" of Jesus. Throughout the ministry this "hour" has not yet come (see 2:5; 7:6, 30; 8:30), but as he turns to the cross and resurrection, "the hour has come" (see 12:23, 27; 13:1; 17:1; 19:25–27). To communicate to the readers and hearers of this unique story of Jesus the message of the hour of the death and resurrection of Jesus, the tradition of a threefold prediction of Jesus' death and resurrection is maintained. However, John does not speak of death and resurrection. He continues the tradition that associated the predictions with "the Son of Man," but on three occasions foretells his future death and resurrection by using a double-meaning verb: *to be lifted up* (see 3:14; 8:28; 12:32–34). Again the passive is used, indicating something that will be done to him by others, but John continues to insist, as in Mark 8:31, 9:31 and 10:32–34, that the Son of Man *must* be lifted up (Greek: *hypsōthēnai dei*). The double meaning of the verb instructs the reader/listener that Jesus will experience a physical "lifting up" on a cross that will be at the same time a "lifting up" in exaltation. Although written in an entirely different key, Jesus' death and resurrection fulfill the promises of the Johannine Jesus.

Resurrection Generates Doubt and Fear

One of the most encouraging features of the gospel stories is the realistic narrative portrayal of fragile disciples. These stories of disciples who struggle to respond to Jesus' demands, found in all four Gospels, reflected the lived experience of the earliest Christians. Paul captured it in his exhortation, based on his own experience, to the Corinthians: "For the sake of Christ, then, I am content with weaknesses, insults, hardships, persecutions and calamities; for when I am weak, then I am strong" (2 Cor 12:10). For Paul, the death and resurrection of Jesus transform pre-Christian persons who struggle in vain to do what they know should be done but are unable to put these ideals into practice (see Rom 7:7–25). In the midst of his anguished reflection upon the dilemma of those without Christ, "captive to the law of sin which dwells in my members" (v. 23), he spontaneously cries out: "Thanks be to God through Jesus Christ our Lord."[82] It is this experience that has been captured in the gospels' portrayal of the disciples, a portrait that continues to the end of each story. It is told with narrative vigor in the resurrection accounts.[83]

In Mark and Matthew, Judas betrays Jesus and hands him over (Mark 14:43–46; Matt 26:47–50), and the disciples of Jesus abandon Jesus at his arrest (Mark 14:50; Matt 26:56). Peter remains, but he denies Jesus three times (Mark 14:54, 66–72; Matt 26:58, 69–75). Only the women remain, looking on "from afar" (Mark 15:40–41; Matt 27:55–56).[84] From that point on Mark continues his relentless presentation of human failure, even in the face of God's saving intervention in the resurrection. At the tomb the young man announces the Easter message and instructs the women to tell the disciples and Peter that he is going ahead of them into Galilee, as he had told them (see 14:28). There they will see him (16:7). But the women are so overcome with fear that they run away from the tomb and say nothing to anyone (v. 8).[85] Matthew rehabilitates the women, despite their amazement and fear (see 28:5, 8). He meets them as they leave the tomb and are on the way to announce the Easter message to the disciples. The rehabilitation of the disciples begins in that encounter, as he instructs them to tell his "brethren" that he is going before them into Galilee (vv. 8–10). In the final commission, however, despite the solemnity of the occasion, as Jesus assembles the Eleven on the mountain he had indicated to them, some worship him, "but some doubted" (v. 17). It is a group of believers and doubters that is sent out to all nations (vv. 18–20).[86]

The Lukan story of the journey to Emmaus tells of two disciples who set off from Jerusalem to Emmaus, *away from* the time and the place established by God as the center of saving history. They *know* everything, but they *understand* very little, because their hopes had been dashed by the death of Jesus. Jesus accompanies the failing disciples, instructs them by unfolding the scriptures, showing that the death and resurrection of Jesus *had to take place*. Finally, at the breaking of the bread their eyes are opened. Jesus disappears, and they return immediately to the city they never should have left. There they hear the Easter proclamation: "Jesus has risen and he has appeared to Simon" (Luke 24:13–35). Even Jesus' sudden appearance to all the disciples, who are hiding behind locked doors, does not convince them. They are startled, surprised, and think that they are seeing a spirit (v. 37). Not even the presentation of his pierced hands and feet convinces them. As with the Emmaus disciples, he must share a meal with them and instruct them on the need for the Christ to fulfill all the scriptures. Only then can he leave them, as they return to Jerusalem and the Temple, praising God (vv. 52–53).

Despite the majesty of the Johannine resurrection narrative, it is strongly marked by doubt and unbelief. Mary Magdalene cannot imagine a resurrection and can think only of a stolen corpse (John 10:1–2, 11–18). Thomas will not believe that Jesus has risen from the dead *unless* he is able to put his fingers into the wounds of his hands and his hand in Jesus' pierced side (20:24–29). Eventually, Mary Magdalene and Thomas experience the physical presence of the risen Jesus, come to faith, and proclaim him as "Lord" (vv. 18, 29), but they have "seen" Jesus. The final words of the risen Jesus are a blessing of all who have not seen and yet believe (v. 29). This blessing and this story are directed toward the generations of post-Easter disciples, readers, and listeners to this scripture (Greek: *graphē*: "writing"). They must all become beloved disciples, like the original Beloved Disciple of vv. 2–9, who did not see and yet believed.[87]

Resurrection Grants Forgiveness and Initiates Mission

With the exception of Jesus' threefold questioning of Peter's love for him (John 21:15–17), there are no explicit indications from the risen Jesus that the disciples who have failed to believe, or have denied or fled in fear, are forgiven. Forgiveness is not even explicit in John 21:15–17; it is generally (but not always) taken for granted.[88] Nevertheless, forgiveness is implied by each commissioning. In more theological language, what is outlined below as "forgiveness and mission" should be read as the story of God's gift of "salvation" in and through Jesus. The gift of "salvation" through the death and resurrection of Jesus is central to the message of Christianity. In the gospel narratives, however, explicit reference to salvation is limited to the mocking of Jesus on the cross. In Mark (15:30, 31), Matthew (27:40, 42; see also v. 49), and Luke (25:35, 37, 39) those who have crucified Jesus mock his earlier promises of salvation (Mark 15:30; Matt 27:40; Luke 23:37) or ask him to save himself, as he has saved others (Mark 16:31; Matt 27:42; Luke 23:35, 39). As we have seen, these moments of mockery are ironic presentations of the truth. Jesus' promise of salvation is realized on the cross. Jesus must not come down from the cross to prove that he is King and Messiah, the Savior. It is on the cross that he exercises his royal messianic role and saves (see Mark 15:31–32; Luke 23:35, 39). The resurrection is a story of Jesus' vindication by God and the rehabilitation of the disciples. The narratives of Mark, Matthew, and Luke focus upon this dimension of salvation. The Gospel of John insists that acceptance of Jesus' revelation of God, present throughout his entire presence among us (see 1:1–18), brings eternal life (see 20:30–31). The presence of the incarnate Word (1:14) creates a situation where salvation is possible even now for all who believe in him (see 3:16–21, 31–36; 5:19–30; 6:45–48; 11:25–26; 12:44–50). This is part of what is known as Johannine "realized eschatology." Life and salvation are available *now* in the revealing presence of Jesus Christ. Jesus of Nazareth *is* the "Savior of the world" (4:42). Nevertheless, his saving presence is perfected in "the hour" of his death and resurrection (see 4:34; 13:1; 17:4; 19:30–37). Belief in the crucified and risen Jesus, the Christ and the Son of God, brings eternal life (John 20:30–31).[89]

In the Gospel of Mark the young man's mandate to the women at the tomb that they tell the disciples and Peter that he is going before them into Galilee, where they will see him, as he promised (Mark 16:7), is an indication that discipleship is being rehabilitated.[90] The fact that the women fail (v. 8) does not nullify Jesus' promise of a future meeting in Galilee in 14:28, despite the flight of the disciples and the denials of Peter. Earliest Christian tradition reports appearances (1 Cor 15:3–8), and the gospel traditions consistently report that the women communicated the Easter message to the failing disciples (Matt 28:8; Luke 24:8–9; John 20:18). Mark has reworked this tradition into a frightened silence to make his theological point clear: discipleship is not rehabilitated by any human success, not even by the courageous women who have been at the cross (15:40–41) and at the burial (v. 47). But Jesus has gone ahead of them into Galilee, and they have seen him. There would be no Christian community, and especially no Markan community with its Jesus story, unless the promise of Jesus had come true. There will be a gathering in the "Galilee of the Gentiles" (see Isa 9:1), because God will see to it, not the failed disciples (14:50) or the frightened women (16:8). There the mission of Jesus began, and there fragile disciples will take up that mission, preaching the Gospel to all nations (see 13:10) in the in-between time. Eventually, at the end time, the angels sent out by the Son of Man coming on the clouds of heaven as judge (see 13:26; 14:62) will gather the elect "from the ends of the earth to the ends of heaven" (13:27). Despite its brevity, the Markan resurrection story rehabilitates the fragile disciples and indicates that they will begin a mission from Galilee to preach the Gospel to all nations.

Matthew 28:16–20 develops this Galilean tradition. In the solemn episode that closes the Gospel of Matthew, the risen Jesus exercises his lordship in a gathering of the Eleven on the mountain in Galilee that Jesus has indicated to them (v. 16). The mandate given to the women by the angels in the tomb, to go to Galilee where they will see Jesus (28:7), repeated by the risen Jesus as he meets the women on their way to the Eleven (vv. 8–10), has been obeyed. The Easter message has reached them, and now they have gathered in Galilee.[91] There they will see him (see 26:32). Despite this fulfillment of Jesus' promises, and the obedient response of the Eleven to the women's communication of the command of the angel and Jesus himself, which has brought them to this moun-tain in Galilee, they worship him, "but some doubted." (v. 17). Jesus reveals himself as the Lord of heaven and earth to a mixed group of believers (v. 18), worshipers, and doubters, known throughout the Gospel of Matthew as "people of little faith" (see 6:30; 8:26; 14:31; 16:8; 17:20).[92] Despite their frailty, they are sent out on mission to make dis-ciples of all nations, bringing them into the community of the Father, the Son, and the Spirit by means of the new initiation rite of baptism and by teaching them all the things that Jesus has taught the disciples (vv. 19–20a). What was implicit in Mark has become explicit in Matthew. The disciples are sent out from the "Galilee of the Gentiles" (Isa 9:1) to the ends of the earth. The risen Jesus will be with them in their mission to the close of the age (v. 20).

Luke 24 presents a series of frail disciples. The women at the tomb are perplexed and frightened (vv. 4–5), looking for Jesus in the wrong place (v. 5). They have forgotten the prophet Jesus' promise to them while they were with him in Galilee (v. 6). On remembering his words (v. 8), they report the Easter message to the apostles. But they regard "these words" as an "idle tale" (v. 11). The two disciples journeying to

Emmaus are abandoning God's journey from Galilee, through the paschal events in the city of Nazareth, to the ends of the earth. Jesus' death has discouraged them; he did not fulfill their hopes (vv. 13, 21). The risen Jesus' appearance to the gathered disciples does not generate faith but fear and questions in their hearts, for they think they are seeing a ghost (vv. 36–38). Not even his invitation to see his wounded hands and feet, his flesh and bones, leads to belief. Instead, "they still disbelieved with joy" (vv. 39–41). This intense focus upon the lack of faith of all the characters who play a role in Luke 24 throws into relief the compassion of Jesus who reaches out to them in his failure. The women remember the words of Jesus (v. 8). Jesus accompanies his failing disciples who are abandoning God's journey. He opens the scriptures for them, indicating that their disappointment over Jesus' death is a misunderstanding of God's design. By sharing God's word with them and by breaking bread with them, he brings them back to Jerusalem, the place they should never have abandoned. There they hear the Easter proclamation: "The Lord has risen indeed, and has appeared to Simon" (vv. 25–35). It is within the narrative context of this fragility that Jesus returns to share meals with them (vv. 30, 41–43). Once he has reestablished his bond with them he can commission them to preach "that repentance and forgiveness of sins be preached in his name to all nations, beginning from Jerusalem" (v. 47). It is as apostles who have experienced Jesus' compassion, his call to repentance, and the forgiveness of their failures and sins that they are sent out: "You are witnesses of these things" (v. 48). As Luke's Easter narrative has made clear, they are indeed witnesses of the forgiveness of sin.

The same motif is found across John 20. Mary Magdalene does not suspect that Jesus had been raised from the dead. She is only interested in a stolen corpse (vv. 1–2, 11–15). The risen Jesus must call her by name and tell her to abandon her desire to cling to him (vv. 16–17). She eventually confesses to the disciples: "I have seen the Lord" (v. 18). Thomas will not believe unless Jesus responds to his "fleshly" conditions (vv. 24–25). He too is summoned by the presence of the risen One and arrives at faith in his confession, "My Lord and my God!" (v. 28). These foundational disciples, one a woman and the other a man, have their own agenda, unwilling to accept the fact that Jesus is now risen from the dead, and must return to his Father and their Father, to his God and their God (v. 17). They still seek the "fleshly Jesus." The command to Thomas, "Do not be faithless, but believing" (v. 27) is directed to all who fail to accept what God has done in and through the risen Jesus. He must go away, in order to establish a situation marked by his absence and the presence of the Spirit/Paraclete. Blessedness is found in belief without seeing (v. 29), as the Beloved Disciple believed without seeing Jesus (v. 8). The commission given to frightened disciples behind locked doors also points to the possibility of ongoing failure to accept God's presence in and through Jesus and in his Spirit-filled post-Easter community. The disciples are to be the presence of the divisive, critical, and judging presence of Jesus in a world of unfaith (vv. 21–23).

John 21 also portrays a gathering of disciples who seem to have forgotten everything they have experienced. "I am going fishing," says Simon Peter (v. 3a). They laconically respond, "We will go with you" (v. 3b). Only the Beloved Disciple recognizes the presence of the Lord by the side of the lake: "The disciples did not know that it was Jesus" (v. 4). The amazing catch of fish changes this, but fear returns as a theme in this Easter story: "Now none of the disciples dared ask him, 'Who are you?' They knew it was the Lord" (v. 12). Behind Simon Peter's threefold confession of love lies his threefold denial of Jesus. Despite failure, Peter is appointed the shepherd of the flock (vv. 15–17). He will eventually glorify God with his self-gift unto death (vv. 18–19). The only person who has not failed, the Beloved Disciple, is the one "who has written these things" (v. 24).

The Risen Jesus Gives the Spirit

The risen and departing Jesus promises and gives his Spirit to the disciples to guide and strengthen them in his absence. In the Lukan resurrection narrative the reader/listener is left with the promise. As we have already seen, in Luke 24:49, just before his departure, Jesus tells his disciples: "And behold, I send the promise of my Father upon you; but stay in the city, until you are clothed with power from on high." The reader/listener will need to read on into Luke's second volume before this promise is fulfilled, as the power from on high descends upon the assembled disciples "when the day of Pentecost had come" (Acts 2:1).[93] The Jewish celebration of Pentecost recalled the gift of the Law at Sinai. The Lukan scene has strong reminiscences of that foundational experience for the people of God at Sinai. The promised power from on high given to the apostles tells again of the presence of God with his people

(Acts 2:1–4). Sounds from heaven and fire accompany them as they "were all filled with the Holy Spirit" (v. 4). After encountering God at Sinai, amid heavenly noise and fire (see Exod 19:18–19), Moses came down from the mountain with the Law for Israel, a covenant between God and his people. In Jerusalem "men from every nation" are present to hear the disciples speak in all the known languages, reversing the curse that began at the Tower of Babel (see Gen 11:1–9). A new and universal people of God has been founded at a new Pentecost (Acts 2:5–13).[94]

The Gospel of John, as we have seen, promises the gift of the Spirit/Paraclete (7:37–39; 14:15–17, 26; 15:26–27; 16:7–11, 12–15). Jesus gives it abundantly in his "hour," as he makes God known by bringing his task to its perfect accomplishment (19:30), and in his commission to the disciples so that they might continue his critical, revealing, and judgment presence in his absence (20:21–23). The association of the gift of the Spirit with the risen Jesus (John), and with the risen and departing Jesus (John and Luke) brings to closure the need for Jesus to remain with his infant community. He will be with them always in the gift of his Spirit; his God and Father is their God and their Father.[95]

Conclusion

The narrative reporting of the early Church's convictions about the resurrection of Jesus displays a remarkable fertility of theological imagination. Beginning from an indescribable occurrence that followed the ignominious death of Jesus of Nazareth, early Christians began to articulate, as best they could, their impressions of what happens when the eschatological intervention of God touches the events of human history. As Christian readers early in the third Christian millennium we look back to these stories with some justified puzzlement. There is much in these stories that defies our scientific control, but perhaps that is the way things should be.

There are many wonders scattered across the gospel stories. But none of them surpasses the way the story of Jesus of Nazareth begins and ends.[96] The Gospel of Matthew and the Gospel of Luke report a virginal conception (Matt 1:18–25; Luke 1:26–38). The Gospel of John claims that the man who came to be known as Jesus Christ preexisted before all time in a loving union with God as the very Word of God that would be "spoken" into the world (John 1:1–18). All four Gospels end the story with the documented historical fact that Jesus was executed by the Romans, most likely in some sort of collusion with Jewish authorities. However, that ending is not the end, as a further wonder brings all four stories to an end. Jesus is raised by God from death, and in Luke and John he ascends to his Father.

Christians believe that God entered the human story in and through his Son, Jesus of Nazareth. It is right that we are unable to explain *how* the human presence of the Divine in our history began and ended, even though we live in the faith *that* this happened. In John 12:43, as Jesus closes his public ministry, John plays on a Greek word that has two meanings. The Greek word is *doxa*. It can mean achievable, measurable, human success, or it can mean the revelation of the Divine. The former meaning is found throughout Greek literature, and in everyday Greek usage. The latter is only found in the Bible. It is used in the LXX to speak of the visible presence of God in such wonders as the gift of the Law on Sinai (see Exod 19:16; Deut 5:24), the fire in the desert, the gift of the manna (Exod 16:7), other numinous visions of God's presence (see Exod 14:4, 17, 18; 16:10; 24:16, 17; 33:18, 22; 40:34–35), and even the beauty of the skies (Ps 19:1). These were all human experiences that defied explanation but were regarded as revelations of God's care for his people.[97] The narrator asks why the leaders of Israel would not accept Jesus. His response is that they preferred the *doxa* of men rather than the *doxa* of God (John 12:43).[98] The mysterious entry and exit of the Divine from our human history lies beyond our human or scientific control, measurable human success. But as believing Christians we affirm our right to claim that in Jesus we have been granted sight of the glory of God.

Belief in the resurrection of Jesus was born because the earliest Christians found that it "made sense" of their experience of Jesus.[99] However, it was more than that, as is obvious from the rich interpretation of what the resurrection of the Messiah meant for them, communicated through the four gospel narratives. The imaginative telling and retelling of the story of Jesus' death and resurrection provided the basis for two thousand years of Christian faith and practice. It is a further wonder that by the end of the first Christian century unforgettable narratives emerged from an understanding of what happened to the crucified Messiah, to tell what it meant—first for Jesus, and then for all who choose to follow him. It is only a beginning. Subsequent Christian life and thought have taken this further, as they should.[100] Believers can only wonder at what God has done for Jesus, but we rejoice in what Jesus has done for us in and through the resurrection. This is especially true in our current era, when Christian institutions and practice are under threat from many sides, and also from the way Christianity is lived by many of us.[101] The stories of the resurrection of the Messiah assure us that Jesus' promises come true, that our fears, doubts, failures, and sin are overcome, as we are sent out again and again on mission, accompanied by the never-failing presence of Jesus in the gift of his Spirit.

Notes

1. As the narrator in Yann Martel, *Beatrice and Virgil* (Edinburgh: Canongate Books, 2010), 7, comments: "Stories—individual stories, family stories, national stories—are what stitch together the disparate elements of human existence into a coherent whole. We are story animals."

2. On this question, see also Gerald O'Collins, *Believing in the Resurrection: The Meaning and Promise of the Risen Jesus* (Mahwah, NJ: Paulist Press, 2012), 29–34.

3. Courageously faced in 1973 in a balanced, critical, and eminently readable fashion by Raymond E. Brown, *The Virginal Conception and Bodily Resurrection of Jesus* (New York: Paulist Press, 1973).

4. There is some conflict in the Gospels about the nature of the Friday on which he was crucified (14 Nisan: the day of rest of the Passover feast [John]; 15 Nisan: the first day of the feast [all the Synoptics]), but his death is well documented. See the surveys by Ed Parish Sanders, *The Historical Figure of Jesus* (London: The Penguin Press, 1993), 249–75; John P. Meier, *A Marginal Jew: Rethinking the Historical Jesus*, 4 vols., ABRL/AYBRL (New York: Doubleday/New Haven, CT: Yale University Press, 1991–2009), 1:386–406; Gerd Theissen and Annette Merz, *The Historical Jesus: A Comprehensive Guide* (Minneapolis, MN: Fortress, 1996), 157–61.

5. For a full-scale introduction to a contemporary critical reading of the Gospels, see Francis J. Moloney, *The Living Voice of the Gospel: The Gospels Today* (Peabody, MA: Hendrickson, 2007).

6. For a tracing of the earliest confessions of the resurrection of Jesus, see, among many, Brown, *The Virginal Conception and Bodily Resurrection of Jesus*, 78–96; Xavier Léon-Dufour, *Resurrection and the Message of Easter*

(London: Geoffrey Chapman, 1974), 5–59; Dale C. Allison, Jr., *Resurrecting Jesus: The Earliest Christian Tradition and Its Interpretation* (New York: T. and T. Clark, 2005), 228–39.

7. For example, a reconstructed source that provided material for both Matthew and Luke and may be earlier than Mark ("Q"), has no trace of a passion and resurrection narrative. However, suffering and ultimate vindication are presupposed, even if not narrated, by the Q document. See, for example, Christopher M. Tuckett, *Q and the History of Early Christianity: Studies on Q* (Edinburgh: T & T Clark, 1996), 283–323; John S. Kloppenborg, *The Earliest Gospel: An Introduction to the Original Stories and Sayings of Jesus* (Louisville, KY: Westminster John Knox, 2008), 73–84. The relevant texts are discussed there. It is generally accepted that a pre-Markan passion narrative did not contain a resurrection story. For suggested reconstructions, see Marion Soards, "The Question of a Premarcan Passion Narrative," in Raymond E. Brown, *The Death of the Messiah: From Gethsemane to the Grave: A Commentary on the Passion Narratives in the Four Gospels,* 2 vols., ABRL (New York: Doubleday, 1993), 2:1492–1524 (Appendix IX). See also Adele Y. Collins, *Mark,* Hermeneia (Minneapolis, MN: Fortress, 2004), 819, for a recent tentative reconstruction of the narrative.

8. This is not to discount the possibility of "experiences" that have been reported, over the centuries, by people who claim to have extraordinary encounters with deceased people. For a well-documented presentation of these experiences, including one of his own, see Allison, *Resurrecting Jesus,* 269–99. Allison, among many, will not discount the possibility of these encounters but cites Hugh Montefiore's conclusion concerning an experience of the risen Christ that led him into Christianity: "I cannot account for my vision of Jesus by any of the psychological or neurophysiological explanations on offer" (269). They are beyond scientific probing. See also the reflections of O'Collins, *Believing in the Resurrection,* 175–91, on recent research into encounters between grieving widows and their beloved dead.

9. In pre-critical times, nothing was made of these differences, and everything was gathered into a large unified narrative, regarded as a report of what actually happened. This provided a rich tapestry for the Church's liturgy and preaching, and should not be discounted, but the theological and christological depth that is given to Christian origins by respecting the differences across the fourfold gospel tradition must be recognized.

10. For a well-documented survey of these proposals, see Allison, *Resurrecting Jesus,* 199–213.

11. Several of these highly critical scholars were marginalized within their Christian traditions, and some lost their academic positions. Outstanding among these were David Strauss (1808–74) and Albert Loisy (1857–1940).

Strauss was the first systematically to introduce the notion of "myth" into the interpretation of the Gospels' presentation of Jesus' life, teaching, death, and resurrection. See David F. Strauss, *The Life of Jesus Critically Examined*, ed. Peter C. Hodgson, trans. George Eliot, Lives of Jesus (Philadelphia: Fortress, 1972 [original German: 1835]). Loisy claimed that the resurrection was not historical but the product of the faith of the first Christians. See, for example, *The Birth of the Christian Religion*, trans. Lawrence P. Jacks (London: George Allen and Unwin, 1948 [original French: 1933]). For further background and their experiences in their respective Christian communities, see William Baird, *History of New Testament Research*, 2 vols. (Minneapolis, MN: Fortress, 1992–2003), 1:246–58 (Strauss); 2:163–72 (Loisy).

12. For more background, see Horton Harris, *The Tübingen School* (Oxford: Clarendon Press, 1975). The approach of the school is associated with its founding figure, Ferdinand Christian Baur. On Baur and other members of the school, see also Baird, *History of New Testament Research*, 1:258–78. Baird captures the spirit of the German universities at that time: "Having eaten at the tree of *Wissenschaft*, they had become like God, knowing the difference between fact and fable" (2:86).

13. Brooke Foss Westcott, *The Gospel of the Resurrection: Thoughts on Its Relation to Reason and History* (London: Macmillan, 1906), 6.

14. Ibid., 139.

15. The founding fathers were Karl Ludwig Schmidt, Martin Dibelius, and Rudolf Bultmann. For more detail, see Francis J. Moloney, *Mark: Storyteller, Interpreter, Evangelist* (Peabody, MA: Hendrickson, 2004), 19–28.

16. Rejection of an empty tomb and the affirmation of resurrection faith has been made popular by Rudolf Bultmann, one of the founding figures of form criticism (see below). He has many followers, although not all would follow his existentialist/theological agenda.

17. Founding figures were Hans Conzelmann, Willi Marxsen, and Günther Bornkamm. For more detail, see Moloney, *Mark: Storyteller, Interpreter, Evangelist*, 28–31.

18. This approach dominates much contemporary Gospel scholarship. For more detail, see Moloney, *Mark: Storyteller, Interpreter, Evangelist*, 31–37; Moloney, *The Gospel of John*, 13–20. See also Francis J. Moloney, "Mark as Story: Retrospect and Prospect," 1–11, and the broader discussion reported there.

19. There are, of course, an increasing number of historians and neo-atheists who would continue the age-old claims that Christianity is based upon a lie. This position is not represented by the scholarship under discussion and need not bother us.

20. See Rudolf Bultmann and Five Critics, *Kerygma and Myth*, ed. Hans Werner Bartsch, trans. Reginald H. Fuller (New York: Harper and Row, 1961), 38–43.

21. Bultmann and Five Critics, *Kerygma and Myth*, 41.

22. Willi Marxsen, *The Resurrection of Jesus of Nazareth*, trans. Margaret Kohl (London: SCM Press, 1970), 77. What this meant in the earliest Church is described by Marxsen in his chapter: "The Miracle of the Resurrection" (112–29). He states: "For 'Jesus is risen' simply means: today the crucified Jesus is calling us to believe" (128). For an extensive negative review of Marxsen's study, see Gerald O'Collins, *The Heythrop Journal* 12 (1971): 207–11. O'Collins concludes: "We meet here a sharp distinction between the historian and the believer, an unwarranted separation of the cognitive side of faith from the decision to commit oneself—in a word, a radical isolation of faith from reason" (211). There is more to it, however. As O'Collins himself recognizes ("He shows himself definitely cut from traditional Lutheran cloth" [211]), Marxsen takes the Lutheran agenda of "by faith alone," which had been further radicalized on the basis of the New Testament texts by Rudolf Bultmann, to its logical conclusion. Only faith in Jesus Christ is of redemptive value. The search for historical support is an act of unfaith. This is a serious theological position, even if unacceptable to many. It must be respected.

23. For an up-to-date and exhaustive study that surveys opinions from every side, see Allison, *Resurrecting Jesus*, 198–375.

24. These two positions have been combined by Adele Y. Collins, "Apotheosis and Resurrection," in *The New Testament and Hellenistic Judaism*, ed. Peder Borgen and Søren Giverson (Peabody, MA: Hendrickson, 1997), 88–100. See also: Collins, *Mark*, 781–94. On Markan creativity, see John Dominic Crossan, "Empty Tomb and Absent Lord," in *The Passion in Mark: Studies on Mark 14–16*, ed. Werner H. Kelber (Philadelphia: Fortress, 1976), 134–52.

25. Variations of this position have been adopted by the significant Catholic scholar Rudolf Pesch, "Zur Entstehung des Glaubens and die Auferstehung Jesu," *Theologische Quartalschrift* 153 (1973): 103–17. Pesch's work has influenced Hans Küng, *On Being a Christian*, trans. Edward Quinn (London: Collins, 1977), 343–81, esp. 370–73; and Edward Schillebeeckx, *Jesus: An Experiment in Christology*, trans. Hubert Hoskins (London: Collins, 1979), 320–97. Pesch, in turn, depends upon the research into pre-Christian Jewish materials by Klaus Berger, *Die Auferstehung des Propheten und die Erhöhung des Menschensohnes: Traditionsgeschichtliche Untersuchungen zur Deutung des Geschickes Jesu in früchristlichen Texten*, SUNT 13 (Göttingen, Vandenhoeck und Ruprecht, 1976). For a more detailed survey of this discussion, see Francis J. Moloney, "Resurrection and Accepted Exegetical Opinion," *ACR* 58 (1981): 191–202. See also O'Collins, *Believing in the Resurrection*, 76.

Like Strauss and Loisy, these scholars have also had to deal with censure from church authorities. More recently, Pesch has withdrawn his support for this proposal. See Rudolf Pesch, "Le genèse de la foi en la resurrection de Jésus. Une nouvelle tentative," in *La Pâque du Christ: Mystère de salut,* ed. Martin Benzerath (Paris: Cerf, 1982), 51–74.

26. See Allison, *Resurrecting Jesus,* 312.

27. See especially Adele Y. Collins, *Mark,* Hermeneia (Minneapolis, MN: Fortress, 2004), 782–94; Daniel A. Smith, *Revisiting the Empty Tomb: The Early History of Easter* (Minneapolis, MN: Fortress, 2010). See the critical discussion of Smith's book by O'Collins, *Believing in the Resurrection,* 17–19. With reference to Adele Collins, O'Collins rightly points out that evidence for disappearance/assumption is not even vaguely present in Mark 16:1–8 (see 19). Also see his more general discussion of assumption and exaltation theories (55–59). The introductory chapter to O'Collins's recent book also appeared as "The Resurrection: Nine Recent Approaches," *AeJT* 18 (2011): 1–18, available online at aejt.com.au.

28. Not all would accept the following argument, and for some there is no need to defend the historicity of empty tomb (or the appearances). Like Westcott, they regard the trustworthiness of the gospel accounts as sufficient proof. Others would be more aggressive in their affirmation of the historicity of the empty tomb and the appearances on a more scholarly basis. See, for example, Wolfhart Pannenberg, *Jesus—God and Man,* trans. Lewis L. Wilkins and Duane A. Prieve, 2nd ed. (Philadelphia: Westminster, 1977), 88–114; Gerald O'Collins, *Jesus Risen: An Historical, Fundamental, and Systematic Examination of Christ's Resurrection* (Mahwah, NJ: Paulist Press, 1987); Nicholas T. Wright, *The Resurrection of the Son of God* (Minneapolis, MN: Fortress, 2003). For what follows, I am guided by Allison, *Resurrecting Jesus,* 299–352.

29. See Allison, *Resurrecting Jesus,* 303–7.

30. On this, see the older but important essay of Hans von Campenhausen, "The Events of Easter and the Empty Tomb," in *Tradition and Life in the Church: Essays and Lectures in Church History,* trans. A. V. Littledale (London: Collins, 1968), 42–89.

31. See the documented discussion of this issue in Allison, *Resurrecting Jesus,* 326–31. It is the argument that leads his extremely critical survey of the many possible solutions, both for and against the existence of an empty tomb, to state that this "remains a decent argument for some real memory there—especially when one keeps in mind that 'the resurrection narrative is the only place in the whole Bible where women are sent by the angels of Yahweh to pronounce his message to men,'" citing Tibor Horvath.

32. The Beloved Disciple accompanies Peter in John 20:2–10, but for historical purposes that can be regarded as a uniquely Johannine theological motif (see esp. 20:8: "He saw and he believed").

33. Allison, *Resurrecting Jesus*, 321. See also Craig A. Evans, *Mark 8:27–16:20*, WBC 34B (Nashville, TN: Thomas Nelson, 2001), 530–32. Even Rudolf Bultmann admits that Mark 16:1-8 is "extremely reserved" (*History of the Synoptic Tradition*, trans. John Marsh [Oxford: Blackwell, 1968], 286).

34. On the later interest in tombs, see Peter Brown, *The Cult of the Saints: Its Rise and Function in Latin Christianity* (Chicago: Chicago University Press, 1981). The lack of interest in a tomb site is discussed by Allison, *Resurrecting Jesus*, 312–14, but he questions it, pointing to the existence of the Holy Sepulchre Church in Jerusalem. This is surprising from the highly critical pen of Allison. That particular building replaced the pagan Capitoline temple, flanked by a temple to Aphrodite, erected by Hadrian in AD 135. Holy Sepulchre Church was not constructed until Constantinian times (fourth century), under the direction of Constantine's mother, Helena. The link between the site of Jesus' burial and the Constantinian church, associated with the relic of the "true cross," is the stuff of legend, however close it may be to the truth. On this, see Jerome Murphy-O'Connor, *The Holy Land: An Oxford Archaeological Guide from Earliest Times to 1700*, 4th ed. (Oxford: Oxford University Press, 1998), 45–57. Murphy-O'Connor claims that Christians held liturgical celebrations on the site till AD 66, and that the site was protected after the walls were built outside it (AD 41–43). He suggests that the building of Hadrian's temple was "probably reinforced with bitterness" (45–46). He offers no evidence for these claims.

35. As Raymond E. Brown, *The Virginal Conception and Bodily Resurrection of Jesus*, 127, puts it: "Modern fundamentalist statements such as 'Our faith depends on the empty tomb' or 'we believe in the empty tomb' are not only open to ridicule about the emptiness of one's faith, but also misplace the emphasis in resurrection faith. Christians believe in Jesus, not in a tomb."

36. O'Collins, *Believing in the Resurrection*, 80–99, reflects both historically and theologically in order to develop a very positive understanding of the message of an empty tomb.

37. To claim, as do some scholars (for example, Bultmann), that these reports are crassly materialistic misses the point entirely. It is not "apologetics" for Christian faith but an affirmation that the risen Jesus is the same person as the pre-Easter Jesus.

38. O'Collins, *Believing in the Resurrection*, 14–15. O'Collins has long defended the possibility of determining historical facts surrounding the appearances. Most recently, see Gerald O'Collins, "Peter as Witness to Easter," *TS* 73 (2012): 263–85. Gerald O'Collins has made a remarkable contribution to Christian reflection upon the resurrection. To the best of my knowledge, his first book on the question was *The Easter Jesus* (London: Darton, Longman, and Todd, 1973). Since then he has written more than a dozen books on the

resurrection, and an equal number on fundamental theology and Christology, where the resurrection is a central issue. His most recent publication, *Believing in the Resurrection,* continues his passionate attention to this central aspect of Christian life.

39. O'Collins, *Believing in the Resurrection,* 16.

40. See especially Dale C. Allison, *The Historical Christ and the Theological Jesus* (Grand Rapids, MI: Eerdmans, 2009). Worth noting is Allison, *Constructing Jesus: Memory, Imagination, and History* (Grand Rapids, MI: Baker Academic, 2010), 462: "If my deathbed finds me alert and not overly racked with pain, I will then be preoccupied with how I have witnessed and embodied faith, hope and charity. I will not be fretting over the historicity of this or that part of the New Testament."

41. See the still useful analysis of the various forms of the appearance stories in Charles H. Dodd, "The Appearances of the Risen Christ: An Essay in Form-Criticism of the Gospels," in *More New Testament Studies* (Manchester: Manchester University Press, 1968), 102–33.

42. For a lucid discussion of the problems generated by these various recipients of appearances, see Raymond E. Brown, *The Virginal Conception and Bodily Resurrection of Jesus,* 81–113.

43. See, for example, Brown's speculations on the nature of the risen body: "A corporeal resurrection in which the risen body is transformed to the eschatological sphere, no longer bound by space and time—a body that no longer has all the natural or physical characteristics that marked its temporal existence" (ibid., 85 n. 145). Does that help? Probably not much more than Allison's use of paranormal encounters with the deceased, lamented by O'Collins, *Believing in the Resurrection,* 14–16.

44. At the heart of this question is the steady use of Greek verbs associated with "seeing," especially the passive form (Greek: *ōphthē*) in crucial appearance passages (1 Cor 15:5; Luke 24:34; Acts 13:31). It is used in a dative construction, that is, it means "appeared to." The other verb used is *to be made manifest* (passive forms of the Greek verb *phaneroō*). The latter is more generally associated with a divine revelation, and the former is widely used across the LXX in association with a number of ways in which the divine presence or activity is "made visible to" human beings. See the excellent synthesis in Brown, *The Virginal Conception and Bodily Resurrection of Jesus,* 89–92. See also O'Collins, *Believing in the Resurrection,* 61–66.

45. On this, see Brown, *The Virginal Conception and Bodily Resurrection of Jesus,* 89–92.

46. Ibid., 91.

47. O'Collins, *Believing in the Resurrection,* 16.

48. See Brown, *The Virginal Conception and Bodily Resurrection of Jesus*, 126.

49. As Allison rightly assesses the situation: "Contrary to the gung-ho apologist, it is possible in theory that Jesus awakened from death, that the tomb was empty, that he appeared to some of his followers, and that historians cannot prove any of this to anyone. And contrary to the evangelistic sceptic, it is equally possible, again in theory, that when Jesus died he died for good, that the appearances were altogether illusory, that his tomb remained forever full, and that historians cannot establish any of this" (*Resurrecting Jesus*, 339).

50. Again, Brown, *The Virginal Conception and Bodily Resurrection of Jesus*, 127–28, is most helpful. He insists that Christians should continue to speak of the *bodily* resurrection of Jesus. However, what that means is more difficult to ascertain. Looking back to the beginnings of the tradition, Brown writes: "Our earliest ancestors *in the faith* proclaimed a bodily resurrection in the sense that they did not think that Jesus' body had corrupted in the tomb. However, and this is equally important, Jesus' risen body was no longer a body as we know bodies, bound by the dimensions of space and time" (italics mine). He recommends that we take seriously Paul's insistence that risen bodies are no longer natural or physical but rather spiritual (see 1 Cor 15:42–44). On this, see 86–87 n. 147.

51. Sanders, *The Historical Figure of Jesus*, 280.

52. The theological establishment of the risen Jesus as "Lord" by means of the resurrection is much earlier than the gospel narratives. See, especially, the pre-Pauline formula embedded in Romans 1:3–4. On this, see Brendan Byrne, *Romans*, SP 6 (Collegeville, MN: The Liturgical Press, 1996), 39–40, 43–45. Other very early formulas can be found in 1 Cor 12:3; Phil 2:9–11; Rom 10:9, 12–13. This study, however, is limited to the gospel stories, where later narrative forms of affirming the lordship of the risen Jesus can be found (see especially Luke 24:34; John 20:18, 28; 21:7, 15–17. Matt 28:16–20 does not use the expression *Lord*, but the commission reflects the lordship of Jesus over heaven and earth).

53. Karl Marx's famous dictum, "Religion is the opium of the people," is an example of this point of view.

54. See Roger Haight, *Dynamics of Theology*, 2nd ed. (Maryknoll, NY: Orbis Books, 2001), 16–19. On Haight's presentation of "faith," see Phillip D. Gleeson, "Today: A Study in the Theological Method of Roger Haight" (D.Theol. diss., MCD University, Melbourne, 2012), 22–29. See further, the parallel stimulating reflection on faith from a Girardian perspective in Joel Hodge, *Resisting Violence and Victimisation: Christian Faith and Solidarity in East Timor* (London: Ashgate, 2012), 69–118: "Faith…is not a gap in human

knowledge but the fundamental substance of human being that is not seen and that results in the communion and fulfilment for which we hope" (105).

55. Haight, *Dynamics of Theology*, 17 (parenthetic addition mine).

56. Ibid., 18. As Gleeson, "Today," 23, explains: "Faith is also a key element in life because human beings choose objects of faith which provide unity, order and intelligibility to their lives. Whether such objects are nothing more than merely the pursuit of selfish pleasures, the fact remains, Haight argues, that a chosen path or direction can be discerned in people's lives on which their hearts have been set. An object of faith is always operative within the sum total of people's decisions."

57. The strength of the work of Rudolph Pesch, Hans Küng, and Edward Schillebeeckx lies in the fact that they look back to the disciples' experience of the pre-Easter Jesus as the birthplace of faith in the resurrection. While they fail to give due credit to the eschatological event of the resurrection itself, they are right in claiming that the memory of the pre-Easter Jesus would have been an important factor that led to their faith in Jesus as their risen Lord. It "made most sense" to the disciples because it "made sense" of their memory of Jesus.

58. Once they found that faith in the risen Jesus was the expression of the universal and transcendent experience that made most sense to them, its articulation in confessions of faith and in faith-filled stories became an expression of their "beliefs." See Haight, *Dynamics of Theology*, 26–29. He points out: "Beliefs may be considered expressions of faith that are distinct from faith itself" (26). The *unique* early Christian experience of *faith* in the risen Jesus as Lord and Savior transcends its various expressions, but the *beliefs* articulated in Mark, Matthew, Luke, and John are, as we have seen, *pluriform*.

59. What follows depends upon the narrative commentaries in chapters 1 to 4. It does not pretend to be an exhaustive list. Relevant discussions of textual problems and critical scholarship will be found in earlier chapters and will not be repeated below. For some parallel reflections on each of the gospel traditions, further amplified with more theological considerations, see O'Collins, *Believing in the Resurrection*, 100–119.

60. As we have seen, the use of the Greek expression *dei* is important in Luke 22—24. This way of indicating the presence of the divine plan is continued in the Acts of the Apostles. The expression appears twenty-two times.

61. The same focus upon the angel in the empty tomb is found in the mandate to tell the disciples that Jesus is going before them into Galilee: "Lo, I have told you" (28:7). Mark has "as he told you" (Mark 16:7).

62. We have already seen that this passage is textually doubtful but nowadays widely accepted as authentic. See above, 88.

63. On the theme of meals and eating in the Gospel of Luke, see Robert J. Karris, *Luke: Artist and Theologian: Luke's Passion Account as Literature* (New York: Paulist Press, 1985), 47–78.

64. These very physical Lukan and Johannine descriptions of hands and feet and sharing meals no doubt played a role in the early Church's preaching of the resurrection. For some commentators it is little more than a crass materialism. This misses the point. The evangelists stressed that the Jesus they once knew was truly risen. The risen Jesus was the Jesus of their pre-Easter experience.

65. The establishment of Jesus as Messiah and Lord "in holiness by his resurrection from the dead" (Rom 1:3–4) is a very primitive Christian confession. See above, 176 n. 52.

66. This is the literary and theological function of the so-called messianic secret. See Moloney, *The Gospel of Mark*, 173–74, 304–5.

67. On Mark's presentation of Jesus as the Messiah, see Moloney, *Mark: Storyteller, Interpreter, Evangelist*, 130–36. For an understanding of 14:61–62 and 15:2 as Jesus' acceptance of a royal messianic role, see Moloney, *The Gospel of Mark*, 304–5, 310–11.

68. See Jeremy Camery-Hoggatt, *Irony in Mark's Gospel: Text and Subtext*, SNTSMS 72 (Cambridge: Cambridge University Press, 1992), 175–76.

69. On Mark's presentation of Jesus as the Son of Man, see Moloney, *Mark: Storyteller, Interpreter, Evangelist*, 143–52.

70. Ibid., 152.

71. Some have suggested that the presentation of Jesus as the messianic Son of God in whom the Father is well pleased in the Markan prologue (1:1–13; see vv. 1, 11; see also 9:7) reaches a climax in the Easter proclamation of Jesus, the crucified One, now raised by God (16:6). In this reading, even though there is no explicit reference to messianic terms, the theme of Jesus as the messianic Son of God from 1:1–13 returns in 16:1–8. See, for example, Jack Dean Kingsbury, *The Christology of Mark's Gospel* (Philadelphia: Fortress, 1983), 153–54.

72. For the development of this theme within the passion narrative, see David L. Tiede, *Prophecy and History in Luke-Acts* (Philadephia: Fortress, 1980), 97–125. In the light of the above sketch, it is clear that, for Luke, the Messiah must not only die but also be raised from the dead. For Luke T. Johnson, *The Acts of the Apostles*, SP 5 (Collegeville, MN: The Liturgical Press, 1992), 23–32, Luke also presents the ascension of Jesus as "Jesus' enthronement as King, and therefore as Messiah." Jesus is not a corpse or a ghost, but "one living in power, 'at the right hand of God' (LXX Ps 109:1; Acts 2:34–36; 7:55)" (30).

73. For an interpretation of these texts and contexts from the Gospel of John in support of this claim, see Francis J. Moloney, *The Gospel of John*, at the various places cited. See also the older study, Francis J. Moloney, "The Fourth Gospel's Presentation of Jesus as 'the Christ' and J. A. T. Robinson's 'Redating,'" *The Downside Review* 95 (1977) 239–53.

74. It is widely accepted that 17:3 is a redactional clarification added to 17:1–5. One of the reasons for this suggestion is that Jesus calls himself "Christ." This is the only such occurrence in the Gospel. Whatever one makes of this, it must be read and interpreted within its present Johannine context. See the discussion in Moloney, *The Gospel of John*, 460–62, 464.

75. The close association between "Christ" and "Son of God" is important for Johannine Christology. It is only insofar as Jesus is the Son of God, as indicated by 1:1–18, that Jesus is "the Christ." On John 20:31, see especially Rudolf Schnackenburg, *The Gospel according to St. John*, trans. Kevin Smyth et al., 3 vols. (London: Burns and Oates; New York: Crossroad, 1968–82), 3:338–40: "The bringer of revelation, come in the flesh, the Son of God, is the bringer of life for mankind who has succumbed to death, and he is, in this sense, the Messiah" (339).

76. Not every use of "Lord" in John 20 (especially vv. 2, 13, and 15) is a confession of the lordship of the risen Jesus. However, they all play into John's narrative strategy, as Mary Magdalene moves from the use of the Greek expression *kyrios* as a respectful address (vv. 2, 13, and 15) to a confession of faith (v. 18).

77. It is too significant theologically for the all-too-common portrayal (often found in Christian iconography) of Jesus disappearing into the clouds, head first. For some Old Testament background to an "assumption" of a significant figure into heaven (e.g., Enoch, Elijah, Moses), see Fitzmyer, *The Gospel according to Luke*, 1:828. It was also a familiar theme in Hellenistic literature. See Johnson, *Acts*, 30. This is not the place to discuss the slightly different timetable and description of the ascension in Acts 1:6–11. For some it is literary and theological, for others it is the result of the division into Luke and Acts from an originally unified text into two separate documents. See, among many, Christopher F. Evans, *Saint Luke*, 927–28; Joseph A. Fitzmyer, *The Acts of the Apostles*, AB 31 (New York: Doubleday, 1997), 191–94, 195–96.

78. See, for this translation of the Greek, Fitzmyer, *The Gospel according to Luke*, 1:827–28.

79. For a very useful chart, showing the similarity in message between John 14 and 16, see Raymond E. Brown, *The Gospel according to John*, 2 vols., AB 29–29A (Garden City, NY: Doubleday, 1966–70), 2:589–91.

80. Although best known as a Lukan motif, Luke never uses the word *to ascend*. It is only John who uses the word that describes a physical going up in ascension (Greek: *anabainō*).

81. On John's rich theology of the cross, see Francis J. Moloney, *Love in the Gospel of John: An Exegetical, Theological, and Literary Study* (Grand Rapids, MI: Baker Academic, 2013).

82. This passage has often been incorrectly taken as biographical. It is a profound reflection upon the hopelessness of the situation of the person prior to Christianity. For a full explanation of the passage along these lines, see Byrne, *Romans*, 216–34.

83. Each evangelist handles this theme differently, but it is present in them all. Mark is most severe in his portrayal of failing disciples. See Moloney, *Mark: Storyteller, Interpreter, Evangelist*, 160–67. On a number of occasions Matthew rewrites his Markan source to soften the severity, but it remains. See Jack Dean Kingsbury, *Matthew as Story*, 2nd ed. (Philadelphia: Fortress, 1988), 129–45. Luke is even more careful in his presentation of the apostles, as they are a crucial part of his "missionary" agenda. But see Robert C. Tannehill, *The Narrative Unity of Luke-Acts: A Literary Interpretation*, 2 vols. (Philadelphia: Fortress, 1986), 203–74. For an illustration of John's presentation of struggling disciples, see Francis J. Moloney, "Can Everyone Be Wrong? A Reading of John 11:1–12:8," *NTS* 49 (2003): 505–27.

84. For the literary pattern developed by Mark in 14:1–72 to highlight the tragic failure of the disciples in the passion narrative, largely followed by Matthew, see Moloney, *Mark: Storyteller, Interpreter, Evangelist*, 276–78.

85. The message of failure and unfaith, despite the resurrection, is very present in the later ending to Mark, in 16:9–14 ("they would not believe it" [v. 11]; "they did not believe them" [v. 11]; "he upbraided them for their unbelief and hardness of heart" [v. 14]).

86. Although the expression "people of little faith" (Greek: *oligopistoi*) is not found here, this Matthean theme is present. See below, n. 92.

87. Lack of recognition also appears in John 21:4, and fear in v. 12.

88. Although the majority position, not everyone accepts that Peter's threefold confession of love is linked with the threefold denial of Jesus. See, for example, Rudolf Bultmann, *The Gospel of John*, trans. George Beasley-Murray (Oxford: Blackwell, 1971), 712–13. But that is the majority position. For Schillebeeckx, *Jesus*, 379–92, it is especially the disciples' experience of the grace of conversion and forgiveness that is an important element in the generation of Easter faith. The textual evidence is not strong.

89. A biblical analysis uncovers what *the inspired text* tells us, with its many rich possibilities. A theological reflection is then able to show how this richness plays into a *theology of salvation*. See especially, Anthony J. Kelly, *The*

Resurrection Effect: Transforming Christian Life and Thought (Marknoll, NY: Orbis Books, 2008), 131–52.

90. It was also suggested above that the parallel between the young man who fled naked in 14:51–52 and the young man dressed in a white robe in 16:5 is a further promise of rehabilitation. See above, 10–11.

91. Matthew, Luke, and John continue the earliest tradition of appearances of the risen Jesus (see especially 1 Cor 15:3–8), which Mark has suppressed, for his own theological purposes.

92. See Luz, *Matthew*, 1:343: "This traditional expression has become important for Matthew; it characterizes the situation of the community that stands between unfaith and faith and that in its doubt may once again turn to Jesus' power for help (8:26; 14:31)."

93. See Johnson, *The Gospel of Luke*, 406: "The promise of the Holy Spirit is the final statement of Jesus in the Gospel, and is followed immediately by this first account of the ascension. For Luke, these are two moments of the same process: the 'withdrawal' of Jesus is not so much an absence as it is a presence in a new and more powerful mode: when Jesus is not among them as another specific body, he is acceptable to all as life-giving Spirit."

94. See Johnson, *The Acts of the Apostles*, 41–47.

95. The promise of the risen Jesus in Matthew 28:20 that he will be with them until the end of the ages must be understood in the light of a lived experience of an association between the community and the risen Jesus. As the Matthean community read and listened to its Jesus story toward the end of the first Christian century, its members would have been aware that the risen Jesus was no longer "with them" in the same way that he was to the disciples in the story. Matthew does not introduce the Spirit, but as Luz, *Matthew*, 3:635, puts it: "The evangelist does not need to have the Risen One who has appeared to the disciples disappear, because he remains there in his word, in his commandments and in the experience of the presence of God among those who hear and do this word." See above, n. 93.

96. See Joseph Ratzinger, *Jesus of Nazareth: The Infancy Narratives*, trans. Philip J. Whitmore (New York: Image, 2012), 56: "Karl Barth pointed out that there are two moments in the story of Jesus when God intervenes directly in the material world: the virgin birth and the resurrection from the tomb… These two moments are a scandal to the modern spirit." See Ratzinger's response to this "scandal" on 56–57.

97. For further detail, see Moloney, *Belief in the Word*, 55–57.

98. See Moloney, *John*, 365: "The former will not sacrifice the *horizontal* dimension of all that this world can offer, and rejects the *vertical* inbreaking of God, who sends the Son from above that the world might be saved (cf. 3:16–17)."

99. See Gleeson, "Today," 22–29.

100. I point especially to Kelly, *The Resurrection Effect*. This remarkable study starts from Paul's witness and the gospel stories to show how contemporary biblical, theological, and philosophical thought enables an understanding of the resurrection of the Messiah as "saturating" Christian faith and its practice in a way that could transform the life and thought of believers.

101. O'Collins, *Believing in the Resurrection*, 127–74, devotes valuable attention to these questions that are beyond the scope of the present study.

Bibliography

Commentaries on the Four Gospels

The Gospel of Mark

Anderson, Hugh. *The Gospel of Mark*. New Century Bible. London: Oliphants, 1976.

Byrne, Brendan. *A Costly Freedom: A Theological Reading of Mark's Gospel*. Collegeville, MN: The Liturgical Press, 2008.

Collins, Adele Y. *Mark*. Hermeneia. Minneapolis, MN: Fortress, 2007.

Culpepper, R. Alan. *Mark*. Smyth & Helwys Bible Commentary. Macon, GA: Smyth & Helwys, 2007.

Donahue, John R., and Daniel J. Harrington. *The Gospel of Mark*. Sacra Pagina 2. Collegeville, MN: The Liturgical Press, 2002.

Dowd, Sharyn. *Reading Mark: A Literary and Theological Commentary on the Second Gospel*. Reading the New Testament. Macon, GA: Smyth & Helwys, 2000.

Evans, Craig A. *Mark 8:27—16:20*. Word Biblical Commentary 34B. Nashville, TN: Thomas Nelson, 2001.

Hooker, Morna D. *The Gospel according to St. Mark*. Black's New Testament Commentaries. London: A. and C. Black, 1991.

LaVerdiere, Eugene. *The Beginning of the Gospel: Introducing the Gospel according to Mark*. 2 vols. Collegeville, MN: The Liturgical Press, 1999.

Marcus, Joel. *Mark: A New Translation with Introduction and Commentary*. Anchor Bible/The Yale Anchor Bible 27–27A. 2 vols. New York: Doubleday; New Haven, CT: Yale University Press, 1999–2009.

Moloney, Francis J. *The Gospel of Mark: A Commentary*. Grand Rapids, MI: Baker Academic, 2012.

Schweizer, Eduard. *The Good News according to Mark*. Translated by Donal H. Madvig. London: SPCK, 1971.

Taylor, Vincent. *The Gospel according to St. Mark*. 2nd ed. London: Macmillan, 1966.

The Gospel of Matthew

Byrne, Brendan. *Lifting the Burden: Reading Matthew's Gospel in the Church Today*. Collegeville, MN: The Liturgical Press, 2004.

Davies, William D., and Dale C. Allison. *The Gospel according to Matthew*. International Critical Commentary. 3 vols. Edinburgh: T & T Clark, 1988–97.

Garland, David E. *Reading Matthew: A Literary and Theological Commentary*. Macon, GA: Smyth & Helwys, 2001.

Hagner, Donald A. *Matthew*. Word Biblical Commentary 33A–33B. 2 vols. Dallas, TX: Word, 1993–95.

Keener, Craig S. *A Commentary on the Gospel of Matthew*. Grand Rapids, MI: Eerdmans, 1998.

Luz, Ulrich. *Matthew*. Translated by James E. Crouch. 3 vols. Hermeneia. Minneapolis, MN: Fortress, 2001–7.

Meier, John P. *Matthew*. New Testament Message 3. Wilmington, DE: Michael Glazier, 1980.

Nolland, John. *The Gospel of Matthew*. New International Greek Testament Commentary. Grand Rapids, MI: Eerdmans, 2005.

Patte, Daniel. *The Gospel according to Matthew: A Structural Commentary on Matthew's Faith*. Philadelphia: Fortress, 1987.

Schweizer, Eduard. *The Good News according to Matthew*. Translated by David E. Green. London: SPCK, 1976.

Senior, Donald. *Matthew*. Abingdon New Testament Commentaries. Nashville, TN: Abingdon, 1998.

The Gospel of Luke

Bovon, François. *Luke*. Translated by Christine M. Thomas and James Crouch. 3 vols. Hermeneia. Minneapolis, MN: Fortress, 2002–2013.

Byrne, Brendan. *The Hospitality of God: A Reading of Luke's Gospel*. Collegeville, MN: The Liturgical Press, 2000.

Ellis, E. Earle. *The Gospel of Luke*. New Century Bible. London: Oliphants, 1974.

Evans, Christopher F. *Saint Luke*. Trinity Press International New Testament Commentaries. London: SCM Press, 1990.

Johnson, Luke T. *The Gospel of Luke*. Sacra Pagina 3. Collegeville, MN: The Liturgical Press, 1991.

Fitzmyer, Joseph A. *The Gospel according to Luke*. 2 vols. Anchor Bible 28–28A. Garden City, NY: Doubleday, 1985.

Marshall, I. Howard. *The Gospel of Luke: A Commentary on the Greek Text*. New International Greek Testament Commentary. Exeter: Paternoster Press, 1978.

Schweizer, Eduard. *The Good News according to Luke*. Translated by David E. Green. London: SPCK, 1984.

Talbert, Charles H. *Reading Luke: A Literary and Theological Commentary on the Third Gospel*. New York: Crossroad, 1982.

Tannehill, Robert C. *Luke*. Abingdon New Testament Commentary. Nashville, TN: Abingdon, 1996.

———. *The Narrative Unity of Luke-Acts: A Literary Interpretation*. 2 vols. Philadelphia: Fortress, 1986–1990.

The Gospel of John

Barrett, C. Kingsley. *The Gospel according to St. John*. London: SPCK, 1978.

Beasley-Murray, George R. *John*. Word Biblical Commentary 36. Waco, TX: Word, 1986.

Brodie, Thomas L. *The Gospel according to John: A Literary and Theological Commentary*. New York: Oxford University Press, 1993.

Brown, Raymond E. *The Gospel according to John*. 2 vols. Anchor Bible 29–29A. Garden City, NY: Doubleday, 1966–70.

Bultmann, Rudolf. *The Gospel of John: A Commentary*. Translated by George Beasley-Murray. Oxford: Blackwell, 1971.

Haenchen, Ernst. *John 1—2*. Translated by Robert W. Funk. 2 vols. Hermeneia. Philadelphia: Fortress, 1984.

Hoskyns, Edwyn C. *The Fourth Gospel*. Edited by Francis N. Davey. London: Faber and Faber, 1947.

Keener, Craig S. *The Gospel of John: A Commentary*. 2 vols. Peabody, MA: Hendrickson, 2003.

Lincoln, Andrew T. *The Gospel according to Saint John*. Black's New Testament Commentaries. New York: Crossroads, 2005.

Lindars, Barnabas. *The Gospel of John*. New Century Bible. London: Oliphants, 1972.

Moloney, Francis J. *Belief in the Word: Reading John 1—4*. Minneapolis, MN: Fortress, 1993.

————. *Glory Not Dishonor: Reading John 13—21*. Minneapolis, MN: Fortress, 1998.

————. *The Gospel of John*. Sacra Pagina 3. Collegeville, MN: The Liturgical Press, 1998.

Schnackenburg, Rudolf. *The Gospel according to St. John*. Translated by Kevin Smyth, Cecily Hastings, Francis McDonagh, David Smith, Richard Foley, and G. A. Kon. 3 vols. Herder's Theological Commentary on the New Testament IV/1–3. New York: Crossroads, 1968–82.

Other Studies Cited

Aland, Kurt and Barbara. *The Text of the New Testament: An Introduction to the Critical Editions and to the Theory and Practice of Modern Textual Criticism*. Grand Rapids, MI: Eerdmans, 1987.

Allison, Dale C. *Constructing Jesus: Memory, Imagination and History*. Grand Rapids, MI: Baker Academic, 2010.

————. *The End of the Age Has Come: An Early Interpretation of the Death of Jesus*. Philadelphia: Fortress, 1985.

————. *The Historical Christ and the Theological Jesus*. Grand Rapids, MI: Eerdmans, 2009.

————. *Resurrecting Jesus: The Earliest Christian Tradition and Its Interpreters*. London: T & T Clark, 2005.

————. *Studies in Matthew: Interpretation Past and Present*. Grand Rapids, MI: Baker Academic, 2005.

Aus, Roger David. *Simon Peter's Denial and Jesus' Commissioning of Him as His Successor in John 21:15-19: Studies in Their Judaic Background*. Studies in Judaism. Lanham, MD: University Press of America, 2013.

Baird, William. *History of New Testament Research*. 2 vols. Minneapolis, MN: Fortress, 1992-2003.

Berger, Klaus. *Die Auferstehung des Propheten und die Erhöhung des Menschensohnes: Traditionsgeschichtliche Untersuchungen zur*

Deutung des Geschickes Jesu in frühchristlichen Texten. Studien zur Umwelt des Neuen Testaments 13. Göttingen: Vandenhoeck and Ruprecht, 1976.

Best, Ernest. *Following Jesus: Discipleship in the Gospel of Mark.* Journal for the Study of the New Testament Supplement Series 4. Sheffield: JSOT Press, 1981.

Betz, Hans Dieter. "Apostle." In *The Anchor Bible Dictionary,* edited by David Noel Freedman, 1:309–11. New York: Doubleday, 1992.

Blaine, Brad B. *Peter in the Gospel of John: The Making of an Authentic Disciple.* Academia Biblica 27. Atlanta: SBL, 2007.

Boomershine, Thomas E. "Mark 16:8 and the Apostolic Commission." *Journal of Biblical Literature* 100 (1981): 213–23.

Bovon, François. "The Lukan Story of the Passion of Jesus (Luke 22–23)." In *Studies in Early Christianity,* 74–105. Wissenschaftliche Untersuchungen zum Neuen Testament 161. Tübingen: Mohr Siebeck, 2003.

———. *Luke the Theologian: Fifty-five Years of Research.* 2nd ed. Waco, TX: Baylor University Press, 2006.

Brown, Peter. *The Cult of the Saints: Its Rise and Function in Latin Christianity.* Chicago: Chicago University Press, 1981.

Brown, Raymond E. *The Birth of the Messiah: A Commentary on the Infancy Narratives in Matthew and Luke.* Garden City, NY: Doubleday, 1977.

———. *The Death of the Messiah: From Gethsemane to the Grave: A Commentary on the Passion Narratives in the Four Gospels.* Anchor Bible Reference Library. 2 vols. New York: Doubleday, 1994.

———. "John 21 and the First Appearances of the Risen Jesus to Peter." In *Resurrexit: Actes du Symposium International sur la Résurrection de Jésus,* edited by Eduard Dhanis, 245–65. Rome: Editrice Libreria Vaticana, 1974.

———. *The Virginal Conception and Bodily Resurrection of Jesus.* New York: Paulist Press, 1973.

Brown, Sherri. *Gift upon Gift: Covenant through Word in the Gospel of John.* Pittsburgh Theological Monograph Series. Eugene, OR: Wipf and Stock, 2010.

Bultmann, Rudolf. *History of the Synoptic Tradition.* Translated by John Marsh. Oxford: Blackwell, 1968.

————. *Theology of the New Testament.* Translated by Kendrick Grobel. 2 vols. London: SCM Press, 1955.

Bultmann, Rudolf and Five Critics. *Kerygma and Myth.* Edited by Hans Werner Bartsch. Translated by Reginald H. Fuller. New York: Harper and Row, 1961.

Burge, Grant M. *The Anointed Community: The Holy Spirit in the Johannine Tradition.* Grand Rapids, MI: Eerdmans, 1987.

Byrne, Brendan. "The Faith of the Beloved Disciple and the Community in John 20." *Journal for the Study of the New Testament* 23 (1985): 83–97.

————. *Lazarus: A Contemporary Reading of John 11:1–46.* Zacchaeus Studies: New Testament. Collegeville, MN: The Liturgical Press, 1991.

————. *Romans.* Sacra Pagina 6. Collegeville, MN: The Liturgical Press, 1996.

Camery-Hoggatt, Jeremy. *Irony in Mark's Gospel: Text and Subtext.* Society for New Testament Studies Monograph Series 72. Cambridge: Cambridge University Press, 1992.

Chennattu, Rekha M. *Johannine Discipleship as a Covenant Relationship.* Peabody, MA: Hendrickson, 2006.

Coleridge, Mark. *The Birth of the Lukan Narrative: Narrative as Christology in Luke 1—2.* Journal for the Study of the New Testament Supplement Series 88. Sheffield: JSOT Press, 1993.

Collins, Adele Y. "Apotheosis and Resurrection." In *The New Testament and Hellenistic Judaism,* edited by Peder Borgen and Søren Giverson, 88–100. Peabody, MA: Hendrickson, 1997.

————. *The Beginning of the Gospel: Probings of Mark in Context.* Minneapolis, MN: Fortress, 1992.

Coloe, Mary. "Theological Reflections on Creation in the Gospel of John." *Pacifica* 24 (2011): 1–12.

Conzelmann, Hans. *The Theology of Luke.* Translated by Geoffrey Busswell. London: Faber and Faber, 1960.

Crossan, John D. "Empty Tomb and Absent Lord." In *The Passion in Mark: Studies on Mark 14–16,* edited by Werner H. Kelber, 134–52. Philadelphia: Fortress, 1976.

Culpepper, R. Alan. *John, the Son of Zebedee: The Life of a Legend.* Studies on Personalities of the New Testament. Columbia: University of South Carolina Press, 1994.

————. "Peter as Exemplary Disciple in John 21:15–19." *Perspectives in Religious Studies* 37 (2010): 165–78.

Dahl, Nils Alstrup. "The Passion Narrative in Matthew." In *The Interpretation of Matthew*, edited by Graham Stanton, 42–55. Issues in Religion and Theology 3. London: SPCK, 1983.

Davies, William D. *The Setting of the Sermon on the Mount*. Cambridge: Cambridge University Press, 1963.

Deines, Roland. "Not the Law but the Messiah: Law and Righteousness in the Gospel of Matthew—An Ongoing Debate." In *Built on the Rock: Studies in the Gospel of Matthew*, edited by Donald M. Gurtner and John Nolland, 53–84. Grand Rapids, MI: Eerdmans, 2008.

De la Potterie, Ignace. *The Hour of Jesus: The Passion and Resurrection of Jesus according to John: Text and Spirit*. Slough, UK: St. Paul Publications, 1989.

Dibelius, Martin. *From Tradition to Gospel*. Translated by Bertram Lee Wolf. The Library of Theological Translations. London: James Clark, 1971.

Dillon, Richard J. "Easter Revelation and Mission Program in Luke 24:46–48." In *Sin, Salvation and the Spirit: Commemorating the Fiftieth Year of the Liturgical Press*, edited by D. Durkin, 240–70. Collegeville, MN: The Liturgical Press, 1979.

————. *From Eye-Witnesses to Ministers of the Word*. Analecta Biblica 82. Rome: Biblical Institute Press, 1978.

Dodd, Charles H. *The Interpretation of the Fourth Gospel*. Cambridge: Cambridge University Press, 1963.

Donaldson, Terence R. *Jesus on the Mountain: A Study in Matthean Theology*. Journal for the Study of the New Testament Supplement Series 8. Sheffield: JSOT Press, 1985.

Dupont, J. "The Meal at Emmaus." In *The Eucharist in the New Testament*, edited by J. Delorme et al., 115–21. London: Geoffrey Chapman, 1965.

Dumm, D. R. "Luke 24:44–49 and Hospitality." In *Sin, Salvation, and the Spirit: Commemorating the Fiftieth Year of the Liturgical Press*, edited by D. Durkin, 230–39. Collegeville, MN: The Liturgical Press, 1979.

Finegan, Jack. *Encountering New Testament Manuscripts: A Working Introduction to Textual Criticism*. London: SPCK, 1975.

Fitzmyer, Joseph A. *The Acts of the Apostles*. Anchor Bible 31. New York: Doubleday, 1997.

————. *Luke the Theologian: Aspects of His Teaching*. London: Geoffrey Chapman, 1989.

Frankemölle, Hubert. "Pharisäismus im Judentum und Kirche." In *Gottesverächter und Menschenfeinde?*, edited by Horst Goldstein, 123–89. Düsselforf: Patmos, 1979.

Friedrichsen, Timothy A. "The Commissioning of Women Disciples: Matthew 28:9–10." In *Transcending Boundaries: Contemporary Readings of the New Testament: Studies in Honor of Francis J. Moloney*, edited by Rekha M. Chennattu and Mary L. Coloe, 265–79. Biblioteca di Scienze Religiose 187. Rome: LAS, 2005.

Garrett, Susan R. *The Temptations of Jesus in Mark's Gospel*. Grand Rapids, MI: Eerdmans, 1998.

Genette, Gérard. *Narrative Discourse: An Essay in Method*. Translated by Jane E. Lewin. Ithaca, NY: Cornell University Press, 1990.

Gleeson, Phillip D. "Today: A Study of the Theological Method of Roger Haight." D.Theol., diss., MCD University, Melbourne, 2012.

Green, Mark D. "Mountain." In *The New Interpreter's Dictionary of the Bible*, edited by Katherine Doob Sackenfeld et al., 4:159–60. Nashville, TN: Abingdon, 2006–9.

Gurtner, Daniel M. *The Torn Veil: Matthew's Exposition of the Death of Jesus*. Society for New Testament Studies Monograph Series 139. Cambridge: Cambridge University Press, 2007.

Haight, Roger. *Dynamics of Theology*. 2nd ed. Maryknoll, NY: Orbis Books, 2001.

Hare, Douglas R., and Daniel J. Harrington, "'Make Disciples of All the Gentiles' (Mt 28:19)." In Daniel J. Harrington, *Light of All Nations: Essays in the Church in New Testament Research*, 110–23. Good News Studies 3. Wilmington, DE: Michael Glazier, 1982.

Harris, Horton. *The Tübingen School*. Oxford: Clarendon Press, 1975.

Heil, John Paul. *The Death and Resurrection of Jesus: A Narrative Critical Reading of Matthew 26—28*. Minneapolis, MN: Fortress, 1991.

Hodge, Joel. *Resisting Violence and Victimisation: Christian Faith and Solidarity in East Timor*. London: Ashgate, 2012.

Hooker, Morna D. *Endings: Invitations to Discipleship*. Peabody, MA: Hendrickson, 2003.

Iverson, Kelly R. "A Further Word on Final *Gar.*" *The Catholic Biblical Quarterly* 68 (2006): 79–94.

———. "Orality and the Gospels: A Survey of Recent Research." *Currents in Biblical Research* 8 (2009): 71–106.

Jeremias, Joachim. *The Eucharistic Words of Jesus.* Translated by Norman Perrin. London: SCM Press, 1966.

Johnson, Luke T. *The Acts of the Apostles.* Sacra Pagina 5. Collegeville, MN: The Liturgical Press, 1992.

Juel, Donald. *Luke-Acts: The Promise of History.* Atlanta: John Knox Press, 1983.

Kähler, Martin. *The So-Called Historical Jesus and the Historic, Biblical Christ.* Translated by Carl E. Braaten. Philadelphia: Fortress, 1964.

Karris, Robert J. "God's Boundary-Breaking Mercy." *The Bible Today* 24 (1986): 24–29.

———. *Luke: Artist and Theologian: Luke's Passion Account as Literature.* New York: Paulist Press, 1985.

Kealy, Sean P. *Mark's Gospel: A History of Its Interpretation.* New York: Paulist Press, 1982.

Kelhoffer, James A. *Miracle and Mission: The Authentication of Missionaries and Their Message in the Longer Ending of Mark.* Wissenschaftliche Monographien zum Neuen Testament 2.112. Tübingen: Mohr Siebeck), 2000.

Kelly, Anthony J. *The Resurrection Effect: Transforming Christian Life and Thought.* Maryknoll, NY: Orbis Books, 2008.

Kingsbury, Jack Dean. *The Christology of Mark's Gospel.* Philadelphia: Fortress, 1983.

———. *Matthew as Story.* 2nd ed. Philadelphia: Fortress, 1988.

Kloppenborg, John S. *The Earliest Gospel: An Introduction to the Original Stories and Sayings of Jesus.* Louisville, KY: Westminster John Knox, 2008.

Koester, Craig R. *The Word of Life: A Theology of John's Gospel.* Grand Rapids, MI: Eerdmans, 2008.

Küng, Hans. *On Being a Christian.* Translated by Edward Quinn. London: Collins, 1977.

Lange, Joachim. *Das Erscheinen des Auferstandenen im Evangelium nach Matthäus. Eine traditions- und redaktionsgeschichtliche Untersuchung zu Mt. 2, 16–20.* Forschungen zur Bibel 11. Würzburg: Echter Verlag, 1973.

Lee, Dorothy A. *Flesh and Glory: Symbolism, Gender, and Theology in the Gospel of John.* New York: Crossroad, 2002.

————. "Partnership in Easter Faith: The Role of Mary Magdalene and Thomas in John 20." *Journal for the Study of the New Testament* 58 (1995): 37–49.

Lemon, Joel E. "Scroll." In *The New Interpreters' Dictionary of the Bible,* edited by Katherine Doob Sakenfeld et al., 5:138. Nashville, TN: Abingdon, 2006–9.

Léon-Dufour, Xavier. *Resurrection and the Message of Easter.* Translated by R. N. Wilson. London: Geoffrey Chapman, 1974.

Lightfoot, Robert H. *The Gospel Message of St. Mark.* Oxford: Clarendon Press, 1950.

Lincoln, Andrew T. *Truth on Trial: The Lawsuit Motif in the Fourth Gospel.* Peabody: MA: Hendrickson, 2000.

Loisy, Albert. *The Birth of the Christian Religion.* Translated by Lawrence P. Jacks. London: George Allen and Unwin, 1948.

Luz, Ulrich. *The Theology of the Gospel of Matthew.* Translated by J. Bradford Robinson. New Testament Theology. Cambridge: Cambridge University Press, 1995.

Malbon, Elizabeth S. *In the Company of Jesus: Characters in Mark's Gospel.* Louisville, KY: Westminster John Knox, 2000.

Martel, Yann. *Beatrice and Virgil.* Edinburgh: Canongate Books, 2010.

Marxsen, Willi. *The Resurrection of Jesus of Nazareth.* Translated by Margaret Kohl. London: SCM Press, 1970.

Meier, John P. *Law and History in Matthew's Gospel.* Analecta Biblica 71. Rome: Biblical Institute Press, 1976.

————. *A Marginal Jew: Rethinking the Historical Jesus.* Anchor Bible Reference Library/Anchor Yale Bible Reference Library. 4 vols. New York: Doubleday; New Haven, CT: Yale University Press, 1991–2009.

————. "Nations or Gentiles in Mt 28:19." *The Catholic Biblical Quarterly* 39 (1997): 94–102.

————. *The Vision of Matthew: Christ, Church, and Morality in the First Gospel.* Theological Inquiries. New York: Paulist Press, 1978.

Mlakhuzhyil, George. *The Christocentric Literary Structure of the Fourth Gospel.* 2nd ed. Analecta Biblica 117; Rome: Gregorian and Biblical Press, 2011.

Moessner, David P. *Lord of the Banquet: The Literary and Theological*

Significance of the Lukan Travel Narrative. Harrisburg, PA: Trinity Press International, 1989.

Moloney, Francis J. *A Body Broken for a Broken People: Eucharist in the New Testament*. Revised edition. Peabody, MA: Hendrickson, 1997.

————. "Can Everyone Be Wrong? A Reading of John 11:1—12:8." *New Testament Studies* 49 (2003): 505–27.

————. "The Fourth Gospel's Presentation of Jesus as 'the Christ' and J. A. T. Robinson's 'Redating.'" *The Downside Review* 95 (1997): 239–53.

————. "The Gospel of John as Scripture." *The Catholic Biblical Quarterly* 67 (2005): 454–68.

————. "The Gospel of John: The 'End' of Scripture." *Interpretation* 63 (2009): 356–66.

————. "Johannine Theology." In *The New Jerome Biblical Commentary*, edited by Raymond E. Brown, Joseph A. Fitzmyer, and Roland E. Murphy, 1417–26. Englewood Cliffs, NJ: Prentice Hall, 1989.

————. "John 21 and the Johannine Story." In *Anatomies of Narrative Criticism: The Past, Present, and Futures of the Fourth Gospel as Literature*, edited by Tom Thatcher and Stephen D. Moore, 237–51. SBL Resources for Biblical Study 55. Atlanta: Scholars Press, 2008.

————. *The Living Voice of the Gospel: The Gospels Today*. Peabody, MA: Hendrickson, 2007.

————. *Love in the Gospel of John: An Exegetical, Theological, and Literary Study*. Grand Rapids, MI: Baker Academic, 2014.

————. "Luke 24: To Be Witnesses of the Forgiveness and Compassion of Jesus." In *Apostolic Passion "Give Me Souls,"* edited by Rafael Vicent and Corrado Pastor, 183–95. Bangalore: Kristu Jyoti Publications, 2010.

————. "Mark as Story: Retrospect and Prospect." *Pacifica* 25 (2012): 1–11.

————. *Mark: Storyteller, Interpreter, Evangelist*. Peabody, MA: Hendrickson, 2004.

————. "Matthew 5:17–18 and the Matthean Use of *dikaiosunē*." In *Unity and Diversity in the Gospels and Paul*, edited by Christopher W. Skinner and Kelly R. Iverson, 33–54. Early Christianity and Its Literature 7. Atlanta: SBL, 2012.

————. "Resurrection and Accepted Exegetical Opinion." *Australasian Catholic Record* 58 (1981): 191–202.

Moran, Stuart. *A Friendly Guide to Luke's Gospel.* Mulgrave: Garratt Publishing, 2012.

Murphy-O'Connor, Jerome. *The Holy Land: An Archaeological Guide from Earliest Times to 1700.* 4th ed. Oxford: Oxford University Press, 1986.

O'Collins, Gerald. *Believing in the Resurrection: The Meaning and Promise of the Risen Jesus.* Mahwah, NJ: Paulist Press, 2012.

————. *The Easter Jesus.* London: Darton, Longman and Todd, 1973.

————. *Jesus Risen: An Historical, Fundamental, and Systematic Examination of Christ's Resurrection.* Mahwah, NJ: Paulist Press, 1987.

————. "Peter as Witness to Easter." *Theological Studies* 73 (2012): 263–85.

————. "The Resurrection: Nine Recent Approaches." *Australian eJournal of Theology* 18 (2011): 1–18.

————. Review of *The Resurrection of Jesus,* by Willi Marxsen. *The Heythrop Journal* 12 (1971): 207–11.

Pannenberg, Wolfhart. *Jesus—God and Man.* 2nd ed. Translated by Lewis L. Wilkins and Duane A. Priebe. Philadelphia: Westminster, 1977.

Parsons, Mikael C. *Luke: Storyteller, Interpreter, Evangelist.* Peabody, MA: Hendrickson, 2007.

Perrin, Norman. *The Resurrection Narratives: A New Approach.* London: SPCK, 1977.

Pesch, Rudolf. "Zur Entstehung des Glaubens und die Auferstehung Jesu." *Theologische Quartalschrift* 153 (1973): 103–17.

Ratzinger, Joseph. *Jesus of Nazareth: The Infancy Narratives.* Translated by Philip J. Whitmore. New York: Image, 2012.

Rimmon-Kenan, Schlomith. *Narrative Fiction: Contemporary Poetics.* New Accents. London: Methuen, 1983.

Sanders, Ed Parish. *The Historical Figure of Jesus.* London: The Penguin Press, 1993.

Schaberg, Jane. *The Father, the Son, and the Holy Spirit: The Triadic Phrase in Matthew 28:19b.* Society for Biblical Literature Dissertation Series 61. Chico, CA: Scholars Press, 1982.

Schillebeeckx, Edward. *Jesus: An Experiment in Christology.* Translated by Hubert Hoskins. London: Collins, 1979.

Schneiders, Sandra M. "The Raising of the New Temple: John 20.19–23 and Johannine Ecclesiology." *New Testament Studies* 52 (2006): 337–55.

———. "The Resurrection (of the Body) in the Fourth Gospel: A Key to Johannine Spirituality." In *Life in Abundance: Studies in John's Gospel in Tribute to Raymond E. Brown*, edited by John R. Donahue, 168–98. Collegeville, MN: The Liturgical Press, 2005.

———. "Touching the Risen Jesus: Mary Magdalene and Thomas the Twin in John 20." In *The Resurrection of Jesus in the Gospel of John*, edited by Craig R. Koester and Reimund Bieringer, 153–76. Wissenschaftliche Untersuchungen zum Neuen Testament 222. Tübingen: Mohr Siebeck, 2008.

Schnelle, Udo. *The Human Condition: Anthropology in the Teachings of Jesus, Paul, and John*. Translated by O. C. Dean, Jr. Minneapolis, MN: Fortress, 1996.

Schubert, Paul. "The Structure and Significance of Luke 24." In *Neutestamentliche Studien für R. Bultmann*, edited by Walther Eltester, 165–86. Beihefte zur Zeitschrift für die neutestamentliche Wissenschaft 21. Berlin: Töppelmann, 1954.

Senior, Donald. "The Death of Jesus and the Resurrection of the Holy Ones (Matthew 27:51–52)." *The Catholic Biblical Quarterly* 38 (1976): 312–29.

———. *The Passion of Jesus in the Gospel of Luke*. The Passion Series 3. Wilmington, DE: Michael Glazier, 1989.

———. *The Passion of Jesus in the Gospel of Mark*. The Passion Series 2. Wilmington, DE: Michael Glazier, 1984.

———. *The Passion of Jesus in the Gospel of Matthew*. The Passion Series 1. Wilmington, DE: Michael Glazier, 1985.

———. "The Struggle to Be Universal: Mission as Vantage Point for New Testament Investigation." *The Catholic Biblical Quarterly* 46 (1984): 63–81.

Shepherd, David. "'Do You Love Me?' A Narrative-Critical Reappraisal of *agapaō* and *phileō* in John 21:15–17." *Journal of Biblical Literature* 129 (2010): 777–92.

Sim, David. *The Gospel of Matthew and Christian Judaism: The History and Social Setting of the Matthean Community*. Studies in the New Testament and Its World. Edinburgh: T & T Clark, 1998.

Smith, D. Moody. *John Among the Gospels.* 2nd ed. Columbia: University of South Carolina Press, 2001.

———. "When Did the Gospels Become Scripture?" *Journal of Biblical Literature* 119 (2000): 3–20.

Smith, Daniel A. *Revisiting the Empty Tomb: The Early History of Easter.* Minneapolis, MN: Fortress, 2010.

Soards, Marion. "The Question of a Premarcan Passion Narrative." In Raymond E. Brown, *The Death of the Messiah: A Commentary on the Passion Narratives in the Four Gospels,* 2:1492–1524 (Appendix IX). Anchor Bible Reference Library. 2 vols. New York: Doubleday, 1993.

Stendahl, Krister. *The School of St. Matthew.* 2nd ed. Philadelphia: Fortress, 1968.

Strauss, David F. *The Life of Jesus Critically Examined.* Edited by Peter C. Hodgson. Translated by George Eliot. Lives of Jesus. Philadelphia: Fortress, 1972.

Streeter, Burnett H. *The Four Gospels: A Study of Origins.* London: Macmillan, 1924.

Tannehill, Robert C. "The Gospel of Mark as Narrative Christology." *Semeia* 16 (1980): 57–95.

Tiede, David L. *Prophecy and History in Luke-Acts.* Philadelphia: Fortress, 1980.

Telford, William R. *The Theology of the Gospel of Mark.* New Testament Theology. Cambridge: Cambridge University Press, 1999.

Theissen, Gerd, and Annette Merz. *The Historical Jesus: A Comprehensive Guide:* Minneapolis, MN: Fortress, 1996.

Trobisch, David J. "Codex." In *The New Interpreters' Dictionary of the Bible,* edited by Katherine Doob Sakenfeld et al., 1:697. Nashville, TN: Abingdon, 2006–9.

Tuckett, Christopher M. *Q and the History of Early Christianity: Studies on Q.* Edinburgh: T & T Clark, 1996.

Von Campenhausen, Hans. "The Events of Easter and the Empty Tomb." In *Tradition and Life in the Church: Essays and Lectures in Church History,* translated by A. V. Littledale, 42–89. London: Collins, 1968.

Weeden, Theodore. *Mark: Traditions in Conflict.* Philadelphia: Fortress, 1971.

Westcott, Brooke Foss. *The Gospel of the Resurrection: Thoughts on Its Relation to Reason and History.* London: Macmillan, 1906.

Wright, Nicholas T. *The Resurrection of the Son of God.* Minneapolis, MN: Fortress, 2003.

Zumstein, Jean. "Jesus' Resurrection in the Farewell Discourses." In *The Resurrection of Jesus in the Gospel of John,* edited by Craig R. Koester and Reimund Bieringer, 103–26. Wissenschaftliche Untersuchungen zum Neuen Testament 222. Tübingen: Mohr Siebeck, 2008.

Index of Names

What does this Summer
study meant to you?